# LEAVES FROM A

# L·E·A·V·E·S
## FROM A SUFI JOURNAL

With a foreword by
## Shaykh Fadhlalla Haeri

ELEMENT BOOKS
*in association with*
ZAHRA PUBLICATIONS

© Zahra Trust 1988

First published in 1988 by
Element Books Limited
Longmead, Shaftesbury, Dorset

Printed and bound in Great Britain

Designed by Clarke Williams

Cover design by Max Fairbrother

British Library Cataloguing in Publication Data

Leaves from a Sufi journal.
1. Sufism – Arabic texts
I. Boase, 'Abd al-Wahhab
297'.4

ISBN 1–85230–057–4

# Contents

# Foreword

Sufism is the art and the science of correct living which results in success. Mankind strives towards success, and although success is differently defined from time to time and from place to place, we all seek a way of existence that brings the minimum of trouble and the maximum of happiness and joy. The art of achieving this is the core of all spiritual endeavours and, therefore, Sufism can be considered the heart of Islam.

Since it is a comprehensive art of living, Sufism is concerned with integrity and the integration of all things and instils a full understanding of the meaning behind life. However, unless it is applied by those who have attained fulfilment and inner awakening, it is most likely to end up being of palliative use, or at best, distorted.

The Sufi is he who is constant in his equilibrium; he is analytically aware of the causal world in which he is living and is spontaneously aware of his awareness and his state of being. The Sufi is he who is in the right place at the right time doing the right thing. The Sufi is he who does not look back in time with regret and does not look forward with desires and expectations. The Sufi is he who is living the present fully – outwardly responsible and active and inwardly free and watchful. The heart of the Sufi in its purity reflects the truth behind creation and is constantly polished and purified as he journeys towards higher consciousness.

Because Sufism is concerned with life, the Sufi has to relate and connect with all aspects of life in a totally integrated fashion. Therefore the objective of Sufism is the identification and the tuning to the unific reality that underlies all known and unknown, visible and invisible creation. So it is such a wide web that there is nothing that does not come under its sovereignty or jurisdiction. Therefore the topics in this volume cover a broad spectrum, reflecting most aspects of life.

The present volume is a collection of numerous classical writings as well as contemporary discourses concerning the path of spiritual awakening which was compiled in a manner to benefit those who desire to catch a glimpse of the meaning of Sufism. The articles have been arranged in a logical system to make it easier for the modern mind to assimilate them. They give a foretaste of that state which can be the outcome of following a true programme of self-awakening. Articles covering various phases and aspects of such a programme had appeared over the years in a journal called Nuradeen, a quarterly journal formerly published by the Zahra Trust.

I would like to express my gratitude to all those who have contributed over the years in helping to bring about this book. Special acknowledgement is to be given to Abbas H. Bilgrami for his administrative services, Batal Havri Mazandarami for editorial compilation of this volume and to Dr. Abdul Wahhab Boase for editing the text.

*Shaykh Fadhlalla Haeri*

# SECTION 1

## Man

*Lift up your face to the [one true] faith, turning away from all that is false, in accordance with the natural disposition which Allah has instilled into man [at birth]: for, not to allow any change to corrupt what Allah has thus created – this is the purpose of the one [true] faith; but most people know it not.* (30:30)

———— ★ ————

The Prophet Muhammad (peace be upon him) said:

'Every child is born with a natural disposition to worship Allah; it is only his parents who later turn him into a Jew, a Christian or a Magian?'

# The Nature of Man

## By 'Abd al-Haqq Sayf al-Ilm

Every baby born is an expression of absolute purity. Anyone who has been present at a birth must acknowledge this. Each new birth is a bursting out of life-itself. Every baby is a container for the re-emergence of raw life-energy – unadulterated, undifferentiated. However, each container has a definite form and each is contained in an environment. Each baby has genetic coding determining its physical shape and temperamental balance. Each is born into surroundings of a particular nature, both physical and emotional. These circumstances, together with the chain of events that make up its early life, bring about the individualization of the new child. They combine to make the child, in its own unique way, begin to feel itself separate from its surroundings. Some receive affirmation and satisfaction and so view the world as a friendly, warm, safe place. Others are negated and denied and experience the world as hostile, alien and fearful. Between these two are millions of possibilities and variations different for each child. On the other hand, the kinds of human situations confronted by the child are quite limited and predictable, just as its own specific temperament is of a given type. The end result is a being in every case unique, and at the same time falling within a clearly recognizable category, just as no two individuals are sick in the same way, and yet a particular illness can be diagnosed.

At a certain point after roughly two years, a picture built up of all the various elements mentioned above takes on a more or less definite shape, and the child says, 'This is me!' This 'me' is in fact by no means solid, changing from one minute to the next, but it is established enough as a shape to be claimed as an identity. It is vitally important to realize that this 'identity' has no real existence. What has happened is that the pure life energy and undifferentiated consciousness of the new born baby have, over a period of time and through exposure to a particular environment, become identified in a particular way with their body-container so that they are limited and individualized in it. Through the process of existing the child has acquired a more or less fixed image of itself which it calls 'me', completely losing sight of the unconstrained, undefined, pure life-energy which was its birthright. This assumed identity is accidental, made up of contingent circumstances and passing time. Given a different environment, a child would adopt a different self-form. The reality of the child lies in the pure life energy and undifferentiated consciousness it starts with, not the limited and constricted self-picture it later develops.

This circumstantially constructed, and quite arbitrarily imposed first self-image now becomes for us the basis of all our future dealings with ourselves and with the world which surrounds us. It dictates to us the pattern of our life which is, from now on, spent preserving and perpetuating the existence of this assumed identity with which we have inextricably associated ourselves. As far as we are concerned, it is what we are. However, just look at any two year old and you will find a very unbridled raw-edged being; wilful, autocratic, demanding, easily angered, often destructive, attention seeking, extremely selfish – in a word, monstrous! In its naked form this 'self' is obviously not acceptable. Gradually we learn, by experience, to negotiate with existence. We find out how much we can get away with, what needs to be honed down, what we can express, what we must hold back, what brings about desired reactions and so on. In other words, we try to find a balance between the raw material of our acquired self-picture to which we have given absolute reality, and the hampering social environment in which we find ourselves where total 'self' expression is not permissible or possible. In this way, the original self-picture becomes covered over, layer upon layer, according to the demands of different situations.

Our lives continue to be the playing-out of the first patterning, more and more refined and in an ever larger arena. In cases
where a completely free rein is given to the inclinations of the
primary self-image, the individual will return to his infantile
form as in the recent case of the fabulously rich man who
reverted absolutely to a tyrannical infant, concerned only with
the gratification of his capricious whims and unbounded
appetites. It also occurs to some extent in senility when the old
person loses grip on the cover-up which has been so successfully maintained for so many years. This is the inevitable
description of one who has given absolute reality to his acquired
self-picture. If this was all there was, we would have no other
option than to be slaves to our own assumed identities, our lives
spent hopelessy trying to assuage the appetites and gratify the
desires of a two-year old child. And this is in fact the lot of a
large proportion of the human race.

If you look about you at the phenomena of existence in the
universe, or inside you at the workings of your own body, you
will find clearly discernible laws at work, holding everything in
harmony and balance – in the vastness of the galaxies and the
overwhelming beauty of the stars with their patterns and
movement; in the solar system and the wonderful way the
planets keep to their orbits held by an unbelievably intricate
system of forces; in the Earth's atmosphere and how it provides
exactly the right conditions for the life on its surface; in the
climates and how they preserve the animal and vegetable life in
their different zones; in the forest and the desert and how each
is a delicately balanced ecological system providing everything
necessary for its continued existence; in the separate organisms,
each with its own inexplicable breathtaking beauty and its own
perfectly balanced cycle of growth and decay; in our own bodies
with their perfect co-ordination. You will find that laws govern
the senses, each with its own field of perception; the digestive
system and its extraction of what is beneficial and rejection of
what is superfluous; the brain and its ability to store information
and release it in the right situation; the way the body naturally
sets right any disruption of its equilibrium. The examples are
endless, but the indications are quite clear. Whether you look at
the whole universe or a particular system or a single organism or
the smallest subatomic particle, it is abundantly apparent that
there is a universal law at work tending to order and balance in
every situation.

Apart from the case of man, it is quite apparent that everything submits involuntarily and unconsciously, just by being what it is, to the universal order manifest in existence, or we could say by extension, to the divine reality which it indicates. Each thing in its own unique way, contributes to the upholding of the balance and is itself in itself an indication of its Creator/Source – in the same way that any artifact indicates the person who made it. It is this activity of submission and participation in the unfolding of existence, this acknowledgement, even if unconscious, of the source of existence that constitutes real worship. At this point you must jettison any concept you may previously have held of worship being connected to 'religion'. Worship is organic, inevitable. It is an integral part of all existence. By fulfilling its natural function for which it is perfectly adapted, every creature is at the same time performing an act of worship by playing its own part in manifesting and indicating the one reality. All things, in spite of the diversity of their different forms and activities, have this one thing in common. This is the common denominator in existence. This is the common purpose.

Now we come back to the human species, to ourselves. By use of the intellect, we must arrive at the conclusion that what is true for everything else in the universe must also be true for us, since we are an inseparable part of the whole structure. Just as the basic function of everything in the universe is worship, so worship must also be the keynote of our own existence. However, whereas everything else does so outwardly by its natural unconscious submission to the way things are, we have the capacity of both outward submission to, and inner awareness of, the one reality. This then is our purpose, our reason for being here, and also what defines our outward form – that we both outwardly conform to the natural boundaries imposed on us by the form which we have been given and that we inwardly realize our capacity for decoding what we see around us and accept that existence is what it is, a generous and compassionate out-pouring, the self-manifestation of the essence of the One God, the Lord of the heavens and the earth and everything between them.

These boundaries delineating the natural form of man, showing what it is to be a human creature, have always been available to people, accepted by some, rejected by others, together with the knowledge of the true picture of existence. All creatures except man have their form indelibly stamped in them so that they have no need of external stimulae to bring it out of them. But in our case we have to choose to be human. We have to choose the form that is in reality our nature. It is very important to grasp this. Even though we have to learn what it is to be human, all we are doing is removing ignorance and uncovering what is in fact our organic natural pattern. Recognized morality is not something imposed on man out of social convenience, but something that is inherent in us and required by our form for the proper functioning of the human social nexus. It is a natural patterning coming from within them and appearing in a social context. Unlicensed behaviour, the unrestricted giving way to the infantile appetites which is the present hallmark of the human situation is in fact unnatural. It constitutes a covering-up of the simple morality which is the true reality of human nature and leads inevitably to the total disruption of human social order.

We have noted that every creature knows its form and it is not in the evidently compassionate nature of existence that we, the human species, should alone be left with no way to know the form we should assume to truly fulfil our humanness and of course the simple fact is that we have not been neglected. At regular intervals, throughout the time that human beings have inhabited the earth, we have been reminded of the total knowledge we are capable of containing and have been shown the form which is naturally ours by men directly inspired by the Reality Itself to carry out this task. These teachings have in part survived to this day in the form of the so-called 'religions'. And this explains the clear similarities that exist between them. But they are, for the most part, just archeological fragments of the original teaching which have been distorted, vitiated, pieced together and adapted to man's lower nature. This has made them separate and antagonistic to each other, thus obscuring the fact that they are in reality successive manifestations of one continuously repeated teaching – men sent to men by their Creator to show them and tell them how to be human. Show and tell. The teaching has been both by example and by word. The two must go together for the necessary transformation to take place. In each case, a transmission took place from the Messengers to the human communities where they appeared, whereby communities, who had relapsed into ignorance and squalid sensual gratification, who had on a mass scale allowed their infantile self-form to take over and become the dominant influence in their society, were purified, lifted up, and transformed by the transmitted process into radiant examples of true humanity. They were communities where generosity, justice, compassion and humility were the rule rather than the exception and the people lived within clear moral limits.

It is these messengers from Reality and their followers who gave rise to what are now known as the 'world religions' which have in every case, in one way or another, been altered beyond recognition, so that the original purpose, to show humans how to be human, has been completely obscured. Two examples briefly illustrate how the original clear teachings has disappeared. They are what are now called Judaism and Christianity. In Judaism, the word of the Messenger has been exalted above the example so that the humanizing, transformative process brought and demonstrated by Moses to his people has become the rigidly structured hair-splitting laws of the rabbinical tradition which are inhuman and tyrannical rather than compassionate and liberating. In Christianity, the example of Jesus was romanticised almost to the exclusion of what he said (it must be remembered that he was always a practising Jew and nowhere renounced the Mosaic law, but came to breathe into it the humanity and compassion that had been squeezed out), but what has transpired is that his clear example was made into a mystery and the moral parameters blurred, allowing the amorphous moral chaos which now exists in the so-called 'Christian' countries. Examination of each one of the 'religions' will reveal the same thing – how an original pure teaching has been perverted and distorted leading, in most cases, to the very opposite of what was originally intended.

The final complete version of the pure human teaching was the one revealed to Muhammad in Arabia in the early seventh century of the Christian era. It was transmitted by him to some of those around him and practised by them in Medina. It is known as Islam. This is where we must look if we desire to find the picture of the true human form and to know the knowledge that we are capable of containing since, of all the teachings, it is the only one that we know for certain to be completely intact.

The message is there, unchanged by a single word, in the form of the Qur'an, giving us directly from Reality Itself the picture of the whole of existence and telling us exactly our part in it. The example of the Messenger himself was minutely recorded showing us the perfection of the human form and how those around him took it on and therefore how we ourselves can do the same. This is not to say that the Muslims have not gone the way of previous communities and distorted and misapplied and misunderstood the original teaching. They clearly have. But the original teaching is still totally available and accessible for those who want it. The chain of transmission leading from the last of the Messengers, Muhammad, is unbroken and continues to this day.

Awareness of our predicament is an essential step but it is only the first step. To escape from the tyranny we have imposed on ourselves, the endless appeasement of our insatiable infantile self-forms, which is all that we have allowed ourselves to be, a basic transformation is necessary. What has to be transformed is the heart and there is no way to it except by embarking on action – immediately. The action that is necessary is the taking on of the truly human form which was recorded for the last time in the revelation of the Qur'an and perfectly demonstrated in the life of the last of those sent for that purpose by the One God, the Messenger Muhammad. This will give us real inner awareness and acceptance of the true nature of the universe and what is beyond it and hidden within it. The two together, the practice and the acceptance, will lead to the liberation which we all desire; the overwhelmingly intoxicating experience of tasting the timeless spaceless presence of the One from Whom we have come and to Whom we inevitably must return. Set out and you will arrive.

# SECTION 2

## Family and Society

*Marry those among you who are single and those who are fit . . . if they are needy, Allah will make them free from want out of His grace.* (24:32)

*He it is Who created you from a single being, and of the same did He make his mate that he might find comfort and solace in her.* (7:189)

---
★
---

*Hadith*: 'Marriage is my tradition and whoever seeks other than my tradition is not with me.'

★

*Hadith*: 'The widow shall not be married until she is consulted, and the virgin shall not be married until her consent is obtained.'

★

*Hadith*: 'Everyone of you is a ruler and everyone of you shall be questioned about those under his rule . . . the man is a ruler in his family and he shall be questioned about those under his care; and the woman is a ruler in the house of her husband, and she shall be questioned about those under her care; and the servant is a ruler so far as the property of his master is concerned, and he shall be questioned about that which is entrusted to him?

# Marriage and Family in Islam

## By Abu al-Fadhl Ezzati

Islam has been introduced by the Qur'an to be the religion of balance, a balance in the widest sense of the term covering the entire area of human thought and life. It is a balance between reality and ideals. A Muslim's notion of Allah's Oneness is or should be reflected in his own striving towards a co-ordination and unification of the ideals and realities of spiritual and physical motives and tendencies, of body and mind, of nature and man, of the cosmos and man, and of various aspects of human life. Islam teaches man, first, that the permanent worship of Allah in all the manifold actions of human life is the very meaning of life; secondly, that the achievement of this purpose remains impossible so long as we divide our life into two parts, the spiritual and the material. They must be bound together, in our consciousness and action, into one harmonious entity. The unity of Allah in Islam has influenced all of its ideals and realities. Man has not been divided into two contradictory parts, spiritual and material. If the object of our life as a whole is the worship of Allah as is suggested by the *ayah*, *I have not created the jinn and men except that they should worship Me* (51:56), then we must necessarily regard this life in its totality as one complex of religious, moral and spiritual responsibilities.

Everything which truly helps the individual, society and mankind as a whole can be regarded as worship, and is rewarded if well performed or punished if not fulfilled. On the other hand, anything which is harmful to the divine nature of the individual, society and mankind is regarded as disobedience to God, is forbidden and must be punished. Thus all our actions, even sexual ones, must fulfil a divine purpose and must be performed as acts of worship, that is, performed consciously as constituting a part of God's universal plan. Worship of Allah in the widest sense constitutes, according to Islam, the meaning of life and vice versa. The dichotomy between body and mind, religion and politics, spirit and matter, between the spiritual and the material life is completely rejected by Islam. On the basis of balance, Islam establishes absolute harmony amongst all human spiritual and physical motives, tendencies, and potentials. The natural conclusion is that Islam rejects celibacy and monastic life, and looks upon marriage as a holy contract, a divine institution, and even an act of worship. So much so that it is reported that the Prophet, peace be upon him, has said: 'He who marries has saved half of his faith'; and 'Marriage is my institution, he who disregards it is not a follower of mine.'

The love of spouse and the love of members of a family for each other is required in Islam because the Prophet, peace be upon him, is reported to have said: 'Is Islam anything other than love [love of Allah for the sake of Whom one loves others]?' Islam is nothing but love; love of Allah for the sake of Allah, and love of spouse, parents, children, relatives, fellow human beings, love of other creatures and of the entire universe for the sake of Allah and as a means to earn the love of Allah. We can thus see that there is no contrast between the love of Allah and the love of His creatures.

The concept of the family (*ahl*) in Islam is broader and more inclusive than in western society, that is, the parents and children always remain as members of one's family. It covers even distant relatives, so much so that the maintenance, welfare, respect and love of them is regarded as a religious responsibility. The term *ahl*, which also means people, semantically covers more than one's immediate relatives or even near of kin. The term used in the Qur'an for near and distant relatives is *dhaw al-qurbah* and the general term used in Islamic literature for

one's duty towards them is *salat al-rahim*. There are many verses
in the Qur'an making it the duty of every Muslim to provide
maintenance (in the case of need), love and respect for all near
and distant relatives (2:83,177; 4:36; 8:41; 16:90; 17:26; 30:38). For
instance:

> Surely Allah commands you to justice and good and to give to kindred [their
> due]. (16:90)

It is thus appropriate to conclude that the term family in western
society covers only a small portion of the family suggested by
Islam. Maintenance, love and respect of one's distant relatives is
as obligatory as to one's own immediate family, though the
obligation to one's immediate family is the first in the line of
priority. The Prophet, peace be upon him, is reported to have
said: 'On the Day of Judgement, one's relatives stand at the gate
of heaven to certify whether one has been good to them'
(Kulayni in *Al-Kafi*, chapter on faith and unbelief). He is also
reported to have said: 'The quickest reward is for the good done
to one's relatives (*salat al-rahim*).'

As far as love and respect of one's parents is concerned, the
Qur'an states:

> Your Lord has commanded that you shall not worship [any] but Him, and
> goodness to your parents [it comes next to serving Allah] . . . say not to
> them [so much as] ugh, nor chide them [and always] talk to them with
> respect. Make yourself submissively gentle [and humble] to them with
> compassion, and [pray for them] saying: 'Oh Lord, have compassion on
> them, as they brought me up [when I was] little . . . and give to the relatives
> their due'. (17:23–26)

The Prophet is reported to have said: 'The key to heaven is
under the feet of the mother.' A person asked the Prophet:
'What is the best thing I can do?' He replied: 'Serve your
mother,' He asked: 'And what is the second best?' He replied
again: 'Serve your mother.' He asked again, and the reply was
the same. He asked for the fourth time: 'Who comes next?' The
Prophet replied: 'Your father, then your relatives in order of
relationship.' Respecting and serving one's parents is frequently
commanded by the Qur'an (46:15, 31:14). It is suggested that
difference of religion (non-Muslim parents) does not release one
from the religious obligation of maintenance. Even *jihad* (war in
the name of Allah) is not allowed without the mother's
permission. One of the cardinal sins in Islam is to be disrespect-
ful and disobedient to one's parents.

Just as respect, obedience, and the maintenance of one's parents have been strongly commanded and enjoined upon children, so the parents also have duties towards their children which must be fulfilled. Both parents and children have rights and responsibilities over each other. Although parents' love for children is natural, the Qur'an and Sunnah (the traditions of the Prophet) have still laid guidelines regarding children's rights (16:58–59, 43:17, 6:152, 2:233).

Islam regards marriage as a constitution in its own right, and thus rejects strongly anything challenging its constitution or the rights and responsibilities which it entails. The Qur'an suggests cornerstone of the society is two persons:

> *I exhort you only to one thing, that you stand and rise up for the cause of Allah in twos and singly.* (34:46)

Thus, Islam recognises the authority of the family as the constitutional genesis and fundamental basis of human society.

As far as the constitution of marriage is concerned, Islam regards it not as a sacrament but as a contract and thus subject to the conditions and stipulations concluded between the two sides of the marriage. But the marriage contract involves three parties, the first being Allah. The stipulations, therefore, should not contradict the divine law (*shari'ah*) of Allah and the holy nature of the marriage.

> *Men are responsible for women because Allah has given them more than the other and because they spend out of their property; the good women are therefore obedient . . .* (4:34)

Is is suggested that man provide for the wife (maintenance) though the wife may have financial means. Thus, a married woman is a person in her own right with a financially independent status, even after marriage. (This explains the position of women in the Islamic law of inheritance). It is in regard to women's more delicate, sensitive and emotional nature that Islam allows this financially independent status. The nature and biology of men and women are not the same, consequently they have been treated independently and have been entrusted with particular roles, functions, rights and responsibilities in Islam. The Prophet, peace and blessings be upon him and his family, is reported to have said: 'Everybody is responsible. The ruler is responsible. The husband is responsible for his home and his family. The wife is responsible for her husband, his home, family and children. And thus, you are all responsible.'

The most important role of the Muslim woman is to be a good wife and a good mother. For this she is innately suited. Islam recognises the immense value and position of women in educating and shaping future generations.

> *And we have enjoined upon man concerning his parents: his mother carries him in weakness upon weakness, and his weaning is in two years. Therefore show gratitude to Me and to your parents.* (31:34, 46:15)

The welfare and maintenance of the family is the religious responsibility of the husband and father – the education and moral training of the children has been made the obligation of both parents. Inside the family the principles of love, sincerity, discipline, security, respect, mutual understanding, mutual responsibility, and equality within the divine law should rule. The Prophet was an ideal and a paradigm in the matter of treatment towards family members. He used to stand up on the arrival of Fatimah and would make her sit by his side. He often carried Hasan and Husayn, his grandchildren, on his back and shoulders. The Prophet is reported to have said: 'The best of you is he who is best to his family.' It is also reported that he said: 'Whoever dies while her husband is pleased with her will enter paradise.'

Love for the members of family should be looked upon as a means to the love of Allah, and they should not contradict each other. However, the main principle of marriage is mental security, solace, comfort, and relaxation:

> *One of His signs is that He created mates for you from yourselves that you may find solace and rest in them, and He put between you love and compassion. Surely there are signs in this for a people who reflect.* (30:21)

The duties of the spouses towards each other are very important in Islam. The Qur'an devotes a chapter entitled *Al-Nisa* (The Women) to the rights and responsibilities of the spouses. The Qur'an prescribes disciplinary measures in cases of violation of rights and responsibilities, namely, admonition and separation of bed (4:16).

As for safeguarding the state of marriage and solving marital difficulties, the Qur'an asks the believers to seek a reconciliation amongst the spouses themselves, but if a breach is still feared, *then appoint an arbitrator from his people and an arbitrator from her people. If they both desire peace and agreement, Allah will establish harmony and peace between them. Surely Allah is Knowing, Aware* (4:35). Thus, all necessary measures should be taken to re-establish peace and harmony between the two, both by themselves and by their relatives and people. This is because the Prophet, peace be upon him, is reported to have said: 'The most detestable thing for me and in my religion is divorce.' Thus divorce, as the last thing to do, is the most hated permissible measure to be taken. This is why, by and large, marriage in the Muslim community is more stable compared with western society. The other factors contributing to the stability of marriage in the Muslim community are: (a) the definition of the rights and responsibilities of the spouses in the *shari'ah* (the body of Islamic law); (b) the general Islamic moral and ethical values and measures which regulate differences of culture, race, colour and nationality, thus putting marriage in its correct perspective; and (c) the Islamic concept of family, home, relationships of near and distant kin, as well as the Islamic relationship between human beings and marriage partners.

# Man/Woman

## By Umm Husayn

The purpose for which we are created is that we may come to know Allah. One much quoted Hadith or saying of the Prophet states that: 'He who knows himself, knows his Lord.'

Seekers of self-knowledge must thus define their role in this existence and understand the boundaries within which they have to function if they are to behave correctly. If this is to happen it is crucial that men and women know the nature of the relationship that Allah has ordained between them. This is revealed in the following *ayat*:

> And one of His signs is that He created mates for you from yourselves that *you may find rest in them, and He put between you love and compassion;* *most surely there are signs in this for a people who reflect.* (30:21)
> O people! Be careful of [your duty to] your Lord, Who created you from a *single being and created its mate of the same [kind] and spread from these* *two, many men and women; and be careful of [your duty to] Allah, by whom* *you demand one of another [your rights] and [to] the ties of relationship.* (4:1)

From these *ayat* we come to know that woman is man's pair, created like him from a single self and that their destiny is to live in harmony together. Elsewhere in the Holy Qur'an it is revealed that in his existence men are the custodians of women:

*Men are the maintainers of women because Allah has made some of them to excel others and because they spend out of their property: the good women are therefore obedient, guarding the unseen as Allah has guarded; and [as to] those on whose part you fear desertion, admonish them, leave them alone in the sleeping-places and beat them; then if they obey you, do not seek a way against them; surely Allah is High, Great. (4:34)*

Yet, while man has authority over woman in this world, her potential for reward in the next is identical:

*And whoever does good deeds whether male or female and he [or she] is a believer – these shall enter the garden, and they shall not be dealt with a jot unjustly. (4:124)*
*Whoever does good whether male or female and is a believer, We will most certainly make him live a happy life, and We will most certainly give them their reward for the best of what they did. (16:97)*

Like man, woman is dependent on her correct transaction in this world if she is to enjoy the fruits of the next. So woman's fulfilment of her covenant with Allah is that she must obey and serve the man under whose care her Creator has entrusted her, be it husband, father, brother, son, or in the absence of any of these, a relative or righteous man in the community.

Allah's greatest gift to woman is the opportunity she has to be fulfilled spiritually through serving a man. By dedicating herself wholeheartedly to her husband, she can annihilate her lower tendencies in his service. This course of action ensures not only a correct life here and now, but also the rewards of the life to come.

The Blessed Prophet spoke of woman's station in relation to man as follows: 'Had it been permissible for a human being to prostrate in obeisance before another human being, I would have ordained that women should prostrate before their husbands.' On another occasion, he described the 'best women among you' as being 'those who bear children, have feelings of love, and are of pure character; in their own family they have a fair social standing, and before their husbands they are humble and submissive; they adorn themselves for their husbands and hide themselves from others; they lend careful ear to what their husbands say, obey their orders and while in privacy they comply with their wishes.' And He considered a loving, giving wife as a man's most valued treasure: 'After the blessings of Islam, the most precious gift of God for a Muslim man is his having a Muslim partner, because whenever he sees her, her appearance provides a joy for him, and she obeys his orders and is the custodian of his wealth and honour.'

In return for this love and devotion man is enjoined both in the Qur'an and the Hadiths to treat women with tenderness and respect:

*And treat them kindly.* (4:19)

In his address at Mina, during the last year of his life, the Blessed Prophet said: 'You should advise others to behave well towards women, because they have come to live in your houses; they are dependent on you; they are God's trust whom you have voluntarily made your partners.'

Another Hadith states: 'The best men among my followers are those who are not harsh upon their family but treat them with benevolence and kindness.' 'Ali, the Commander of the Faithful, in a letter written to one of his sons, recommended that, 'Woman is like a sweet smell and is of tender nature, not hard-hearted like a tyrant, so always placate her and treat her gently, so that you may lead a peaceful life.'

While man is considered the head of the family, the running of the house and the upbringing of the children is considered the woman's domain. Indeed her husband is as an honoured guest in her home. A Hadith says: 'Verily, man is the head of the family and woman is the head of the house.'
'Ali, the Commander of the Faithful, speaking about the importance of a woman's contribution to her family, said: 'An educated woman educates a family, a community, a nation.'

The Blessed Prophet divided the work between his daughter, Hazrat Fatimah Zahrah, and her husband 'Ali in this way: the work of the household was assigned to her and the work outside the house to him. Hazrat Fatimah Zahrah is said to have been very satisfied with this division.

Marriage is only worthwhile if it helps the husband and wife, their earthly desires satisfied, to explore their full spiritual potential. If the relationship is not conducive to the spiritual development of both, the one helping the other, it will be a miserable affair. The most fortunate woman is she whose passion and devotion for her husband has expanded to such a point that she can use it as a springboard to dive into the eternal love of the Creator. So she can truly say to her beloved: 'We are but one, for the love of you is the love of One.'

Woman's role must accordingly be seen as one of submission to whatever circumstances destiny has decreed for her. For some this involves a quiet life in the home, for others an arena of dynamic action. The important factor is her transaction with the man into whose care Allah has entrusted her. It is this thread of devotion that links the lives of the three great ladies of Islam, the wife, daughter and granddaughter of the Blessed Prophet – Hazrat Khadijah, Hazrat Fatimah Zahrah, and Hazrat Zaynab. Their lives were very different, but all three dedicated themselves selflessly and with unquestioning devotion to the men who were their custodians.

Hazrat Khadijah recognised her husband's shining star and willingly gave him not only her constant support, in the face of much opposition, but also all her worldly wealth. When confronted by his opponents, she replied that her wealth came from Allah, how better could it be spent than in the service of the Prophet of Allah. She was the foremost business woman of her time, having employed the service of the Blessed Prophet before their marriage. Her modesty and the correct behaviour for which she was famed gives Muslim women a model of how they can transact correctly in the world of affairs.

Hazrat Fatimah Zahrah's short life was spent serving her father, husband and children quietly in the home. Her consideration for her husband was such that once when she was sick, and 'Ali asked her what he might bring her, her reply was nothing. When he pressed her for a reply, she said that the Blessed Prophet had told her not to request anything from her husband in case he could not provide it and would feel ashamed. Imam 'Ali continued to beg her for an answer, and finally she asked for a pomegranate.

Hazrat Zaynab is the example of a woman forced by events into outer action, at a time when there were no men to protect her. Amid darkness and danger, she stepped forth as a tigress to protect the life of her sick nephew, Imam 'Ali Zayn al-'Abidin, and the honour of her family. For Hazrat Zaynab, the strongest masculine influence in her life had been her brother, Imam Husayn. Her husband, knowing this, permitted her to accompany the Imam to Karbala, where she was to leave her mark on history.

All three were women of loyalty and passion; all three showed by their devotion and sacrifice that woman's greatest fulfilment comes from obedience and service to her man.

### A Letter of Shaykh al-Darqawi

Women should leave what does not concern them and perform what Allah has made obligatory for them. They only perform what supererogatory things they are able to do. Then they will be happy, Allah willing, and not wretched or burdened because they grind flour, sieve, plait, knead, season, bandage, untie, sweep, give water, gather firewood, spin, milk, go into labour, bear their children, and raise them. These are all great deeds and well-known striving. With these deeds, they only need the prayer, fasting, and what Allah has made obligatory, like *zakat* for the one who has the minimum of property subject to *zakat*, or the *Hajj* for the one who is able to make it.

. . . I am only reminding you about what I have mentioned concerning women so that you can inform them. Most of them do not consider this to be action. By Allah, it is among the greatest of actions. Allah wipes out evil deeds by it and elevates degrees. Tell them about it so that they can leap up to it, and so they will not resent it. It is very great with Allah. That is absolutely definite.

From *The Darqawi Way* (The letters of Shaykh Mawlay al-'Arabi ad-Darqawi)

# Raising Children

## By 'Allamah Baqir al-Majlisi, translated by Shaykh Abu 'Ali Fattaah from *Hilyat al-Muttaqin*

### Introduction

The Prophet Muhammad has indicated to us in a very clear manner that the *din* (life transaction) of Islam is entirely based on the knowledge of proper behaviour in any given situation. He said (may Allah bless him), 'The *din* is [the knowledge of] proper behaviour, entirely.'

It is this knowledge of the proper bounds and limitations, as well as acting upon this knowledge, that will bring us goodness in this world and the next. It is through the knowledge of proper behaviour that we are able to act in harmony, the natural tendency of each person being toward goodness. Each one of us knows what kindness and goodness is. Each one of us knows how we ourselves like to be treated; however, unfortunately, many of us act contrary to this innate knowledge in our dealings with others.

The Prophet Muhammad taught us that each human being is born in goodness, that is, that the natural state of humanity is goodness. Nobody is born in sin as some would have us believe. It is only at a later period in our lives that we are taught by our surroundings i.e. family, culture, and so forth, to behave in a manner contrary to our nature.

The Prophet said that each child is born in the natural state of submission (*Islam*), and it is the parents who introduce the child to various beliefs and dogmas going against this natural tendency. Muslims today, particularly in the West, may be generally unaware of proper behaviour in many living situations. This stems from the cultural environment in which they exist.

Much of the problem for the Muslim who is unaware of the proper behaviour stems from the cultural and family environment in which he was raised. In spite of the fact that many of us came from homes in which there was love and respect, there may have been little knowledge. In the traditions of the Prophet and the Imams of his household, we are told that action without true knowledge brings about more corruption than good.

The materialistic (*kafir*) society which surrounds us lacks this essential knowledge, so it is not passed down through the generations from father to son and mother to daughter. Behaviour is instead handled in a 'hit or miss' fashion, and is at best a mixture of proper and improper traditions and customs which have generally descended to the level of material considerations and survival techniques.

Those of us who have entered into the *din* as adults must be particularly careful in our actions, scrutinizing every act to ensure that it is in accordance with the limitations and laws established for all time in the Qur'an, and explained in the traditions of the Prophet. Allah has given us guidelines by which we must live in order to find success in this world and the next. He has informed us of our responsibilities as Muslims towards those who are closest to us, that is our families, as well as informing us of our responsibilities regarding our brother Muslims.

The Prophet said: 'Those closest to you (in relation) are more deserving of your love.' For this reason we must pay particular attention to the proper upbringing of our children. Being members of our families, they are the most deserving of our love and care. We must strive to instil in them behaviour and values which will bring them joy in this life as well as the next. Each one of us is held responsible for their proper education and upbringing.

Allah has instructed us in the Qur'an in the following manner regarding the behaviour of children:

> And Luqman said to his son while he admonished him: O my son! Do not associate anything with Allah; most surely association [of others with Him] is a great wrong.

> And We have enjoined man to respect his parents – his mother bears him with frailty upon frailty and his weaning takes two years – saying: Be grateful to Me and to both your parents; to Me is the eventual coming.

> And if they contend with you that you should associate with Me what you have no knowledge of, do not obey them. Keep company with them in this world kindly, and follow the way of he who turns to Me; then to Me is your return; then I will inform you of what you did.

> O my son! Surely if it is the very weight of the grain of a mustard seed, even though it is in [the heart of] a rock, or [high above] in the heaven or [deep down] in the earth, Allah will bring it [to light]; surely Allah is the Subtle, the Aware.

> O my son! Keep up prayer and enjoin the good and forbid the evil; and bear patiently what befalls you; surely these acts require courage.

> And do not turn your face away from people in contempt, nor go about in the land exulting overmuch; surely Allah does not love any self-conceited boaster.

> And pursue the right course in your going about and lower your voice. Surely the most loathsome of voices is the braying of the donkey. (31:13–19)

Stemming from these general instructions came more specific instructions which have been recorded in the Hadith literature attributed to the Prophet and the Imams of his household. Following is a translation from the book *Hilyat al-Muttaqin*, by 'Allamah Majlisi. The compiler of this book has gathered together many important traditions concerning the proper upbringing and care of children. The chapter quoted begins with the very early life of the child and continues through various stages of the child's growth and development.

## The Period of Nursing and its Adab

The maximum period a child may be nursed is two years. It is not permissible to nurse a child for more than two years unless there is a valid reason for doing so. A child should not be nursed for less than twenty-one months unless it be for reasons of the mother or child's health, or for other valid reasons which make it absolutely necessary to discontinue. For example, if the mother no longer has milk and the parents do not have the means to procure a wet nurse or a wet nurse is not available, then the period of nursing may be less than the prescribed twenty-one months.

A number of scholars consider it to be obligatory for a mother to nurse her child from her own breast immediately after the birth of the child. The first three days are very important for the proper functioning of the baby's digestive system. The scholars say that if she does not nurse her own child for that period, the child may very possibly not have the strength that it should have for growing properly. The Commander of the Faithful, 'Ali, peace be upon him, said: 'The best milk for a child is the milk from its own mother.' Imam Ja'far al-Sadiq saw a woman who was nursing her child and he said to her, 'O woman, do not favour one breast over the other when you are nursing (your child). Switch back and forth equally, so that the nutrition and the amount of water that the child takes in will be balanced. Do not nurse for less than twenty-one months. If you do so without a valid reason you will wrong the child.'

He says in another Hadith: 'Do not let a woman who rejects Islam nurse your child. However, a woman who is a Christian or a Jewess may do so. You should not allow them to take the child to their homes and nurse it. If they are going to nurse the child, then forbid them from drinking wine, eating pork, and all the other things *haram* (forbidden) in Islam which they consider to be *halal* (permitted).'

The Commander of the Faithful, 'Ali ibn Abi Talib, said: 'Allow only a woman whose outward and inward courtesy is proper to nurse your child, because the child will take on those qualities from her.'

## The Upbringing of the Child

Imam Ja'far al-Sadiq said: 'Let your child busy himself with play until he is seven years old. After that, educate him for seven years. If those seven years have been successful, then continue to educate him, but if you were unsuccessful, then there is no hope for him. If you have not taught him good manners by the time he is fourteen, then it will be very difficult to do.' In another Hadith, he says: 'You should allow him to play until he is seven years old. You should teach him to read and write in the next seven years. After that you should teach him the specifics of what is *halal* (permitted) and *haram* (forbidden) by Allah.' (This does not mean that you should not be teaching your children all of the time, but when they are fourteen you should go into a deep study of it.)

In a Hadith, 'Ali (peace be upon him) said: 'For the first seven years take care of your child and give him the proper training with regard to his physical situation (cleaning his body, etc.). Then for the next seven years teach him *adab* (proper courtesy). Then have him serve you until he is twenty-three years old. He will continue to develop his intellect (*'aql*) until he is thirty-five years old. After that he will be tested, tried, and receive more experience. Generally, one's intellect is in the process of development until one reaches thirty-five, and from then on one gains experience which adds to it.'

In another Hadith, it says: 'Boys who are six years old and older should not sleep under the same sheet in the same bed. Boys and girls who have reached the age of ten should not sleep in the same bed with each other.'

It is reported from the Messenger of Allah that the right of the child on his father is that the father give him a good name and teach him courtesy (*adab*). He should also teach his son a good way to earn his living.

In another Hadith, it is said that a person named Sukuni came to Imam Ja'far al-Sadiq, and said: 'I am very sad.' The Imam asked: 'Why are you sad?' He replied: 'Because Allah gave me a daughter.' The Imam replied: 'O Sukuni, the earth will carry her and her daily bread is from Allah. She will live without taking anything from your life, and she will not cause your daily sustenance to diminish.'

Then he asked: 'What name did you give her?' Sukuni replied: 'Fatimah.' Then the Imam exclaimed: 'Oh! Oh!' and he put his hands on his forehead. He said: 'The Messenger of Allah, may Allah bless him and his family, said that the right the child has upon his father, if it is a boy, is that the father has found and married a good mother for him (i.e., that the father has chosen a good woman as the son's mother before his birth), that he give him a good name, teach him the Qur'an, make sure that he is circumcised, and that he teach him to swim. If it is a daughter, he must find a good mother for her, give her a good name, teach her *Surat al-Nur* (The Light), not teach her *Surat Yusuf* as a child, not hand her over to any kind of situation which would cause affliction to her, and he should marry her to her husband at an early age.'

Then he said: 'Since you have named your child Fatimah, never say bad things about her nor curse her and do not strike her.'

It is related from the Commander of the Faithful, 'Ali ibn Abi Talib, that the Messenger of Allah, may Allah bless him and his family, said: 'Teach your children to swim and teach them to use the bow.'

Imam Musa said about the child who plays many pranks and is naughty during his childhood, that this is a sign that he will be knowledgeable and patient when he grows up.

It is also related from the Messenger of Allah that the mother and father will also bear the weight of the wrong action if the child is disobedient. He said that Allah will have mercy on the father and mother who encourage their children to goodness.

It is related from Imam Ja'far al-Sadiq that the Messenger of Al ah said that Allah will have mercy on the one who helps his children in goodness. The person who related this said: 'What do you mean by helping them?' The Prophet said: 'That you make things easy for them to do so that they can accomplish them, and accept from them insignificant things that they have done for you as goodness, letting them know that you see it as goodness. Do not give children tasks that will be too difficult for them to do lest they leave them and become discouraged. Do not behave cruelly or abruptly with them.'

In another Hadith, it is said that a person came to Imam Ja'far al-Sadiq and said: 'To whom shall I show goodness?' The Imam replied: 'To your father and your mother.' The man said: 'They have died.' Then the Imam said: 'To your children, be merciful and kind with them, and if you make a promise to them be loyal to your promise, because they think that you are the one who gives them their daily bread, so they trust you.'

Imam Musa said: 'Allah does not become angry with anyone in the same way as He gets angry with the one who wrongs women and children.'

In another Hadith the Messenger of Allah, may Allah bless him and his family, said: 'Kiss your children and Allah will write for you a good action for each time that you have done so. The one who makes his children happy will be made happy by Allah on the Day of Resurrection.'

In another Hadith, it is said that somebody came to the Prophet, and said: 'I have never kissed any of my children.' When that man went away, the Prophet said: 'This person, as far as I am concerned, is a person of the Fire.'

In another Hadith, he said that anyone who has children should play with them like a child plays.

Imam Ja'far al-Sadiq said: 'Allah will be merciful to His slave according to the amount that he loves his children.'

In a Hadith, it is related that the Messenger of Allah saw a person who had two children. With one child he was never affectionate and he never kissed him. The other one was his favourite and he kissed and constantly showed him affection. The Prophet asked: 'Why do you not treat both of them with the

same kindness? Know that it is better not to show any
favouritism towards one child over another unless one is more
of a scholar or more keen in learning. Then favouritism will
encourage the eagerness for knowledge.'

The Prophet also said: 'Every parent who teaches his children
the Qur'an will be called before Allah on the Day of Resurrection
adorned in a garment of light, and that garment will light up the
faces of the people of Paradise.'

In a Hadith, related by Imam Ja'far al-Sadiq, it is said that
when a child is three years old one should say to him seven
times: *La ilaha illa'llah* – there is no God but Allah. When the
child becomes three years, seven months and twenty days, then
say to him seven times: *Muhammadun Rasulu'llah* –
Muhammad is the Messenger of Allah. When the child has
reached four years exactly, you should say to him seven times:
*Allahumma salli 'ala Muhammadin wa ali Muhammad* – O Allah,
bless Muhammad and the family of Muhammad. When he is
five years old, you should make sure that he knows how to
make a *sajdah* (prostration) properly. When he is six years old,
you should teach him how to make *salat* (prayer) and encourage
him to make it. Then, when he is seven years old, you should
show him how to make *wudu'* (ablution) properly. (This does
not mean that you cannot teach him these things earlier if he
shows an interest in or an inclination towards them.) Command
him to make *salat* when he has reached nine years of age, and
make sure that he knows how to perform *wudu'* and *salat*
correctly. Strike him if he refuses to perform them. When he has
learned how to perform *salat*, Allah will forgive his mother and
father.

It is reported from the Commander of the Faithful, 'Ali, that
he forbade that a weapon of war be worn by children or that
they be allowed to handle them.

In another Hadith, it says to make sure that you wash any
grease or dirt off your children's hands and faces at night before
they sleep, because Satan will come and smell them while they
are sleeping and he will frighten them in their sleep. The angels
who write good actions will be annoyed by it.

The Messenger of Allah said: 'Everyone who goes to the marketplace and buys a gift and brings it home to his family, is like one who has given charity to a group of destitute and poor people. The first ones he should give gifts to are his daughters, for indeed, everyone who makes his daughters happy is like one who has freed one of the children of Isma'il from slavery. The one who makes the eyes of his son bright and makes him happy is like the one who has wept through fear of Allah. Allah will cause everyone who weeps from fear of Allah to enter Paradise.'

Imam Ja'far al-Sadiq advised parents to give their children the types of food that cause the flesh in their bodies to grow and their bones to be strong. In another Hadith it is related: 'Have them eat pomegranates and it will help them reach the potential of their youth and strength.'

In the book called *Tibb al-A'immah* (The Medicine of the Imams), it is related from the Commander of the Faithful 'Ali, who said: 'If a child cries incessantly or if a woman is fearful or if someone suffers from the affliction of insomnia, then let them read the *ayah* from *Surat al-Kahf* (The Cave) which says:

> *And so We prevented them from hearing in the cave for a number of years, then We raised them up that We might know which of the two parties was able to compute the time for which they remained.* (18:11–12)

It is also related that a daughter or a girl of six years should not be allowed to be kissed by a man who is not *mahram* to her, i.e., one who is not a member of her family and to whom she would be eligible to be married. Also she should not be allowed to sit on his lap.

In another Hadith, it is related that a girl who has reached six years of age should not be kissed by boys, and a boy who has reached seven years of age should not be kissed by a woman.

In a Hadith which is considered to be trustworthy it says: 'Cursed is the one who neglects his family and does not spend anything on them.'

Imam Musa said: 'The family members of a man are like his prisoners. The person who has been given grace and blessings from Allah, and does not share it and give of it generously with those who are his prisoners, will have those blessings and grace withdrawn from him.'

Imam Ja'far al-Sadiq said: 'Anyone who spends on two daughters or two sisters or two aunts or two women servants or takes care of them financially will be saved by Allah from the Fire.'

The Messenger of Allah, may Allah bless him and his family, says that there are degrees in the Garden which no one will attain except three kinds of people. One is the just Imam, another is the person who is good to his relatives, and the third is the person who has a family, spends on his family, and is patient with the annoying things they do.

From Imam Ja'far al-Sadiq, upon him be peace, it is related that there are five people on whom spending is obligatory: your children, father, mother, wife, and servant. Amongst your children are included your children's children as far as they go. Father and mother include your grandparents and their parents as far back as they are alive.

# Advice to a Son

## Translated by Hajj Abbas Mubarak from *Mirat al-Rashad* by Shaykh 'Abdullah al-Mamaqani.

### Enjoining Obedience to Allah, the Glorified; Warning of Disobedience and Indolence; Spending Life Uselessly and Other Instructions

Know, my son, may Allah grant you the success of obedience to Him and may He preserve you from disobedience to Him, that Allah, the Glorious, loves all of His creation boundlessly. Such is the relationship of every craftsman towards that which he has made. He is the Mighty and the Majestic; establishing the obligatory, the recommended, the proper behaviour, the forbidden and the *makruh* (detestable). He only did this to bring about that which is of benefit to the slaves (mankind) and to keep them safe from that which is harmful. The disobedience of the disobedient does not harm Him, nor does the obedience of the obedient benefit Him.

He did well who said: 'If the entire creation turned against Him in denial they would be but a speck of dust on His hem.'

He, the Exalted, is absolutely without need and His only intention when He established the laws was to improve the state of the slaves (mankind), enjoining them to what is beneficial while safeguarding them from harm in this life and the next. Since this is the situation, it would be foolish to depart from obedience to His commands and prohibitions – even though the requirements of thankfulness to the One Who Bestows and the One Who is the Master is contrary to intellectual independence. It would be leaving that which would bring benefit to the self while inviting harm upon it.

My son, I warn you of disobedience. It attracts to you disappointment in this world and punishment in the next. Do you not see that by one mistake our grandfather, Adam, upon him be peace, was expelled from the garden.

I warn you, my son, about indolence and idleness and what is introduced by them. It has been said: When Satan and the commanding self are unable to make the ugly actions seem attractive or the good actions seem unattractive, they turn towards actions which lead to indolence and idleness by drawing the mind towards excess of what is considered necessary regarding eating, drinking, sleeping, comfort, collecting wealth, spending time in beholding what is beautiful, relaxing, mixing with people, discussing and other things such as that. Satan and the self (*nafs*) make each of these so attractive to the slave that he pursues them, and from them there comes to him laziness, indolence and the wasting of precious time.

Beware, my son, of expending yourself in what is not proper in this life nor of benefit to you in the next. For every moment of your life is a precious jewel, indeed more precious. The means of attaining the jewel is through earning and toiling, unlike the attainment of age. When the appointed time of death comes, it will not be delayed. Beware, my son, of wasting or losing this jewel. Seize your youth before your old age, your health before your infirmity, your strength before your weakness, your wealth before your poverty, your leisure before your preoccupation, your life before your death.

Embark upon your youth before you become senile
And the health of your body before it becomes ill.
Not everyone who has lived [in this life] will be safe in the next.
Offer [your best actions], for everyone will arrive
At that which he has sent ahead.

It is related that the people of the Garden do not regret anything of their life in the world except the time during which they did not remember Allah. There is no self whether pious or shameless who on the Day of Reckoning does not blame itself. If it has done righteous deeds, it says: 'Would that I had done more so that I could have attained a higher station than what I have.' If it has done evil, it says: 'Woe unto me! Would that I had not acted so that I would not be punished.' The Prophet, peace be upon him, said to Abu Dharr: 'Be greedier with your life than you are with your money.'

It is related that the best of the obediences is being mindful of time. He who wastes the days of his sowing will regret the days of his reaping.

I warn you, my son, do not waste your life in anything that is not going to be of benefit to you after death. It is related that the man of intellect is he who works in his day for his tomorrow before the affair leaves his grasp. The shrewd one is he who subjugates himself and works for what is after death. The foolish one is he who follows his whims and wishfully thinks of Allah's forgiveness.

The person who has spent his life in what will not be of benefit to him in the hereafter is like someone who has left valuable jewels strewn upon the face of the earth. He is occupied in picking up [worthless] stones and digging up [useless] pottery, suffering hardship only so that children may play with them.

So, my son, the light of my eye, the delight of my heart, know the value of your life and do not absorb it in what will not save you. Do not be like the silkworm, working hard to destroy itself.

Then I advise you, my son, may Allah grant you success in performing every good deed and keep you from every ill deed, to acquire noble character and the praiseworthy attributes which are the following:

### Safeguarding the Tongue

Hold your tongue from that which does not concern you because most of the mistakes of the children of Adam are from this tongue. There is no organ that has so many sins as the tongue.

Silence is one of the doors to wisdom. Guard your tongue so that you may be led to the Garden. It is related that goodness is written for the believing slave as long as he remains silent and that whoever wants safety in the two abodes should safeguard his tongue. Does man topple over on his nose in the fire except by the reaping of his tongue? When Allah wishes goodness for a slave, he helps him to safeguard his tongue and makes him occupied with his faults, instead of the faults of others. He who decreases his speech perfects his intellect and clears his heart. The faith of a slave does not become sound until his heart becomes sound and, in turn, his heart does not become sound until his tongue becomes sound. This is because the tongue of the believer is behind his heart. If the believer wishes to speak, he considers what he is going to say. If it is good, he manifests it and if it is evil, he hides it. But the hypocrite's heart is not behind his tongue. He says whatever comes upon his tongue and does not care whether what he says is for him or against him.

Surely, silence will not cause you regret, while many a speech will cause you regret in this world and the next. A man is hidden beneath his tongue. So my son, weigh your speech before you utter it and subject it to the scrutiny of your intellect and knowledge. If it is for Allah and in Allah, then say it; otherwise, do not reply, be silent, be mute. He excelled who said: 'A tongue that speaks quickly is given to the winds. As long as a man has not spoken, his faults lie hidden.'

It is related that there is no organ of the body that does not address the tongue saying: 'I beseech you by Allah, do not cause me to be thrown into chastisement.' It is said that if we look at the nature of speech and silence we would say: 'If your speech is of silver, O self, then your silence is of gold.'

In specific situations, however, it could be that speech is as gold and silence as dust, such as when speaking about *fiqh* (Islamic law) and enjoining others to the lawful courtesies and the attributes of a pleasing character. In fact, silence could well be a deadly poison, such as remaining silent from enjoining good deeds, prohibiting the forbidden and guiding those who seek guidance. May Allah give you success in attaining whatever pleases Him and may He make your future state better than your past.

## Taking Account of Oneself

Take account of the self every night. It is up to you, my son, may Allah provide you with good in the two abodes, to take account of yourself before you are asked to account. In the same way as the merchant takes account with his helper in order to know what he has done during the day, you should call yourself to account every night before you sleep in order to know what you have embarked upon during that day. If you see in yourself shortcomings because you have committed a wrong action or been disobedient to Allah, ask His forgiveness and return to Him, imploring Him to wipe it from you. Correct that which has passed by, fulfilling it and asking forgiveness. If you see in yourself lassitude, laziness, distraction and the wasting of capital, discipline yourself with the whip of sincere advice and exhortation. Impress upon yourself the way of obedience, then watch it like a merchant so that its moments are not wasted in distraction or that its life is not sold for too small a price or for a loss. If you see from yourself good conduct and proper taste in the spending of time, thank Allah for that, and ask Him to increase the soul in success and guidance. It is related from them [the Imams], upon whom be peace: 'He is not amongst our people who does not call himself to account every day. If he has done what is wrong, he asks for forgiveness and turns in repentance to Allah.'

It is transmitted by some of the people of knowledge that there was a man of knowledge who would keep a pencil and piece of paper near him, and would write everything that he had said and done from the beginning of the day until the time of his sleep at night. Then he would look at it and thank Allah for any of the good things and for his success with himself. As for those things which were shameful, he would ask Allah's forgiveness.

From the tablets of Abraham, upon him be peace, there is written: 'The man of intellect has four different times within his day, unless his intellect is overcome: a time in which he calls upon his Lord; a time in which he takes account of himself; a time in which he reflects upon what Allah has made for him; and a time in which he takes what is permissible for himself. In this period he takes help for the other times and in it there is an ease for the heart.

## Observing the Self

It is upon you, my son, to notice the presence of your Lord and His awareness of you in all of your states, movements, actions, speeches, breaths, thoughts, steps and moments. So prefer that which the Lord Almighty has preferred and choose what he has chosen. The Prophet Luqman, upon him be peace, said to his son: 'If you were to be watchful of Allah, the Exalted, you would not have the audacity to commit any sin. Simply noticing that He sees you and is aware of you would prevent you from opposing Him.'

## Reflection

I enjoin you, my son, to practise reflection, for it is one of the most important methods of awakening the self and purifying the heart. It has a great capacity to lift away turbidity, break desires, cause the withdrawal from the abode of arrogance and turn one's attention to the abode of eternity and delight. It is at the highest of the acts of worship and at the core of obedience – rather, its spirit. It has been said that the most virtuous act of worship is contemplation or reflection upon Allah, the Exalted, and upon His Power.

Reflection is the means by which the slave is conveyed to Allah. Acts of worship connect the slave to Allah's reward, the Glorious and Mighty, but that which joins to the Exalted Himself is better than that which joins to His reward. Reflection is an act of the heart while *'ibadah* (worship) is an act of the limbs. The heart is the noblest of the various limbs, therefore, an act which it performs is necessarily nobler than the acts of the other limbs or faculties. It has been related that the reflection of an hour is better than the worship of a year, sixty years or seventy

years, according to the different traditions, implying different
degrees of reflection.

Often reflection is what can save man from the Fire, and Hurr
ibn Yazid al-Riyahi [a commander of Ibn Ziyad's army against
Imam Husayn at Karbala who deserted and joined the side of
Imam Husayn] was saved by means of reflection of an hour.
Even if he had performed acts of worship for a year or years, it
would not have been of benefit to him because of what he had
embarked upon. But the reflection of an hour benefitted him
and saved him. Thus, an hour's reflection is made better than
the worship of seventy years. It has been related that no
worship is greater than prayer and fasting except reflection
upon Allah.

First, my son, reflect at times upon the situation of those of
the past. From where did they come and to where did they go?
What did they take with them, what did they leave behind and
with what did they busy themselves. Reflect on how he who
would not touch the dust with his foot, would sleep upon silk
brocade and walk upon the earth insolently was separated from
his wealth, family, offspring, palaces, homes, servants and
retinue. How he took up the shroud and put his delicate cheek
upon the dust; how he became companion to the maggots and
vipers and dwelt in the dark grave alone.

Secondly, at other times, reflect that when death comes it
comes suddenly. Death has its time, and when it comes no one
puts it off by a minute. Be on guard against it at every instant!
Prepare yourself for it before the affair of this world is out of
your hands. Do not take lightly nor be distracted from the
preparation for it through repentence and [corrective] actions.
How many amongst mankind were suddenly overtaken by
death, having no respite in which to remember Allah, the
Glorified, and ask forgiveness: Be on guard against being like
them and becoming one of the people of grief and regret who
having postponed turning to Allah and delegating [their affairs
to Him], say 'My Lord, send me back in order that I may correct
that which I have neglected.'

Thirdly, reflect upon this world, that it is nothing but an
abode of hardship, discomfort, toil, suffering and strain, and

that its purity is mixed with turbidity, its comfort is joined to hardship, and that Allah did not create ease within it, as the Exalted said in a sacred Hadith (*hadith qudsi*): 'My slaves ask Me for something I did not create which is ease in this world. And they fail to ask for that which I created which is eternal happiness.' Surely you, my son, when you reflect upon this, what you endure of misfortune becomes insignificant to you and you prefer the action leading to the next life and notice that if there is no way out of toil and difficulty in this world, enduring hardship for unending ease is more deserving of your efforts and easier.

Fourthly, reflect upon what you will soon meet of the world's after death: of the grave, the interspace, the gathering, the resurrection, the dispatching of the books, the materialising of actions, the declaration of faith, the reckoning, the straight path, the balance, what Allah has prepared for those who are in *taqwa* (fearful awareness) and those who are guilty, of the Garden and its many provisions and the Fire and its divisions of punishments.

Fifthly, reflect that what you own is of no benefit unless it is presented totally in the way of Allah, the Exalted; that you own nothing but the length of your shroud; that your offspring, your dependents, your children, your beloveds, your relatives will be of no use to you except to lay you on your side in your grave to surrender you to your actions; and that what is of benefit to you is only your striving for the face of Allah, the Glorified. It accompanies you and does not separate from you. Surely, if you reflect upon the points mentioned you will increase your good actions and the sincerity in them. You will be saved from destruction and you will prepare for your tomorrow before the affair is out of your hands. It has been related that the most praiseworthy renunciation of the world is the mentioning of death, and that the most praiseworthy reflection is the reflection upon death.

Whoever is distracted from the remembrance of death spends his life in what does not concern him, while he who clings to the remembrance of death spends his life in what is of benefit to him. Surely it is the best of admonishers, the quickest of restrainers and sufficient in goodness. It makes constriction and difficulty seem easy. It ensures that the wealthy man will be generous with his wealth in order to reap the rewards of the hereafter. The slave is held back from busying himself with what is of no benefit to him. Certainly he has excelled who said: 'It will ease tragedies and will make you desire that which is of benefit to you on the Day of Reckoning; it will make you cling to repentence before death; it will cause you to correct your way before it is too late, cutting off hopes, depriving you of the pleasures of maybe and perhaps.'

## Patience

Of the kinds of patience there are: steadfastness while upon trial, thankfulness for favour and contentment with the decree.

My son, I enjoin you to practise patience; it is one of the most important methods of obtaining relief. Surely, by it the worshippers are awarded the highest degree in the two abodes. He who examines the state of those who have gone before would realize this.

Wear the robe of patience upon the vicissitudes of time. You will obtain from the goodness of patience the best of outcomes.

My son, be as good-natured when there are shocks and tribulations as when there is ease. Make whatever Allah chooses for you of health and sickness, well-being and afflictions, youth and old age, strength and weakness, wealth and poverty, and the like thereof, loved by you, because it is what the All-Wise has chosen for you. He knows all of the outcomes, He loves you and is kinder to you than your parents and self. He is the source of goodness for you.

My son, guard yourself against despondency that arises over disasters and adversities and the fear that arises from them. Be content with what the Wise, Compassionate brings forth. Leave the complaint and bad opinion of what befalls you. It has been transmitted that the Master of Prostration (Ali ibn al-Husayn), upon him be peace, said in one of his poems:

When you are tried by a slip, endure it.

The Most Generous is patient, so to endure what you have done
   is more resolute.
Do not complain to created beings for you would only be
   complaining of the Merciful to the merciless.

My son, make yourself as agreeable in times of distress as you
make yourself agreeable in times of ease, in poverty as in
wealth, in times of misfortune as in times of well-being and so
on. About this the Imams, upon whom be peace, have said:
'Patience is enduring the distaste of trial and hardship. More
praiseworthy than that is to be steadfast in obedience to Allah,
the Glorified. More praiseworthy still, is to preserve oneself in
abstention from what Allah the Exalted has forbidden.'

It has been narrated from the Prophet (peace be upon him)
that he said: 'Whoever endures a misfortune with patience until
he regains the goodness of ease, Allah writes for him three
hundred degrees. What is between each degree is as that which
is between the heaven and the earth. Whoever is steadfast in
obedience, Allah writes for him six hundred degrees. What is
between each degree is what is between the outer boundaries of
the earth and the Throne. And whoever perseveres in his
abstention from disobedience, Allah writes for him nine
hundred degrees. What is between each degree is as what is
between the outer boundaries of the earth and the outermost
limits of the Throne.'

# SECTION 3

## Health

*There comes forth from within it [the bee] a beverage of many colours, in which there is healing for men; most surely there is a sign in this for people who reflect.* (16:69)

*Therefore eat the lawful and good things which Allah has provided for you, and render thanks to Allah for His blessings if it is [truly] Him that you worship.* (16:114)

*And He made the balance, so that you might never transgress the measure.* (55:7–8)

———— ★ ————

*Hadith*: 'For every illness there is a remedy.'

# A Discourse on Health

## By Shaykh Fadhlalla Haeri

Man always seeks his own well-being. From the moment he is conscious of his existence he strives towards this end, attempting to improve his condition along a path of many diverse actions and circumstances. However, in order to attain ultimate well-being man must recognize that all these diverse occurrences must converge upon one state – a state of positive neutral consciousness.

In the same way as there is a direction in time moving from moment to moment, along a seemingly certain pattern, so there is a direction in the pursuit of this state of neutrality. Man's direction in the pursuit of health generally begins outwardly and moves inwardly. There is a parallel improvement in either condition. The less concern one has with outer physical health, the more one is free to attend to inner spiritual health; and that can only be achieved if one is fit and healthy.

We want to be free. Freedom, in fact, is another definition of this state of positive neutrality. Material freedom is sought by man so that he may survive and exist as a biological entity that has a prevailing influence over everything else. It is necessary for him to have outer well-being, but that alone is not sufficient in his quest for neutrality, because he is seeking something that is beyond his own horizon. How can he look at that horizon, let alone beyond it, if he is too preoccupied with his own immediate situation.

We are able to recognise the constant shifting from one extreme to another, from illness to wellness, yet we know there is a foundation of neutrality beyond this duality. In fact, the more we are in a state of stable neutrality, the more we see the extreme ends of the scale of duality. It is for this reason that the more the man of *tawhid* (divine unity) gains materially, the more he recognises the necessity to debase himself in order to maintain a healthy balance. The man of wisdom also recognises that the more he has genuinely debased himself, the more he will rise. This is the ecological reality.

Searching for longevity is a proof of the echo of everlasting-ness within man. But often this is misinterpreted and translated into a desire for perpetual youth. There is a contradiction in man's aspirations; he wants to have complete neutrality, yet he knows that every moment is based on turmoil, for time arises out of dynamic movement and flux. It is through the light of his own consciousness that he may recognise the folly of this desire.

The man of wisdom recognises that the solid foundation within him is beyond turmoil, because it is based on timeless-ness, on a cause that is unchanging. Our fixation with the outside is an indication that we are seeking the changeless, but this search lies in the wrong direction for the outside will always change. Our desire for perpetual life is a proof that we contain in us the essence of immortality. This desire, however, is per-verted because it is impossible to preserve our bodies forever. Whether we like it or not, they exist in dynamic flux along the direction of time, from the womb to the tomb.

We have no choice but to seek health, and we should know that the purpose of outer health is to produce inner health, which cannot be maintained unless the immediate environment is in ecological balance with it. We would then realise that our immediate environment is not separate from the outer environ-ment around us, from the overall environment, from the whole earth and from the whole universe. Hence we must recognise a universal health. If we start from the microcosmic health, we end up with the macrocosmic health. Therefore, if we want to be healthy we must want to heal those around us. Balanced outer health will eventually lead to inner health. For the inner self, conviction is its health, vigilance its wakefulness, indifference its slumber; self-knowledge is its life, and self-ignorance its death. If we feed and nourish the self-knowledge, which is already ingrained in each individual, ignorance will vanish. The result will be complete harmony between the outer and the inner.

We find throughout history that a high degree of respect was always shown both to men of inner and outer knowledge. They were often combined in the same men, for those of inner knowledge were also endowed with much outer knowledge, including the knowledge of outer health. They were men who could nourish people's hearts and reassure them that this transitory existence is only an aspect of the endless existence of Reality, that there is One Cause behind all of these effects – Allah, from Whom everything emanates, by Whose Grace everything is supported, and to Whom everything will eventually be returned. This knowledge is connected with the state of equilibrium and neutrality which was mentioned earlier.

Islamic medicine takes you into that state of neutrality. It is all based on the Qur'an, on that which is real and permanent, because we are all seeking permanency. Islamic medicine is the medicine that is going to cure us. The man of submission recognises that this world is a laboratory into which we have come in order to learn the meaning of purity. It is another stage of growth within us. First there is growth in the womb of which we are unconscious, then there is growth outside the womb of which we are conscious. What we are conscious of is the problem; we may, for example, be conscious of nothing other than confusion. We cannot be separate from our cause. The effect has come from that cause. The cause permeates all and is closer to us than our jugular vein.

The seeker of reality views this world as a hospital in which he is a patient. Whether we like it or not, we are here to achieve ultimate well-being, which is to drown in the well of Oneness so that we see nothing other than the One Cause behind what appears to be confusion. The real hakims were seekers of

Reality. They believed that life is from the Most Beneficent, the Most Glorious Creator, and that if we say there is nothing other than His generosity and His all-encompassing mercy, then we take wisdom wherever it comes so long as it is recognisable along the path of *shari'ah*. They therefore collected outer knowledge from many lands – from Egypt, Greece, Rome, India, China – and unified it to obtain the best prescriptions.

These great men of Islamic medicine had the strongest spiritual motivation for their work – they themselves wanted to be cured. They were striving for that state of equilibrium and they recognised that the only way they could reach their goal was by abandoning the so-called 'self' in the path of service. Their work was for them a vocation and an aspect of worship, rather than a profession. They wanted health for themselves, so they also wanted it for others. They were the instruments of the divine justice and love of the Creator, for by bringing people into outer health they enabled their patients to recognise that there is nothing higher than the Health-Giver.

The hearts of these practitioners were motivated by generosity and by the joy of serving others. They were not archivists who wanted to collect what everybody said and categorise it for the sole purpose of creating books. Their books served either to gather the information they themselves needed for their work, or else to disseminate the knowledge to their students. Their knowledge and information was an integrated part of their life, unlike we today who talk about Islamic Studies yet do not live the teachings of Islam. We merely pretend to be the followers of the blessed Prophet, who prayed that Allah give him usable knowledge. Islam is about practicality. Islam is about living fully and joyfully here and now, while retaining that recognition that this existence is temporary and there is a next experience that is beyond time.

If we start from the premise that we, in this world, are moving along a unified direction towards a state of positive equilibrium, we can only be horrified by the current state of medical practice. We find that over the last few decades our doctors have moved more into the area of suppressing symptoms rather than treating the cause of our maladies. The use of 'wonder drugs' minimises the human contact between doctor and patient, reducing the former's role to little more than a dispenser. The arrogance of our medical profession has led to a false emphasis on outer appearance. Everything looks beautiful – the teeth gleam, the hair shines, but if we touch them they fall to pieces because they are not real.

The reason for this movement towards suppression of the symptoms rather than treating the cause is that modern men of medicine do not see the ecological inter-connectedness of everything. This is why they fragment medicine into small individual disciplines. Furthermore, once the profit motive enters medicine it ceases to heal, for the patient's overall cure can only come from those who recognise that they want to be cured themselves. The doctor must recognise that inherently he is sick and that his own and others' ultimate objective must be the knowledge and recognition of the one and only Reality.

At all times man is at a loss. His lower tendencies are always there, dragging him down towards the animalistic levels within him, but he also knows that he contains a higher, divine consciousness which he wishes to reach. The way to that higher self is through the path of service. In the service of others he himself is spontaneously elevated; he moves into the realm of abandonment, into that positive neutrality. He recognises experientially that the more he gives, the more will come to him. The more he is generous, the more the one and only generous Creator will shower him with blessings.

Allah in His Mercy wants to unify what is in us with what is outside us. If we say we believe in Allah, then Allah will afflict us to allow us to witness ourselves, to see whether we truly mean what we say and do what we say we will do. If a person claims to be adhering to the basic tenets of Islamic healing, he must himself profess the abandonment of Islam. If he is in that abandonment he will have total trust in Allah. If he is worried or unhappy, that is his own doing, for at that moment of concern, worry or unhappiness, he is not in a state of full abandonment.

The great hakims would often find the medicine close to where the illness lay. They believed that where there is the action there is also the reaction. There is always a solution close to every problem. These hakims went to the source of the problem, transforming it, rather than treating its outer effect as happens more and more in our system of medicine today. Islamic Medicine is far more difficult to practise. It takes inspiration, perspiration and abandonment to reach the root of the problem and unify the cause with the effect.

Through the publication of *Health Sciences in Early Islam*, Noor Health Foundation hopes to increase the breadth of the platform from which it will serve. It is a platform based on the belief that no one in this creation is separate from the cause of their existence – every effect is a manifestation of its cause. We are all from the one and only Cause. We are all created by one Creator. We are all sustained by His mercy through diverse ways. The more we can share together on that platform, under the umbrella of true submission and following in the footsteps of the blessed Prophet, the more we will have a safer and healthier path through this life. Those of us who are endowed with better health and more time and energy will be given more and more of these delights, provided we adhere to the path of abandonment and service.

We hope that this book will help lead to the practical revitalisation of our heritage. This will only happen if we claim the knowledge of our forefathers in the correct way. If we inherit something whose value we do not fully comprehend, we will end up only talking about it and relegating it to museums. This has hitherto been the fate of the Islamic sciences, which is a contradiction of the spirit in which they first evolved. They were part of a unified approach to knowledge, derived from the inspirations of men of abandonment. They did not come about in the usual, acquisitive, categorising manner. There is nothing wrong in categorisation provided it is used as an instrument through which a desired objective may be achieved. Nowadays, however, the business of writing and researching has become an end in itself. This is why we find such a big difference between the academic arena and the field of action.

This book supports the ultimate goal of man, which is to live a life of spirituality, a life which is in every sense healthy. With this book, Noor Health Foundation hopes to create interest in a unified approach to the healing arts, and to move hearts to recognise the bad situation into which we have inadvertently fallen by ignorantly renouncing the path of those who knew, the path of the seekers of Reality who went before us.

May Allah bless all those who will benefit from our attempts. May Allah purify our intentions and those of our publishers, who have worked with us. May Allah increase the strength of all of those who will be involved in this endeavour along the one and only path of safe conduct. May Allah show them that the knowledge of the way lies from within and that its boundaries are the most glorious. May Allah give us the protection so that we become aware of the one and only Reality behind everything.

# Medical Practice and Institutions in Islam

## By Sami K. Hamarneh

In Islam, highly educated and social-minded physicians faced the challenge of promoting and upholding the ethical commitments and high objectives of their calling. Most of them made good use of available educational opportunities. They enriched their lives with the best possible theoretical and practical training in the various fields of the healing arts, in being exposed to ancient medical writings and commendable methods of clinical and theoretical tutoring and training. Their masters wrote and compiled important manuals, formularies, and treatises which modified and incorporated much of the Greek, Indian and Syriac legacies with valuable additions. Translations, as well as authored medical works, were extensively read, copied and circulated among students, trainees, and practitioners in order to meet and successfully pass rigid requirements and examinations to be licensed to practise the profession legally and with official approval. These regulations and endeavours soon found a counterpart in the West, challenging physicians and generally promoting the healing arts.

Muslim caliphs and rulers inaugurated a forceful and adequate system, supported by public good will, to safeguard and promote better health and social order, safety and security for all citizens. The *hisbah* system, as it is known in Arabic, originated in the early days of Islam and developed into an active bureau to ensure public safety and to guard against fraud in trade, market commodities, weights and measures, and incompetence in professional performance. Thus all practitioners of the healing arts were subject to the supervision and inspection by *al-Muhtasib* and his aides, especially in larger cities such as Baghdad, Cairo and Cordoba.

Although witches were brutally persecuted in the West, charlatans grew in numbers and witchcraft continued to plague the Western social system. In Islam, quack doctors suffered no physical persecution, and made great monetary gains. They deceived the public by propagating their nostrums and 'cure all' remedies. Of these, some were simple preparations or infusions and decoctions of medicinal herbs to which coloured waters or syrups were added. Others were secretly compounded medications prepared in almost the same manner as that in which 'patent medicines' were developed and penetrated drug therapy in Europe and America during the seventeenth and eighteenth centuries.

As early as the third/ninth century, medical and literary critics were vocal in their attacks on medical charlatans and warned the public against their fraud and deception. Also many leading physicians including Yuhanna b. Masawayh (third/ninth century). Ibn Abi al-Ash'ath (fourth/tenth century), Ibn Butlan (fifth/eleventh century) and al-Baghdadi (sixth/twelfth century) exposed the impostures and treachery of these quacks and warned the public against their trickery.

Muslim physicians of the third/ninth and fourth/tenth centuries advanced and enriched medical knowledge in ophthalmology beyond their Greek predecessors, both in personal observations and in experimentations, including surgical operations on the eye. Arabic ophthalmology, as a result reached its highest achievement within the two following centuries. The caliber was so high that Western physicians – after Arabic texts were translated into Latin – admired this transmitted new knowledge and made good use of it in a way that was not surpassed up to the Renaissance. Nevertheless, as was the case in medicine, many charlatan occulists appeared in Islam. They peddled cures and coloured eye lotions at high prices, especially in small towns and out in the countryside. Hunayn, in his ten treatises on the eye, called them highway quack occulists (*attiba' kahhalu al-turuqat*).

In addition to ophthalmology, two other branches of the healing arts, pharmacy and pharmacology, also advanced greatly in Islam, and exerted a profound influence on the West in these same fields. In regard to pharmacy, as was the case in Europe in the pre- and post-Renaissance periods, there were in Islam three classes of apothecaries. The first was the professional educated and social-minded pharmacist, whom al-Biruni (364–443/973–1051) called *al-saydalani* (the pharmacist), *al-natasi* (the well informed and skilled). He called pharmacy *saydalah* and preferably *saydanah*, as it is derived from the use of sandalwood known as *chandan* or *jandan* in Sanskrit from where it was introduced in the Arabic pharmacopeia. By the beginning of the third/ninth century, this class of professionals in the 'Abbasid capital, its suburbs and military camps nearby and in other larger cities, were instrumental in establishing, on a sound foundation, the profession of pharmacy (*saydanah*) as a separate entity from medicine. These pharmacists ran their privately owned drugstores and dispensed and sold drugs over the counter, or as ordered in written prescriptions (*wasfat*) by licensed physicians. They also served as chief pharmacists of dispensaries in large hospitals where they manufactured and dispensed medications to patients admitted to the hospital as well as to those who visited out-patient clinics. Thus, it was under the patronage of Muslim caliphs, and through their encouragement, that pharmacy as a profession arose, and its art, technique, dosage-form preparations, and literature developed and flourished to influence the worldwide maturing of professional pharmacy.

The second, and possibly the most prevalent of them was the class of regular apothecaries (*al-'attarin*). They usually had a fairly good knowledge of popular *materia medica* simples and the preparing of common medications in the form of syrups, electuaries, ointments, etc., but no formal education in the art. Their know-how was mainly derived from apprenticeships and daily practice at the drugstores or manufacturing firms. This class of apothecaries was known before the triumph of Islam, continued throughout the Middle Eastern countries, and up to modern times. In many commercial centres – such as Baghdad, Damascus, Cairo and Tunis – they would gather in one street which was often named *suq al-'attarin* after them. They sold all kinds of spices and perfumes as well as medicinal herbs. Among these apothecaries there were many who, like Masawayh and Hunayn's father, Ishaq al-'Ibadi, provided opportunities for their children to acquire a good education in the healing arts. Among them also was a specialised group consisting of the sellers of syrups (*sharabiyyin*) and aromated waters who occasionally were manufacturers of perfumes.

The third class consists of the drug peddlers and collectors of medicinal herbs and minerals who traded with these simples as a lucrative commodity of commerce. The attractive prices they were able to get for genuine precious drugs led many among them to adulterate valuable *materia medica* with inexpensive simples for greater profit. They never realised what a burden they added to diligent and honest pharmacists and physicians who sought the best and finest of drugs not only for the benefit of their clients, but also to protect their own reputation. Fearful of adulteration, social-minded practitioners now had to separate, test and identify the genuine drug from the adulterated one. Old methods of assays known to the Greco-Roman practitioners as well as new ones were recorded and are preserved in pharmaceutical compendia and *materia medica* texts. They represent organo-leptic tests based mainly on physical properties and the effect of fire in differentiating the good, 'pure' drug from the inferior and bad, and to check fraud.

While industrious pharmacy students found internship under master pharmacists, the medical students had three types of schools to separate them for a career. Such opportunities in Islamic lands were not available in the same liberal way to their contemporaries in Christian Europe. Arabic medical education was, therefore, secured in one or more of the following institutions:

1. Medical education at hospitals where theoretical and practical teaching took place in the lecture room, library, and at the bedside. Students came to hospitals from near

and far to benefit not only from eminent physician-educators on the hospital staff, but also from the opportunities that only hospitals provided for interns and residents. Al-Razi, for example, gained much experience at the hospital he attended in Baghdad, and encouraged other medical students to make the best of their training in hospitals. During the fourth/tenth century and thereafter, many learned men including the Harrani brothers and others from al-Andalus (Muslim Spain) left their native country and came to Egypt, Syria and Iraq to further their medical education by internship in renowned hospitals in these countries. During the seventh/thirteenth century, Ibn Abi Usaybi'ah, after training at al-Nuri hospital at Damascus, went to Cairo where he obtained further experience while attending lectures and practical training at al-Nasiri hospital. Ibn al-Nafis and many other practitioners did likewise. Suffice it to say that those who wished a rounded medical education found in the hospitals – their staff and facilities – ample opportunity which could be gained in no other place. Here they acquired a theoretical, as well as a practical and clinical training. This early development shows an antecedent to the significance which medical educators place on hospital training in modern times.

2. Privately supported hospitals run by an eminent physician or by a religious or community organisation such as the two hospitals in Antioch. The first such medical institution in Islam was founded by the physician Yuhanna b. Masawayh in Baghdad during the first quarter of the third/ninth century. Others followed. Famous physicians such as al-Razi in Rayy, Ibn Abi al-Ash'ath in al-Mawsil, al-Zahrawi in Cordoba and al-Zahra, Ibn al-Tilmidh in Baghdad, Ibn al-Dukhwar and Ibn al-Quff in Damascus operated such schools to train medical students.

3. Private tutoring by one master for one or two pupils at a time. The trainee accompanied his master on his visits and rounds to homes, or at his own clinic. Under the tutor's instructions and recommendations the pupil

trained to use and even make medical and surgical instruments. Many leading physicians emphasised professional ethics and rules that govern the life and conduct of the ideal physician.

One important aspect of Islamic medicine that should not be overlooked is its emphasis on psychotherapy, what was called *Tibb al-ruh*. Care, in Islamic lands, for the mentally ill can be traced to the early second/eighth century. Invariably, in their medical encyclopedias, such as *Firdaws al-Hikmah* by al-Tabari, *al-Tibb al-Ruhani* by al-Razi, and *al-Qanun fil-Tibb* by Ibn Sina, these and other educators devoted considerable space in their books to psychotherapy and the importance of good counselling by doctors. Significantly, Arabic medical men paid special attention to each of their patients with full consideration of their individual circumstances. They felt that because of personality, habits, vocation and habitat, each patient needs particular attention. The patient, to them, was not a mere label or number, but a living, unique individual whose case, symptoms and treatment should be undertaken carefully according to his situation and condition. The genuine interest of physicians toward their clients led to further emphasis on the family-doctor relationship. Even in the general hospitals, tender care toward patients was practised by the most eminent physicians. It initiated good communication between the physician, on the one hand, and the patient and his family on the other. This important humanistic element of the profession, which was highly recommended and upheld by Muslim physicians, unfortunately, seems to have suffered a great neglect in modern medical practice even in today's civilised countries.

In the health field, Arabic contributions included the following areas: codes of medical ethics based on the Hippocratic oath and other Greek writings on deontology; awareness of the importance and propagation of public and private libraries; the manufacture of paper for use in writing medical texts; the development of hospitals on a more scientific basis; diplomas; and advanced medical and university planning, programming and teaching, especially in the late Middle Ages.

# Doctors of the Heart

## Excerpts from *Openings from Allah* by Shaykh Ahmad ibn 'Ajiba al-Hasani, a commentary on the Andalusian sufic text, *The Basic Research*

He is a herbalist, a pharmacist, an opthamologist,
and a master of kohl, an expert physician.

It is a condition upon the doctor of the hearts to know the composition of the cures of the heart, and its beverages, and the food of the spirits. He must also know the benefits of invocation and its tastes, the results of reflection and its gnosis. Invocation is like food for the hearts, and knowledge is like its drink. Discourse is like food for the spirits, and reflection and the glance are like its drinks. To keep company with the gnostics is of great benefit to the hearts, and the spirits, and the secrets. It is their food and their drink and in it is their cure, every one according to his sincerity and his love and according to his degree and station. Every tribe knows its drinking place.

The Shaykh must know how to cure the inner sight. If it is bad because of doubt or *kufr* (unbelief) or hypocrisy, he must extract from it this impairment of trust. He must give it tranquillity and clear certainty. This cure belongs to the people of great light and great care. They are able to make one independent by a glance, even if the inner eye is apparently sound, but is shut because of the sickness of the sensory and illusory, or is blinded by meanness and disturbance and carelessness. The sign of this is that the one who has this malady struggles to get what has been given to him and does not fulfil what is required of him. The Shaykh cures him with the kohl of the unification of actions until he becomes certain that the one who is singled out to create and form is the one who is singled out to judge and manage. The one who planted the tree is the one who will water it and guard it. At this stage, worry will leave him, and disturbance and carelessness and fear, and meanness and avarice. His heart becomes strongly bonded to his Lord, rich from otherness.'

Inevitably, the practice of the strictly Qur'anic *Tibb al-Nabi* (Prophetic medicine) was developed by practitioners of Sufism (*tassawuf*), who studied deeply at the fountain of Hazrat Ali and applied other features such as numerology (*abjad*) to the healing practices. Again based upon pregnant verses of the Holy Qur'an, those who were considered to by *awliya* (saints, or the beloved friends of God) became much sought after to guide a sick person to good health by applying some aspect of *Tibb al-Nabi*. It is recorded that the Chishtiyya saint Hazrat Baba Fariduddin Ganj-i Shakar used to distribute more than 10,000 healing amulets daily at the height of his activities at Ajvodhan, in what is now Pakistan.

Even today, such persons as Abu Anees Muhammad Barkat Ali, of Darul-Ehsan, Pakistan, sees an endless stream of health-seekers, and applies the principles of *Tibb al-Nabi* most faithfully, even to the point of forming the shape of the word 'Allah' in five-foot high letters, composed of the rose petals and other herbs he uses in his remedies – all derived from the Qur'an, the Hadith and the sacred books of spiritual masters. Repeated recitation of various surahs or *ayat* forms a central feature of this healing; for example, on the authority of the Holy Prophet (peace be upon him), it is considered an infallible remedy for every disease to recite *surat al Fatiha* (the opening chapter of the Qur'an) forty-one times for forty days, at the time between the recommended and obligatory cycles or *raka 'at* of the dawn prayer.

Obviously there are several barriers which slow down the implementation of either of these forms of spiritual medicine in the West. The Western-trained mind often seems to resist contentions of the non-manifest and the unseen realities. Both the concept of humours, and indeed, the notion of the soul itself, often meet with blank stares of puzzlement. To learn this science of healing requires the deepest type of commitment, and a true sense of self-sacrifice and service to humanity.

When the inner eye has opened and the light is manifest to it, and it sees the nearness of the Real, but because of its weakness it cannot witness the light, the Shaykh puts on it the kohl of the unification of attributes. If it is open, and it can witness the light which surrounds it, but its own light is not strong enough to join it with the lights surrounding it, he puts on it the kohl of the unification of the essence – then its light connects with the light of the kingdom of power, and it does not witness anything but the light. Only then is its cure complete and successful. This is the commentary upon what 'Ibn 'Ata 'Illah said: 'The gleams of inner sight allow you to witness the nearness of the Real to you, and the inner eye allows you to witness your non-existence because of His existence, and the truth of inner sight allows you to witness His existence and not your non-existence nor your existence.' 'Allah was, and nothing was with Him. He is now as He was.'

The phrase used by the author, 'an expert physician', means that the Shaykh must have gnosis of all the sicknesses and their cures. The people of his time know this in him, and the people of the art confirm it. This is not really a condition because the people of this art are hidden, and Allah the Exalted knows best.

Then the author goes on to say, concerning the states of the Shaykh,

He has reached expertise in symptoms, and the adverse sicknesses of the stomach, more than Galen or Hippocrates.

He says that the Shaykh must be more expert in the knowledge of hearts than these two famous hakims in their field. What he means by symptoms is everything that becomes a barrier for the disciple (*murid*) in his spiritual journey, like his inclination toward leadership and reputation and his obtaining high position before obtaining perfection. Another example would be attachment to this world as an end rather than a means so that his progress is impeded. What he means by the adverse sicknesses are the low desires and intentions. The Shaykh must recognise the desires of the self and Satan, on the one hand, and angelic or divine desires on the other. He must also know the noble and disgraceful intentions and both the elevated and low yearnings. He must cure the *murid* of confusion and gather his heart on Allah and upon being absent from other-than-Him by complete annihilation in Him so that he has a heart which is completely dedicated to Him. He must cure him by guiding him to the condition of servitude to Allah and to fulfil the divine functions which are required of the gnostics. And Allah the Exalted knows best.

If all these matters are perfect in the Shaykh, then it is appropriate for men to go to him to be cured of their spiritual disorders. The author has explained this by saying,

> When what he has is real, the critically ill and the sick seek him.
> He cures them of sicknesses, and the one whose heart is enraged becomes pleased.

The greatest of these sicknesses are anxiety about provision, fear of creation, then anger and impatience when the decree has taken place. The Shaykh cures him by his yearning, the light of his inner sight, and by his glance until the heart of the sick one is full of the light of certainty. Then he becomes independent, by Allah, of everything else and the lights of reliance upon Allah shine upon him and he rests from the struggle of management and choice.

Then he tastes the sweetness of faith. He is pleased with Allah in every state and time. The Prophet said, 'The one who is pleased with Allah as his Lord, and Islam as his religion, and with Muhammad as his Messenger has tasted faith (*Iman*).' In the *Tanwir*, it is said, 'The one who is pleased with Allah as his Lord submits to Him, and the one who is pleased with Muhammad as a Messenger follows him and the one who is pleased with Islam as a religion acts according to it.' I say that there is no doubt that the heart, when it is sick, does not taste the sweetness of trust, nor does it savour obedience and conversation. If the heart is sound, then he tastes the sweetness of trust. One of the pillars of faith is to trust in the Decree, whether good or bad, sweet or bitter. He must find everything that comes from Allah sweet, however it may be, because it is all from the Beloved. May Allah reward the one who said:

I am pleased with what Allah decrees;
His order is accepted with openness among the pious.
If man is struck by the fire of struggle,
The pure gold is like cast gold.
The one who has patience fears nothing –
He is happy in the two states, without any doubt.

The phrase, 'the one whose heart is enraged becomes pleased' is the sign of the cure. As long as the slave is in contraction, majesty and difficulty or is in expansion, beauty and ease, there is still a remainder of sickness of the heart in him. If all the states are the same with him, that is a sign of soundness and perfection. Then he joins the stations of men.

Dhu'l Nun al-Misri was asked, 'Can you describe the *Abdal* (substitutes, a category of saints)?' He said, 'You ask me about pitch darkness, to unveil it to you. They are people who remember Allah by their hearts, glorifying their Lord because they know His majesty. They are the proofs of Allah exalted over His creation. Allah the Exalted has given them the garment of light from His love. He has raised the banners of guidance to show them how to reach Him, and He has given them the station of heroes by His will, and He has given them some of His fear, and He has purified their bodies with His gaze, and He has perfumed them with the scent of the people of His transactions. He has given them robes from His love and has placed on their heads the crowns of His good care. He has deposited in their hearts rubies of His Unseen, and their hearts are connected by His union. Their yearnings flee to Him, and their eyes in the Unseen are looking at Him. He has established them in the contemplation of Him and He has made them sit on the chairs of the doctors among the people of His gnosis. He said to them, "If one is sick because of losing Me, or because of being separate from Me, then cure him. Or if one comes to you who is sick because of fear of Me, give him victory. If one comes who thinks he is safe, then warn him. If one comes who yearns for union, then let him hope. If one comes who is travelling towards Me, give him provision. If one comes who is a coward in his transaction with Me, then encourage him. If one comes to you who has given up hope in My bounty, then give him hope. If one comes who hopes for My excellence, then give him good news. If one comes who has a good opinion of Me, converse with him. If a lover of Mine comes, unite him. If one comes who glorifies My worth, then glorify him. Or if one comes who has done wrong action after My beneficence to him, reprimand him. If one comes who seeks guidance, then guide him . . . " '

Then the author calls our attention to the purpose of this knowledge, and says,

This is not the medicine of Galen, it is concerned with souls.

Here he draws attention to the fact that this type of medicine is not the medicine of bodies which Galen the hakim used to practise. Rather, it is the medicine of souls, which makes them suitable for the Presence of the Perfectly Pure. This is the medicine of the heart which cures the soul of the sicknesses of forms and prepares it for entrance into the presence of the Knower of the Unseen. It makes it one of those who come to Allah with a sound heart, and offers it a sincere seat for a king of great worth, next to the Generous. May Allah give us the delight of dwelling in His presence in this world and the next.

# Healer's Elixir

## A selection from *The Garden of the Two Winds* by Yafa'i:

'Ali ibn Abu Talib, the Prince of the Believers, once replied when asked what the cure for error and wrong action was:

Rise up from here and go to the Garden of Faith, enter and take some roots from the tree of sorrow, a few leaves from the tree of contemplation with the seeds of humility and the fruits of understanding, a small measure of the branches of certainty and the kernels of sincerity with the bark of strenuous effort with some of the stems of turning away from wrong action with the strong medicine of modesty, blend it with the senses, with a heart full of concentration and understanding filled by the fingers of proof and the palms of success. Pour it in the basin of inquiry and wash it with the water of your tears. Then take it all and put it into the kettle of hope, bring it to a boil with the fire of your longing to the point that the superficial, superfluous elements and the dregs and sediment might be separated. Then you obtain the juice and cream of wisdom. Then put it in the plate of contentment and submission, blow on it with the gentle breeze of your supplication for His forgiveness, cool it so that it will not be spoiled, so that this elixir might be made wholesome. Then drink it in a place where no man can be found and where only Allah can see you.

This is the remedy that will quiet your errors and wrong actions and will heal the injury of disobedience so that not a trace of them will remain.

# Fasting and Health

## By Najma Hakimah

Within the yearly cycle of practices taught to us by the Prophet Muhammad (peace be upon him) is the obligatory one month of fasting. Beyond this are many other days of the year during which fasting is encouraged. During a fast we are made aware of our daily habits of eating and drinking. Withdrawal from the normal routine suddenly highlights those habits upon which we have fixed our emotional and psychological dependencies over and above the needs of our bodies for sustenance. Addictions to such things as tea, coffee and cigarettes become glaringly evident. Fasting grants us the possibility of self-awareness.

We live in a time when excess is easy. The speed and quantity with which we produce commodities allows, and indeed encourages, excess. This is no less true of food than of paper, clothes and other items. In addition, we live and work in buildings which are temperature controlled so that we become less and less attuned to changes in climate and weather. These two factors alone tend to discourage us from keeping a careful balance in our bodies. All illness stems from imbalance. Fasting is a means for redressing excess and establishing balance.

Almost every degenerative illness, including cancer, heart disease and multiple sclerosis results from the habitual excessive intake of extreme foods, either too much contractive food, such as meat, or too much richly expansive food, particularly food heavily laden with sugar and chemical additives.

While modern research has sought in vain for a cure for the common cold, anyone who understands fasting knows that two or three days without sugar, fruit juice, dairy products, ice cream or iced drinks will cure any cold. Colds are merely excess mucus trapped and expelled through the nose. A few days withdrawal from cold, wet expansive foods ends the problem. Bronchitis is an exacerbated cold which develops through extended excessive intake of these foods, especially taken across a change in climate. Pneumonia is a form of illness which strikes a person of strong constitution who regularly consumes a proportionately large amount of meat. Either may be prevented by the fast which cures the cold. Appendicitis is associated with the excessive consumption of meat. Attacks are often brought on by overeating. Fasting for a few days is the natural balancing agent for such a crisis.

One of the most important· health maintaining functions in the body is the elimination of excess and toxic matter. The blood as it circulates is constantly being purified and itself purifies the cells through which it passes. Major waste is eliminated through the lower digestive tract. Toxins and waste are also eliminated through the skin, thus the importance of perspiration. If any of these systems become blocked or overwhelmed, the whole body is endangered.

Excess fat and mucus accumulate first toward the periphery of the body – in the sinuses, inner ear, lungs and breasts, and in the lower part of the body in the intestines and kidneys. Later, if the bloodstream continues to be filled with fat and mucus, the excess begins to accumulate around the heart and other organs. If this accumulation is stored long enough, it will eventually begin to calcify, producing kidney stones, gall stones, hardening (sclerosis) of the arteries, the liver, the heart – any organ or tissue may succumb to the process.

Toxins are normally eliminated through the skin without irritation. Skin rashes are a sign of excessive toxic elimination. When suppressed by topical remedies, the toxins which were being eliminated through the skin must seek other avenues, through the bloodstream and other organs. Often they accumulate in and around the internal organs causing serious problems.

Among the different kinds of fasts that have been explored for detoxification of accumulated excess and toxic substances are two types of fasts commonly recommended by health practitioners. One is a juice fast, the other a whole-grain brown rice fast. The juice fast, which may last three days or longer during which only fruit or vegetable juice is consumed, concentrates on cleansing the digestive and circulatory systems. The juice helps to remove toxins from the body, while the liquid intake reduces the severity of the contraction caused by the fasting. A person whose body is accustomed to expansive foods finds the juice fast more gentle than a brown rice fast. The brown rice fast, consisting of ten days during which whole-grain brown rice and water are consumed is designed to give the body a quiet, steady intake of polysaccharides while eliminating all stimulation either of a contractive or expansive nature. This gives the body a rest and allows it to purify itself from all excess.

Extended fasts go beyond the reduction of yesterday's excess. As day by day passes with little or no intake, the body begins to use excess stores of energy materials, thereby reducing the possibility of serious illness. The fast of the month of Ramadan, requiring abstention from all food and drink as well as smoking from sunrise to sunset during one entire lunar month, is a most useful aid to health. Because it is obligatory on every practising Muslim who is able to fast, it provides a yearly rest physically, emotionally and mentally from habits of consumption. By the end of the month we find ourselves eating less and less and needing less and less sleep. Our bodies are able to reduce accumulations of excess and our minds are able to perceive incorrect habits and patterns.

# SECTION 4

## Knowledge and Education

*Read in the name of your Lord Who created — created man from*
*a germ-cell.*
*Read and your Lord is most Bountiful,*
*Who taught to write with the pen — taught man what he knew*
*not. (96:1–5)*

*Allah will exalt those of you who believe, and those who are given*
*knowledge, to high degrees. (58:11)*

*And say, O my Lord, cause me to grow in knowledge. (20:114)*

*And whoever is granted wisdom has indeed been granted wealth*
*abundant. (2:269)*

# The Sanusi
# Zawiyah System

## By 'Abd al-Jami al-'Alim

Shaykh Sayyid al-Sanusi developed an all-embracing educational system, affecting all aspects of the lives of the people who
took part in it, which started with a single settlement in the
Libyan desert and resulted in the vast network of *zawaya* or Sufi
centres throughout the country, revitalising Islam, unifying the
people and offering strong resistance to colonialism.

Sayyid al-Sanusi was one of the sons of a family noted for its
many learned men, and who were influential in many of the
localities near Mustaghanim in northern Algeria. He was
instructed in, and became adept at, all the traditional studies at
an early age. Under a variety of teachers, many of whom were
relatives, he absorbed the entire Qur'an, and excelled in such
subjects as Hadith, Islamic doctrine, and language. He grew to
be a man of imposing stature, virtuous character, and an expert
horseman and marksman. In the company of his teachers, he
moved about the region, living in such places as Tlemsen,
Mu'askara, and Mustaghanim. The nearest of the great cities of
learning at the time was Fez, in Morocco, and he journeyed
there to enter its famous Qarawiyyin mosque-university. There
he sat with the masters of Qur'anic interpretation and of
unification (*tawhid*). Expending himself to the utmost, Sayyid

al-Sanusi himself became distinguished and sought after. Unwilling to seek any reputation, however, he resolved instead to make the arduous journey to Mecca to fulfil the rites of pilgrimage and expand his inner horizons.

He followed a route through the deserts of North Africa which put him in contact with as many genuine gnostic saints and scholars as possible. He wrote later: 'During the travels which I had occasion to make . . . I had the opportunity of meeting a considerable number of illustrious men of sound knowledge and noble character, amongst whom there were great orators, and eminent imams . . . Some aspired to follow the road which would bring them as near as possible to the King of Kings (i.e. the spiritual path or *tariqah*); others wished simply to study and secure for themselves a license, and obtain the blessing at the hands of the praiseworthy scholars (*'ulama*) . . . I met them all over the country – in places widely separated from each other, in 'Arad and in Jarid, in Tripoli and at localities far and near . . . Some I met in Tunis and its neighbourhood, in towns and countryside, in the *zawaya* of the desert of Cyrenaica. Others I met in the towns of Egypt, and finally near the tomb of Shaykh Zarruq whose teachings have spread both in the East and the West. During the various travels and through numerous conversations, with a language which the common people could not comprehend, where the essence of knowledge was discussed . . . all along I have met with honest groups, faithful brethren and made friendships which are of the highest esteem.'

Sayyid al-Sanusi remained in some locales on his journey for extended periods of time. He became known as a man who departed from many of the more rigidified aspects and customs adopted blindly by many pseudo scholars – to the extent that he was both hated by the more arrogant for his freedom, and loved by many as a being of piercing intellect, wisdom and perception. He always sought to unite all Muslim peoples by following the principles of consensus (*ijma*) and reminding them of their common beliefs, thereby dispelling internal strife and dispute. His freedom of spirit was his conviction that knowledge should be applied in independent reasoning (*ijtihad*) in all matters of Islamic life and practices. He would advise people to 'direct yourself toward God and submit yourself completely to Him both in heart and form, so that you neither see, nor hear, nor witness anything else,' and 'the highest one can reach is following the footpath of the Prophet (peace be upon him) in high and low, matters great and small.'

Shaykh al-Sanusi returned to Libya in 1853, where he designed and commissioned to be built what was shortly to become the great university *zawiyah* at Jaghabub. While the ground at that location was supposedly infertile and the water poor, it also happened to be at the crossroads of two main caravan routes and between two groups of hostile desert tribes. During the ensuing years the Sanusiya *tariqah* grew phenomenally. A key point in this was the large turnover of accomplished students who were constantly being sent out from the *zawaya* to take their practical and spiritual knowledges to people who lived virtually on the edge of existence and many of whom Islam had hardly touched.

The Sanusiya had been heard of far south in the large isolated oasis of Kufra, among the warlike Zwuyya Berber tribe. This tribe sent a request to the Shaykh that he send representatives and establish a *zawiyah* in their midst, and that they were willing to change their way of life for the better. Shaykh al-Sanusi sent one of his finest men there with instructions to construct a *zawiyah* at Jawf, in the Kufra basin, and teach therein. That tribe turned their misdirected energies to productivity and spirituality and became eventually the strongest supporters of the Sanusiya. Sanusi *zawaya* existed in places as far west as Algeria, east to the Hijaz in Arabia, and south to the central Sudan. In fact, for a long period of time, the sultan of Wadai harboured the Sanusis, and was on friendly terms with Shaykh al-Sanusi, as the two had met in Mecca some years earlier.

It was said of Shaykh Muhammad ibn 'Ali al-Sanusi that 'what interested him was work; continuous and productive activity.' This was exemplified in his own tireless activities; lacking means, yet raising great centres of learning in desolate places where the only way people had existed was by pillage and robbery. He had the ability to deal with these unruly desert Arabs – who thereafter became his staunchest supporters and defenders. He acted upon his knowledge of the Book of Allah, the Qur'an, which he had absorbed to such an extent that every *ayah* could be applied practically.

The successor to the Sanusiya *tariqah* was the Shaykh's son Muhammad al-Mahdi, and he was in turn assisted by his brother Muhammad al-Sharif. Their father said of the two: 'Al-Mahdi holds the sword, al-Sharif the pen.' Among the Sanusiya, the two aspects were virtually synonymous – as their primary defence was knowledge and their enemy ignorance. A Turkish emissary inquired into the matter of armaments while touring the main Sanusi *zawiyah*, and was promptly shown the impressive library of 8,000 volumes. This did not mean, however, that any *zawiyah* was not prepared for active defence. On the contrary, the *zawaya* were patterned after the *ribat*, or fortified outpost, that had been originated by the nomadic Berbers of the Western Sahara about 1040 A.D. They came to be known as men of the *ribat*, or *murabitin*, and also *mulathamun*, after the men's desert custom of wearing a face-cover called a *litham*. Their revitalisation of the decadent Islam of their time was as a direct result of their prolonged and concentrated devotion within the defended confines of their *ribat*. The model of the *ribat* is along the following basic lines:

1.  A group of Muslims enclose themselves in the *ribat* for intensive training in submission (*islam*), faith (*iman*) and righteousness (*ihsan*).
2.  They must study and recite the Book of Allah until they are used to handling it, know its basic message, and follow its guidance. They must be able to recognise the pure guidance and not follow infidel models.
3.  They must practise *dhikr* (invocation) of Allah and keep vigil at night.
4.  They must be trained in combat. Tactics are part of war.
5.  When the training in all these elements is complete, the individual then goes into solitary retreat. By that, if Allah wills, his inner eye is opened and he is freed from fear of creation and lack of provision.

These men of the *ribat*, *murabitin*, would thereafter be inwardly and outwardly equipped to establish an Islamic society according to the Medina pattern set by the Prophet Muhammad (peace be upon him) and his noble companions.

The Sanusiya created a network of *zawaya* in such secluded spots as Jaghabub and Kufra, especially during the time of Sayyid al-Mahdi, that extended in every region of the Sahara and beyond its southern fringes. They served to revitalise Islam and also bring it within reach of those who had not known it. Sometimes slaves were purchased from caravans passing through from black Africa, who were trained for a period in a Sanusi *zawiyah*, and then freed to return to their people with what they had gained. A delegation of Sanusi brethren from Senegal, a distant 3,900 kms., came to Kufra to pay their respects to Sayyid al-Mahdi. There was a Sanusi representative active in Constantinople, the seat of the Ottoman Muslim khalifate, who was in direct contact with the sultan there and with the main *zawiyah* in the Sahara. There was in fact a regular courier service carrying post and news between each *zawiyah*. All news would reach the main *zawiyah* from any point within the period of a month.

Shaykh al-Sanusi said, 'Wherever a *zawiyah* is built, its building is accompanied with mercy and growth for the place, and people of town and country benefit from its presence there. It is founded only for the reading of the Qur'an and the spreading of the law of the Master of Adnan (the Prophet).' Each *zawiyah* was the means by which adherents were organised and through which expansion was effected. They also provided people with better methods for improving their resources, and served as models for the populace of that region to follow. The most eminent among the *ikhwan* (brethren) were from all tribes and regions. A unified group emerged from within a tribal society, and could not be identified with any single tribe. The land for a *zawiyah* was entrusted by a particular tribe to the Sanusiya *tariqah* as an endowment (*waqf*) for the sake of God. The tribe paid for and worked on constructing the mosque, school, and quarters for a Sanusi deputy (*muqaddim*) or shaykh. These became the centre of life in that principality.

The central figure of the *zawiyah*, be he a shaykh, trustee of a shaykh (*wakil*), or muqaddim, would administer all the affairs of the *zawiyah*, arbitrate local disputes, and be the ultimate authority in any practical or spiritual matter brought before him. He was entitled to money from the *zawiyah* fund for his personal needs and for travelling in the way of Allah, and a man to serve him. There was a yearly conference with the head of the *tariqah* of all the chosen (*khawass*) among these men, on the occasion of the feast of sacrifice. For every *zawiyah*, the shaykh appointed an imam for leading the prayer and teaching, and a *mu'adhan* for calling to the prayer. *Ikhwan* (brothers) belonging to the *tariqah* and who had been students lived inside the *zawiyah*. People attracted to the *zawiyah* otherwise were of two groups: those who were *mujawirun* (attachees) or students in the school; and the *muntasibin* (affiliates) who were simply sincere supporters of the *ikhwan* and the *zawiyah*. Every man worked one day a week for the *zawiyah* and two days a week during the times of planting and harvesting. *Zakat* (Islamic alms tax) was paid to and distributed by the *tariqah*. Those connected to the *zawiyah* were also eligible to receive gifts (*sadaqah*), sometimes from the more wealthy among their brothers.

Children were taught Qur'an in the school portion of the *zawiyah*. Visitors noted the continuous and beautiful Qur'an recitation that could be heard outside. Older students followed a schedule of classes in Qur'an and its exposition, Hadith (recorded sayings of the Prophet), *fiqh* (science of jurisprudence), language sciences, history and logic; training in the martial arts of horseback riding and shooting and attending to arms; also teaching in the skills of carpentry, metalwork, building, spinning, weaving, dyeing, tanning, bookbinding and mat-making. Usually every Thursday was devoted to craft work and Fridays for martial arts training. All students had an enormous desire to learn and the training was thorough. There were at one time as many as 300 students at Jaghabub during the lifetime of Sayyid al-Mahdi. All of the students were given simple clothing and a staple diet of bread, dates, dried milk, oil, bean or lentil soup, tea, and occasionally meat, though it was rarely available. After a student completed his training and left the school, he was at any time thereafter welcome to return to his school and he considered it his home.

Caravans would come through periodically and merchandise would be bought and sold. The *zawiyah* would often serve as the caravanserai and guests were fed generously and treated to several days of hospitality and refuge. The poorer the traveller, the more generous the treatment afforded to him.

Within the thick defensive walls of a *zawiyah* was a connected complex of rock and mud buildings which included apartments for all those students, *ikhwan* and the shaykh residing there; a large mosque; school rooms; travellers and guest rooms (*mada-*

*fah*); rooms for spiritual retreat and solitary nightly invocation; ovens; workshops; food storage rooms; a library; armory; and a large inner courtyard often with a well or water source. The appearance of the large university *zawiyah* at Jaghabub was as one immense many-storied building, within which was a mosque, rooms and apartments joined by arcades and opening onto a central courtyard. Adjoining the *zawiyah* was a cemetery. The buildings were on high ground, and from one side a flight of steps led down to palm gardens in which a system of channels and reservoirs carried water to the palms and various gardens. Another later centre of the Sanusiya was the *zawiyah* called al-Taj (the crown) in the oasis of Kufra; it appeared from a distance to blend in perfectly with the rock formations of the high ridge it was built upon. From there it commanded a view of the whole oasis. It typified all the other *zawaya* in that it was simple, unadorned and austere – and in that was its beauty. The learning and devotion practised within its walls gave it its cool and peaceful atmosphere which provided a haven from the harshness of its surroundings. Anyone who entered it would be inclined to turn inward and reflect upon his own state of heart.

All Muslim people are forever united in the knowledge that there is nothing worshipped but Allah, and that surely Muhammad is the messenger of Allah. This has always been reflected in their tremendous regard for any true man of knowledge. The most sincere of these men have tapped their inner core, their reserve of innate knowledge, by applying themselves vigorously to seeking out teachers whom they could serve, before whom they would humble themselves in order to gain inner sight. Consequently, in all parts of the Muslim world, the centres of civilisation were even more important as centres of learning than of trade. Beyond that, these cities were also only points of departure toward the focal point of Islamic worship at Mecca. There, devoted men from every land met and shared what they knew and passed it on to seekers wherever they went. Invariably, the spread of knowledge has had a form. The spiritual heirs of the Prophet Muhammad have never ceased to branch out and flourish everywhere in the world. One such man was the Shaykh, Sayyid Muhammad ibn Ali al-Sanusi.

# The Pursuit of Knowledge

The holy Prophet said: 'It is obligatory for every Muslim to acquire knowledge. Acquire it from its proper place and impart it to one who deserves it, because to teach for the sake of Allah is good, to seek knowledge is worship, to discuss it is praise to Allah, to utilise it is *jihad* in the cause of Allah, to teach it to an ignorant person is alms, and to pass it on to knowledgeable persons is the source of proximity to Allah.'

(Translation from al-Majlisi's *Bihar al-Anwar*)

The Prophet said: 'The learned ones are the heirs of the prophets – they leave knowledge as their inheritance; he who inherits it inherits a great fortune.'

He is also reported to have said: 'Seek knowledge even unto China.'

Once ten thousand men approached 'Ali and said, 'We seek permission to ask you a question.'

'Ali replied, 'You are at perfect liberty.'

They said, 'Of knowledge and wealth which is better and why? Please give a separate answer to each of us.'

'Ali gave the following ten answers:

1.   Knowledge is the legacy of the prophets. Wealth is the inheritance of the Pharoahs. Therefore knowledge is better than wealth.

2.    You are to guard your wealth but knowledge guards you. So knowledge is better.

3.    A man of wealth has many enemies while a man of knowledge has many friends. Hence knowledge is better.

4.    Knowledge is better because it increases with distribution. While wealth decreases by that act.

5.    Knowledge is better because a learned man is apt to be generous while a wealthy person is apt to be miserly.

6.    Knowledge is better because it cannot be stolen while wealth can be stolen.

7.    Knowledge is better because time cannot harm knowledge. But wealth rusts in course of time and wears away.

8.    Knowledge is better because it is boundless while wealth is limited and you can keep account of it.

9.    Knowledge is better because it illuminates the mind while wealth is apt to blacken it.

10.    Knowledge is better because knowledge induced the humanity in our Prophet to say to God, 'We worship Thee as we are Your servant,' while wealth engendered in Pharoah and Nimrod the vanity which made them claim godhead.

# SECTION 5

## The Qur' an

*And most surely this a revelation from the Lord of the worlds – the Faithful Spirit (Gabriel) has descended with it upon your heart that you may be of the warners, in plain Arabic language. (26:192–195)*

*Our Lord, lay open the truth between us and our people – for You are the best of Openers. (7:89)*

*Hallowed is He who from on high, step by step, has bestowed upon His servant the standard by which to discern the true from the false, so that to all the world it might be a warning. (25:1)*

———— ⋆ ————

# Introduction

The Qur'an is an exposition of reality. It is a description of your existential reality and that which is beyond it. In the Qur'an you will find those factors which govern your *nafs* – your happiness or unhappiness – laid bare. You will find in it that which governs interaction between people. In it you find the story of creation, how it came about with a big bang and how it will end with a big bang, and also what will happen after the end of this physical creation. It is a vast exposure of the ocean of truth.

# The Opening:
## *Surat al-Fatihah*

### Talk by Shaykh Fadhlalla Haeri

*In the Name of Allah, the Beneficent, the Merciful.*
*All praise is due to Allah, the Lord of the Worlds.*
*The Beneficent, the Merciful.*
*Master of the Day of Judgement.*
*Thee do we serve and thee do we beseech for help.*
*Keep us on the straight path.*
*The path of those upon whom thou hast bestowed favours.*
  *Not [the path] of those upon whom thy wrath is brought down,*
                    *nor of those who go astray.*

This Surah is placed at the beginning of the Qur'an because it signifies the opening of knowledge and so the victory over ignorance. If, in the direction we are taking, there is no door, then we have reached our target – we have won.

*Fataha* means to open, reveal, imbue, conquer. This Surah is so named because if you follow it in your heart, you will be victorious. You will conquer and an opening will come for you.

### *Al-hamdu lillahi rabb il-alamin*

*Hamd* is praise. Praise comes if there is knowledge. You can only praise something if you have knowledge of it. Knowledge of something is an aspect of experience. You praise the *rabb*, the lord-sustainer. *Rabba* means to be master of, to have command over. It also means to raise and bring up. *Rabb* is the attribute of that entity which brings what is under its domain up to its full potential, towards the ultimate end which is *huwa*, He, because it has come from Him, from Allah.

We said that when you praise the Ultimate, you must have some knowledge of it. That knowledge could be that of avoiding the non-Ultimate, which is what we are trying to do now. The way to that knowledge is by avoiding that which is unreal, unconducive, unfulfilling; that which does not permanently rehabilitate our hearts.

Up to a certain point, it is all right to praise an aspect of it since we do not have complete cognizance of *rabb*. If we are true to ourselves, we aim for the ultimate in everything. We only want to praise the Ultimate.

Real praise belongs only to the Lord-sustainer, and this is the basis of *tawhid* (divine unity). When you say, *Al-hamdu lillah*, you are only stating the fact that praise is indeed for Allah. Furthermore, you are only able to praise in the first place because you mirror Allah and His Attributes, since you are the created being, having been created by the Creator, Allah. When you abuse the use of *hamd*, instead of gratitude, you reveal your own shatteredness, for if you have truly witnessed that there is no god but Allah (*La ilaha il Allah*), you will understand that Allah's mercy comes not only in *bast*, expansion, but also in *qabd*, constriction, and you will recognise that above all else Allah is truly *ar-Rahman ar-Rahim*, so that every state reflects the mercy of Allah. This explains why it says: *Al-hamdu lillahi rabb il-alamin*.

*Alamin* encompasses all states, all worlds, in the seen and the unseen, in sleep and in wakefulness, here and in the hereafter.

The man of greater perception sees the *rabb*, Sustainer, even in times of constriction. To use *hamd* as an expression of a mood or feeling is *shirk* (associating other than Allah with Allah). Praise is for Allah at all times and under all circumstances. *Hamd* does not allow for the separation between you as a praise giver and the object of praise: you merely echo *hamd*.

## Ar-Rahman ar-Rahim

The characteristics of the Lord whom we love and adore are *ar-Rahman ar-Rahim*, the all-beneficient, the all-compassionate. There is only mercy, but we not not see it because of our ignorance, expectations and desires which only arise from the use of our intellect. Was the mercy not there when you were in your mother's womb? You stayed there for nine months and yet you were unequivocally content. It is the mercy of Creation that we are able to die, so that there may be breathing and standing space for others to come. It is only we who interfere. It is the ego, the *nafs*, the vanity of expectation which frustrates and sabotages our recognition of Allah's mercy. It is the evil *I* which we hear whispering in our ear. Shaytan (Satan) is only a name. He too is from the Creator. If you know how to tackle Shaytan, then you would see nothing other than *ar-Rahman*. There is a cult in the Middle East of some two to three million people who worship Shaytan. They say that we know the Lord through Shaytan, and that on the Day of Resurrection or *Yawm al-Qiyamah*, Shaytan will be forgiven because he has been testing all the good ones and the bad ones. They say he will be the first to be forgiven. If you see anything other than mercy, it is your own doing. It is your own expectations, desires and illusions. You yourself are the author.

## Maliki yawm ad-Deen

*Malik* means owner, master. We come from the Owner. We own nothing, but are all owned. *Yawm ad-Deen*: the day of the Deen. *Yawm* is not only a day, but also a span of time. *Deen*, life-transaction, finds its root in *dana*, to owe, be indebted to. It is the debt of man to want to recognise reality. It is encumbent upon everyone of us to know how to pay the debt upon us.

The *deen* with Allah is Islam. It is a life-transaction. Our way of behaving towards ourselves and towards others is *deen*. It is the way of correct transaction. But if you cannot discipline yourself, you cannot be of any use to anybody else. If interaction is not at least two-dimensional, nothing will work. You will only accumulate more wealth and cultivate more attachment. Eventually, you will be toppled over. Therefore, you have to exercise yourself in order to discipline yourself. The inner discipline begins with the outer discipline. This is the meaning of *deen*. The outer is easier because if you yourself do not stop from overshooting the limits, someone else will. It is the inner that is more difficult, so we start with the outer in order to gain the inner meaning. We go from the gross to the subtle.

## *Iyyaka na'budu wa iyyaka nasta'in*

Once you recognise that you are in love and you are worshipping the *rabb*, you admit it openly, we worship You and we depend upon You. If you are worshipping and you are in love, then you are in adoration. *'Abada* is to worship, adore, serve, and in its second form, it means to make accessible. You depend upon the Merciful. This is only meaningful if there is knowledge, for otherwise it can be considered a tyranny.

## *Ihdina as-Sirat al-Mustaqim*

Show us the direct way. A straight line is the shortest distance between two points. A straight line is also one point travelling in only one direction. Therefore, you ask to be shown the most direct route towards this knowledge.

## *Sirat al-ladhina an'amta 'aleyhim*
## *Ghayr il-maghdhubi 'aleyhim wa'l ad-dalin*

*Sirat al-ladhina an'amta 'aleyhim*, is the way of those upon whom delight has been bestowed, not those upon whom anger burns. *Na'mah* is delight, happiness. There is no anger in this life. If you do not see mercy, then you have brought darkness upon yourself. Your ignorance is not the fault of someone else. If you do something inane and as a consequence harm comes to you, then Reality is angry with you, angry in the sense that you are not in unification with it. Anger implies a high degree of discontent on the part of one entity with another, which leads to severing of the relationship between the two.

There is only Allah. There is only Reality. Consequently, there is no place for superstition. It is you who decide whether Allah is angry with you. *Rahmah* must encompass everything. Your loss is, in fact, within that *rahmah*. The condition you are in is appropriate because you have brought it about by your heart. This is cosmos, not chaos. It is total ecology. As human beings, we are all occasionally at a loss and often unsure. It is for this reason that we have to keep healthy and correct companionship. Existentially, we need guidance.

*Surat al-Fatihah* can be divided into three sections. The first section includes the opening line up to *Maliki yawm ad-Deen*. It is an exposition of reality. You find yourself awakened suddenly and you say: I am in gratitude, praise to Allah, Who has these attributes. You are inspired after having been in the wilderness and bewildered, so you say, *Al hamdu lillahi rabb il-'alamin*, out of contentment and sanity. In the next section (from *Iyyaka na'budu wa iyyaka nasta'in* to *Ihdina as-Sirat al-Mustaqim*), you are the adorer, the *'abd*. This now is transaction and demand. It is a request, it is action. In this section the heart cries out. The third part is like the echo of reality in order to confirm what you are saying and to answer your question.

*Surat al-Fatihah* is the most important Surah in the Qur'an. If it is completely absorbing, and if every word comes from a pure heart, you will cease to talk about opening and you will recognise that the vastness of Allah's mercy is never-ending, so you can only strive to increase, for after the constriction of ignorance, there can only come the expansion of knowledge. The Prophet is reported to have said: 'If I were to load fifty camels of commentary on the *Surat al-Fatihah*, it still would not be sufficient.'

# The Verse of Light:
# *Ayat al-Nur* (24:35)

## By Khwaja Abdullah Ansari
## Translated by Shaykh Abu 'Ali Fattah

*Allah is the Light of the Heavens and the Earth . . .*

Allah is the illumination and shining light that lights up the heavens and the earth. He is the One who forms and distinguishes objects and enlightens the souls of those who have faith. All lights emanate from Him. Some are manifest and clear, and others are hidden and remain within the Unseen. Manifest, that is, like the light of the sun and the moon. However, this light is dependent upon the hidden light. The light of the sun and moon, even though it is light, is a light which is eclipsed daily and tomorrow on the Day of Resurrection they will both be darkened. But the Sun of Intimate Knowledge and the Light of Unity, which rises from the heart in which there is faith, is never eclipsed nor tarnished nor obscured. It is a sunrise without a sunset, a manifesting without obscurity, a bursting forth of light from the realm of longing.

Know that the inner light in its various stages is differentiated. First there is the light of submission (*islam*), which is combined with the light of sincere Devotion (*ikhlas*). The second is the light of faith (*iman*), which is combined with the light of truthfulness (*sidq*). Third is the light of goodness (*ihsan*), which is combined with the light of certainty (*yaqin*). The illumination of submission is the light of sincere Devotion. The illumination of faith is the light of truthfulness. The illumination of goodness is the light of certainty. These are the stations of the path of *shari'ah* (the revealed law) and the realms of those in *Iman*.

But, in addition to these, the people of *Haqiqah* (Reality), and the courageous men of the *tariqah* (those who seek the Inner Essence and Truth on the Sufi Path), have different lights and states. Their light is the light of Discernment (*farasah*) which is accompanied by the light of Unveiling (*Mushahadah*), and the light of divine unity (*awhid*) which is accompanied by the light of nearness to the Absolute One.

*. . . Light upon Light . . .*
Until the slave has arrived in those regions he is limited and tied to his own way, his own manner. When he arrives here the pull and attraction begins to emanate from Allah, the Most Glorious and Mighty. He is then connected with the Divine Allurement and Drawing Power. The lights then aid and assist him: the light of greatness and glory; the light of subtlety and beauty; the light of awe and astonishment; the light of fervour; and the light of closeness. This condition will reach a point when the worship and adoration will vanish into the Divine Light. All of these lights of nearness to Allah are not manifest in any one person in all the world except Muhammad Mustafa, may the peace and blessings of Allah be upon him. It is he alone who possesses absolute perfection, all beauty and grace.

Mustafa (peace be upon him) has said about this Light: 'All of the worlds were gathered together like a fistful of dust, remaining enveloped in darkness, wandering in the abode of darkness, unaware, behind the veil of creation. Then the rains of eternity began to fall from the heavens of infinity. The dust became fragrant, stones turned into jewels, the colour of the heavens and earth was transformed and changed. The fine and delicate was joined together and changed. Then Allah sprinkled the beams and rays of His own Light upon it.' They questioned him saying, 'What are the signs of this Light?' He replied, 'When the breast is opened and expanded with the Divine Light, the determination and resolution is lifted up and exalted, the aggrieved one becomes tranquil, the enemy becomes a friend, dispersion is transformed into one-pointedness, the carpet of abiding eternity (*baqa*) is spread out, the mat of transience and temporariness (*fana*) is rolled up. The prison cell of sadness is closed and the garden of union is opened. It is at this point that the tongue of helplessness and poverty (before Allah) will say:

O Allah! Your action, independent of us, began in goodness;
Your lantern, independent of us, was ignited by Your Mercy;
The garment of light from the Unseen, independent of us,
Was sent to us through your kindness to your servants.
Since the Pathway has been made clear by your sweet tenderness,
Where then will you in your kindness lead us?'

An Amazing Tale:

It is related in the traditions of antiquity that one of the great learned men of Islam was taken prisoner by the Byzantines in the war with Byzantium. Later he was freed and remained there for some time. One day he saw some men of Byzantium gathered together in a desolate place in the wilderness. He inquired of them as to the reason for their being there. They replied that there was a bishop who comes out of his hermitage but once a year and teaches. They told him that this was that day and that the people had come to listen to him. The learned Muslim decided to wait there with the rest of the people. It is said that there were at least thirty-thousand people there that day.

The bishop ascended to the platform and sat in silence. The people were thirsty for his words and advice. Finally, he said, 'My ability to speak has been taken away. Look and see if there are any of the people of Islam with you.' The people answered, 'We know of no such people among us.' The bishop called out in a loud voice, 'Anyone who is in the religion of Muhammad stand up.' The Muslim was afraid and feigned ignorance. The bishop said, 'Even if you don't know him and he doesn't know himself, I know him.' Then he began to look well into the faces of the crowd. When his eyes fell upon the learned Muslim, he cried out, 'This is he! This is the one I've been looking for. Young man, get up and come here. I want to speak to you.' The man rose and went to the bishop who asked. 'Are you a

Muslim?' The man replied, 'Yes.' 'Are you a knowledgeable or an ignorant one?' the bishop asked. 'I have knowledge of that which I know and I seek the knowledge of that which I do not know and I am not considered to be ignorant.' The bishop said, 'I have three questions to ask you. Will you answer them?' 'I will answer them on two conditions. One, that you tell me how you recognised me, and secondly, that I may ask you three questions also.'

The bishop slowly leaned his head forward to the man's ear and said, 'I knew you from the light of *iman* and *tawhid* which was shining from your face.' Then he continued, 'Your Prophet has said that there is a tree in the Garden whose branches extend to every mansion [in the Garden of Paradise]. What is there like that in this world?'

The learned man replied, 'The likeness of that tree in this world is the sun whose rays fall upon every abode and lane.'
'You've spoken rightly,' said the bishop, and then he inquired, 'Your Prophet has said that the inhabitants of the Garden will eat and drink, yet will not have anything expelled from them that would defile them. What is like that in this world?'
The scholar replied, 'A baby in the womb of its mother eats and nothing is expelled from it which would cause defilement.'
'You have spoken rightly,' said the bishop. 'Your Messenger has also said that one seed given in charity or one atom's weight of goodness will become a mountain on the Day of Resurrection. What is there like that in this world?'
The Muslim replied, 'An object that is small in stature will cast a long shadow at dawn and at sunset.'
Again the bishop said, 'You have spoken rightly.'
The learned man then asked the bishop, 'How many gates are there to the Garden?'
He replied, 'There are eight.'
'How many gates are there to the Fire?'
'Seven,' he replied.
'Then tell me,' said the scholar. 'What is written on the gates to the Garden?'
The bishop remained silent and did not attempt to answer this question. The crowd became impatient, and some people began to cry out, 'Give him an answer so thhat this stranger cannot say that a bishop could not answer his questions.'

The bishop said, 'If I am forced to answer this, my answer will not be in harmony with my crucifix nor my holy vestments.' So he ripped off his vestments and his cross and threw them away and said, *'la ilaha illa'llah Muhammad ar-rasulu'llah* (There is no god but the One God, and Muhammad is His Messenger).'

When the people heard this, they began to curse the bishop and to throw stones at him. The bishop called out to thhe Muslim, 'Recite an *ayah* from the Qur'an!' Thhe man recited the following *ayah*: 'And Allah beckons [you] to the Abode of Peace.'

When the bishop heard the *ayah*, he wept and said, 'Know that the veil has been lifted from our eyes and seven hundred angels have come with litters in order to ascend with us, the martyrs, to the heavens. I am certain that there are seven hundred men among us who will become Muslims and confirm the miracle.'

In that instant a group of people who were watching tore off their crucifixes and vestments and openly declared that they were Muslims. The remainder of the people rose up against them and killed them along with the bishop. In the end, when the bodies were counted, they numbered exactly seven hundred.

The Moral:

The purpose and meaning of this tale is that the light of the one who possesses faith and declares the Absolute Oneness of the True Reality of Allah shines out from among the crowd of those who reject and deny the existence of Allah.

*The likeness of His Light is like a niche in which a lamp is placed . . . (24:35)*

A number of commentators have saaid that this parable describes Mustafa, peace be upon him, who was created from light and adorned in the garment of light, whose witnessing was in light, whose transactions were in light, whose miracles were in light and who was himself, in his essence. 'Light upon Light.'

He was the noble Muhammad, in whose face was the light of mercy, in whose eyes was the light of admonition and caution, upon whose tongue was the light of wisdom, between whose shoulders was the light of the prophethood, upon whose palm was the light of generosity, upon whose feet was the light of service, in whose hair was the light of beauty, in whose breast was the light of contentment, in whose innermost secret was the light of purity, in whose essence was the light of obedience, in whose obedience was the light of divine unity, in whose divine unity was the light of confirmation, in whose confirmation was the light of success, in whose success was the light of reverence and veneration and in whose reverence and veneration was the light of submission.

Husayn Mansur al-Hallaj said: 'Within the head of man is the light of revelation and between his two eyes is the light of his secret pleadings and supplications. Within his ears is the light of certainty and upon his tongue is the light of affirmation. In his breast is the light of faith and within him shines the light of the one who praises Allah for everything that remains in existence. At the instant when one of these lights is intensified and flares up, it overcomes the other lights and maintains them within its authority and dominion. When it relaxes its intensity, the lights that were overcome return to their previous state; however, the light emitting from it becomes more powerful, more perfected and more complete than it was before. If all the lights were intensified at once, then there would be "Light upon Light." '

Allah shows the path to whomever He wills by means of His Light. With His power He causes one to reach the Realms of the Unseen. With this Unseen, which is His, He brings one to the Abode of Infinity and Eternity. By means of His Infinity and Eternity, He brings one to the Absolute One.

*[In those houses there are] men who are not distracted by*
*trading and selling from the remembrance of Allah. (24:37)*

Outwardly such people are in the company of men, and inwardly they are witnessing the Names and Attributes of the Truth, the Most Glorious and Mighty. They are a people who

seek that which is their just due and whose remembrance of
Allah is a guide for them. They are a people for whom the love
of Allah is the pathway. The world is insignificant in their eyes.
Their remembrance of Allah is a garment for them, their love for
Allah is their cloak and the Royal Court of the Lord is their
abode. Their determination and resolution have no other goal.
They are the beauty of the Garden and the adornment of the
Abode of Tranquillity. They are emulated by the Companions
(*muhajirun*) and envied by the Helpers (*ansar*).*

When they walk upon the earth, it honours them. They have
no crown nor diadem upon their heads, and in their hearts there
is nothing but the love for Allah. They stand alone on the street
of their Beloved, extolling the All-Merciful One. Their hearts are
joined with the Truth and they behold Him. They sit in the dust,
they sleep in the ditches, their hands are their pillows and their
homes are the mosques. Poverty and need do not detract from
them, for with one sign from them, one blink of the eye, rain
from the heavens of the universe is showered upon them. With
one glance of their hearts, those in denial of the Oneness are
defeated. They instruct Gabriel with the sadness of their heart,
for they are always watched over and awaiting the bestowal of
inner vision.

Dhu l-Nun, may Allah have mercy upon him said, 'One time
the rains did not come and the people were suffering greatly
from the drought. A number of people went out to pray for rain,
and I agreed to accompany them. I saw an *'arif* (one with
intimate knowledge of Allah and a deep love for Him.) I said to
him. "These people that you see have come together in great
sadness and helplessness, lifting their hands (in prayer) and in
need to the Royal Court of the One who needs nothing. Will you
make some indication or signal to Allah?" At that moment he
lifted his face to the heavens and called out:

*The *muhajirun* were the Companions of the Messenger of Allah
from Mecca who accompanied him from Mecca to Medina on
the *hijrah* (migration). The *ansar* are the Helpers from Medina
who welcomed and helped the Messenger and those who
migrated with him.

"O Allah! By the words which passed between us in the night,
And by the secret which was between us last night." '

Dhu l-Nun said that the '*arif*'s words were not even finished before it started to rain. Know that a sign and an indication between two lovers is indeed mighty.'

*And as for those who deny the truth, their deeds are like a*
*mirage in the desert, which the thirsty man deems to be*
*water. (24:39)*

This *ayah* defines the nature of the believer (*mu'min*) and the unbeliever (*kafir*). The belief of the believer is light, and his action is light; his return on the Day of Resurrection is in the direction of the Light. Allah has stated with regard to him, 'Light upon Light.' The disbelief of the unbeliever is darkness and his actions are darkness; his return on the Day of Judgement is a return to darkness. Concerning him Allah says: 'Layer upon layer of darkness.'

*And for him whom Allah has not given a light, he will have*
*no light. (24:40)*

The poor are not brought into nearness with Allah because of their poverty, nor are the rich kept at a distance from Him because of their wealth. The power is Allah's in the affairs of the universe. He receives neither gain nor loss, whether He joins with one or cuts off the other. If you sacrificed both worlds, this world and the next, for the sake of Him, you could not reach Him. Likewise, if you gathered together everything in the two worlds, you could not use it to cut yourself off from Him. The nearness of one (to Allah) is not accidental, nor is the distance of another accidental. Allah has said, 'Anyone whose heart has not received a light from Allah will never have light.'

# The Folding Up:
## *Surat al-Takwir* (81)

## Commentary by Shaykh Fadhlalla Haeri

(This and the following chapter form part of his book, *Beams of Illumination* from the Divine Revelation : Juz' 'Amma, Zahra Publications, 1985)

*In the Name of Allah, the Beneficent, the Most Merciful*

This surah begins on a cosmic scale: 'When the sun is rolled up, when the stars shrink, and when the mountains are moved...' Next it shifts to a human one: ' And when the girl-child that was buried alive is asked for what sin she was killed.' Then it focuses on the inner life: 'And when all the secrets are opened.' It starts with the cosmos, returns to man, and then refers to the open manifestation of all hidden things in order to expose us inwardly and outwardly so that we find the unity in ourselves.

*1 When the sun is folded up,*

*Kawwara* means 'to make into a ball, to compress, to fold something upon itself, to roll up.' A *kurah* is a 'ball.' *Takwir* is the act of something collapsing upon itself in a spherical manner.

The knowledge that the sun is explosive and expansive was obviously already present at the time of the revelation of the ayah since this is a reference to the reversal of this solar process, the end of the creational expansion. As far as the sun is concerned, it is in constant explosion. The same process occurs in a hydrogen bomb, that is, fusion or constant self-explosion. When the self-exploding creation comes to an end, the sun will completely collapse upon itself.

### 2 And when the stars darken,

*Inkadarat* comes from the verbal root kadura, which means 'to be muddy, cloudy, turbid, swarthy.' According to some sources, inkadara means to shoot or swoop down. Man is expansive, he reflects in his own being the expansiveness of the entire cosmos. The Qur'an is a manual of existence; it is concerned with man's role and state in creation. The Prophet Muhammad's own inner reality pulsated out in words as a revelation for all mankind. Therefore, if the Qur'an is not regarded as a manual of existence, as something we can understand in our current state – or in any other state we may be in – then we have not unravelled it and made it useful to us. We must resonate the Qur'anic reality in our day-to-day existence; we must take from it as much as can be of use to us. At every stage of life, the Qur'an is able to remove some of the tarnish which has covered the source of knowledge in us. That source of knowledge is in us, and the purpose of the Qur'an is to bring us into a state of awareness.

Man intrinsically dislikes collapse, because he is a reflection of the expansion of the cosmos. We are lovers of Allah's Attributes, and only like to succeed, and success nowadays means expansion. Sometimes, however, success lies in contraction. Since man is always dying, his success lies in shrinking away to nothing before he dies. Life, his essence, continues so he should not be concerned with his own personal death. The essence lasts forever; why, therefore, should he be miserable? All that is needed is the right attitude.

This *ayah* refers to the collapse of the stars. The implication here is that the stars are all held together by the centrifugal, electromagnetic, gravitational forces between them, making up one complete entity which is in a state of expansion. When the expansive forces are interfered with – which will occur because of the advent of a certain phase in the process of the whole story of creation – they will collapse. Anything that is created must end in due time, whatever it may be. This surah is a description of how this end will occur on a cosmic scale, starting with the most expansive and general, then shrinking to the scale of the individual.

We can also look at the meaning of the *ayah* from the microcosmic point of view. As far as the individual is concerned, the sun is his *ruh* (spirit), and the *najm* (star) is his *nafs* (self). When the sun, or the spirit, stops giving nourishment to the nafs, or the self, which is the star, and when the star subsequently shrinks or collapses upon itself, the self will submit because at that time it will be darkened, that is, smothered and obliterated.

### 3 And when the mountains are moved,

*Suyyirat* is derived from *sayyara*, which means 'to set in motion, start up, send out.' *Sayyarah* means 'car.' When the mountains begin to move, they will not do so with a single jolt, but in a continuous movement. How will a mountain move in this way, unless the turning and hurtling process of the earth in space stops? Since we are hurtling through space at so many thousands of miles an hour, when the end comes and the earth is seized and brought to a sudden stop, the mountains will, of course, be wrenched from their places and shattered. One only has to stop suddenly in a car going twenty miles an hour to experience this process. This, then, is a description of the end of our little drama on this tiny earth.

### 4 And when the pregnant camels are abandoned,

Mountains moving and animals left untended are unusual occurrences. They depict a picture of opposites instantaneously combining. 'Ishar is a camel that is ten months pregnant. For the desert Arab in those times, it symbolised a most desirable possession. If camels are neglected with nobody to care for them, it means that the normal course of events that usually holds desert life together is no longer in operation. The verbal root of *'uttilat* means 'to neglect, leave without care, discontinue, stop.' *'Utlah* means 'holiday or unemployment,' that is, a break in one's normal routine. When the natural creational processes are disrupted, there will be a total breakdown in the life-process.

There are three phases in the total life-process: creation, maintenance, and destruction. The maintenance phase is particularly characteristic of a woman's inclination. Women usually want to achieve stability, whereas men's roles are, generally speaking, more creative. A man builds the house and starts up the home, and the woman maintains it, because she is responsible for the process of continuation on this earth. Her role is the key – she is the centre of the universe. The word for 'mother' in Arabic is *umm*, which also means 'source, origin, foundation, essence.' *Ummah* means 'community, nation, people,' the linguistic root of which is the same as that of *umm*.

The third phase in the life process is that of destruction, an act of which man is quite capable. The reference in this *ayah* is to the process of stopping. What has been created will also come to an end and stop. In other words, nothing more will occur at an initial creational level: there will be no more pregnancies.When the world comes to its end, no sane person will go to tend a camel!

**5 *And when the wild beasts are herded together,***

All wildlife will gather close to each other. Hashara means 'to gather, assemble, crowd (together).' This again reflects the nature of creation. Everything is by nature expansive. Even though all wild beasts tend to move together in herds and groups, they do not press too closely together; they maintain their wildness, their expansiveness. On the day when all systems of life come to an end, they will act in a way that is against their nature, and out of fright they will not scatter but huddle together.

**6 *And when the seas are set on fire,***

*Sajjara*, the root of *sujjirat*, means 'to swell, overflow,' and in its first form *sajara* means 'to fire up, burn, boil over.' Often when something ends, one gets a glimpse of what it was at its inception. In other words, this *ayah* may mean that there will actually be fires bursting out of the ground at the end of creation just as there were when the earth was first created. The earth began as a fireball which later cooled as the creational process unfolded.

The allusion to water that is on fire may refer to volcanoes erupting from the seas, setting the whole sea on fire or even to the flaming infernos at sea caused by oil-carrying supertankers that have caught fire. Whatever its exact meaning may be, the reference to the sea being set alight implies that the ordinary is replaced by the extraordinary.

Water symbolises coolness and calmness, but here we are told that it is going to boil over. Things that we take for granted as being different and separate are joined to their opposites. All of these occurrences are events which will take place when the on-going process of life ceases.

*7 And when the souls are united,*

*Nafs* (self) here could mean *ruh* (spirit). *Zuwwijat* (united) comes from the root *zawwaja*, which means 'to pair, couple, unite.' The *ayah* could mean that the soul will be united with what it gathered together or with what it has known, or that the ruh will be joined with that with which it appears to be united, that is, the body. In the cosmos, pairing constantly takes place; the opposites meet. Man is made up of two aspects: a bodily form which is part of the entity of the so-called 'I' and something indiscernible which is called *ruh* (spirit or psyche). We may reflect on the *ruh's* existence by asking, 'Where am I in deep sleep? Where am I when I dream?' We say, 'I walked up a steep mountainside while I was asleep,' and yet, the physical body did not move. In other words, the *ruh* is another entity in man which has its own experiences. Perceiving this unification of the two opposites, body and spirit, is one way of looking at the meaning of the *ayah*.

Another way of looking at it is that we are not in a state of unification because of the diverse states arising from our *nafs*. Our various expectations, desires and needs must be fulfilled if we are to be neutralised and to experience unity. That is why, in the most gross way, man has to be rehabilitated by what is called 'marriage.' Marriage is a means of fulfilment and it is not always something wonderful; on the contrary, it is often miserable. Nevertheless, in most cases it is positive, especially when both parties have respect for each other, knowing that human beings have come into the world alone and will go out of the world alone. If they help each other to reach self-fulfilment during this sojourn, they will have achieved something.

Thus, there are two possible ways of looking at this ayah. When one's *nafs* is shattered, it is joined to its opposite. Everything in life exists at the level of duality; there is good, and there is also evil. Everything that can be imagined, touched, tasted or in any way perceived, exists in one of two modes. All of us are searching for the One, because we can never be satisfied by duality.

The implication of this ayah is that duality will come to an end. In this life duality will come to an end when man reaches a state of complete self-abandonment and when nothing can fulfil him because he is already fulfilled. This will also occur when man understands the true nature of reality at the point of death. In reality there is only God, there has been only God, and there will be only God. This knowledge comes through inner, experiential realization; it is not necessary that it be learned.

The Qur'an is concerned with deep spirituality. It is concentrated and absolute; it is like a spring whose source, when reached, is bitter. If a person wants to reach its essence, he can only do so by being willing to abandon everything – and that means death. He has to be in *fana'* (annihilation). If not, he is still caught up in the affliction of duality and the realm of wisdom that is only, at best, superficial and existential. Many men of knowledge, therefore, end up in a little cave somewhere so as to lessen the effects of duality, and truth-seekers must seek them there.

When a person arrives at the Qur'an, he finds that it is vast. The essence of man, however, is itself vast. Understanding depends on how forceful and honest one is. The Qur'an says, *Read what is easy of the Qur'an* (73:20). Read what? What does this mean? We read what is already written, what is written in us. This statement is made only to sharpen us, to unravel what is already in us.

In this *ayah* we read, *And when the souls are united*, meaning when we are united with our opposite or when we are neutralised. At the present moment we are not neutralised. We are always craving something, constantly shifting from one aspect of duality to another by changing our external circumstances. This tendency, however, will ultimately be of no avail. We ourselves must change and that is much more difficult than trying to change the world.

We live in duality, and we seek to neutralise, but how do we neutralise? We neutralise our *nafs* by remaining silent, genuinely and positively. In that silence we have direct knowledge of the meaning of the Black Stone which is set into the corner of the Ka'bah in Mecca.

Few Muslims know the meaning of the Black Stone, even though they perform the rite of circling it and kissing it during the Hajj pilgrimage every year. Black contains all the colours – it symbolises death, from which comes life. Life cannot be understood unless one is willing to die. The meaning of *jihad* (literally, utmost exertion, and by extension defensive war against *kufr*) is not blood and misery; it is the willingness to stand fearlessly for life, the life of the spirit. The Prophet (peace be upon him) did not desire war and the death it brought. He used reason to avoid it. He was fearlessly rational, because he used his intellect (*'aql*), and he departed from the polytheistic heritage of his family to become a guide for seekers of the right path to the one God.

Sayyidna Hasan used reason with the most treacherous man who ever lived, Mu'awiyah, when he abdicated the caliphate. Sayyidna Hasan had 20,000 followers, but he knew they were all rascals. He knew that they were not going to make up a useful army, that it was pointless for them to be killed, and that they would renege and desert him.

Disloyalty will often come from those closest to a person. Man is born wanting to be one, and basically everyone is dependent on the one and only Reality, Allah. The saying 'he bites the hand that feeds him' arose because when a person perceives himself to be dependent upon another, he will often strike out, 'biting the hand' that provides for him, as a means of asserting his independence. The reaction is also due, however, to an inner recognition of our ultimate dependence only on Allah.

Ignorance comes about when one is not being thankful to creation. It is in man's very substance, because everything contains its opposite. The part of man that wants to live also contains his own ultimate destruction. We all will die and must see the beauty of perfection in this fact. Although we may still echo love of the Everlasting, the perfection of man's life and death lies in the knowledge that they are just a cycle from which awakening occurs.

We will know who we truly are when we arrive at the state of true unification. We are, in reality, all seeking *tawhid* (divine unity). There is only Oneness, only Allah, but to reach this realisation we must progress through stages. First comes the stage in which a person believes in unity and is then able to say 'I am beginning to understand!' As long as there is 'I,' however, we are in *shirk* (associating other-than-Allah with Allah). When the 'I' drops away, we see nothing other than Allah, nothing other than His Attributes, and that is the ultimate peace from which action emanates. This peace is dynamic, not static or dead, nor is there any drama and affliction in it. The outsider may see affliction, but the *muwahhid* (the unifier) sees no affliction, he sees nothing other than love. At that point everything else will be acceptable and will be seen as perfection. The outward existential situation may not be desirable as the human being perceives it, but it is perfection. It may not be desirable for us to take a bitter medicine, but its perfection lies in returning us to a state of health, tranquillity and balance. This stage, however, is very subtle and should only be revealed in the most intimate company.

The meaning of this ayah, then, is that man's essence is one, and there is only one essence. He starts by *shirk*, by saying, 'My essence is one,' and then 'There is only essence, there is only Allah.'

**8 *And when the girl-child that was buried alive is asked***

**9 *For what sin she was killed.***

The Arabs at the time of the Prophet (peace be upon him) had such arrogance and outer pride that a woman was always frowned upon. They forgot that man himself was the result of woman! They were afraid women would dishonour them by being unchaste and dishonourable. In looking back at that culture, we see that the ayah talks about the worst thing we suffer from, fear of the unknown. Everything that drains away our energy is fear of the unknown. All of our anxieties come to that one point. If we can say *tawakkaltu 'ala'llah*, `I depend on Allah,' and then recognise our condition of slavery in relation to Reality, all our anxiety will stop.

*Maw'udah* is a young girl or female baby that has been buried alive. *Wa'ada* means 'to bury a girl-child alive.' In old Arabic *wa'ada* also means 'to emit the sound of a wall crumbling down.' The sound of a wall collapsing suggests that the murder of a baby is a very grave crime, and it implies that the world is coming to an end: a life is being finished without letting it fulfil its rightful destiny. In other words, at the end of time, the true nature of everything will be revealed. The *arwah* (the spirits, plural of *ruh*), no longer exercise their wordly right of emitting spiritual light as the sun and the stars do or as the *nafs* (self) in its essence, does. The *ruh*, that spark of inner light, is extinguished by man's crime, by his fear, by his *kufr* (unbelief), by his lack of trust in Allah and the generosity of Reality. Now the soul is being asked, and is asking itself, what crime it has committed. By doing so, it is announcing that it committed no crime, that there was no reason for it to be extinguished. It was man's *kufr* that caused its life to be cut off. The buried girl-child questioning the reason for her death is a mithal (a parable or metaphor) to show that it is impossible in this experience or the next to suppress something and forget about it. We cannot silence something forever simply because it cannot react in this world. Soon everything will be totally out in the open. The spirit is being brought as a witness.

The Qur'an poses the question, 'What have you done to deserve being slaughtered?' From the point of view of the *shari'ah* (the revealed Islamic code of conduct), the Arabs had no right to slaughter girl-children. But what could have been the motive behind it from the point of view of *haqiqah* (the truth)? That motive continues to be a source of dispute even now, although it is covered up as much as possible. According to the *shari'ah*, however, man is accountable for his actions; he cannot escape them. If he kills someone wrongfully, it is final, no matter what the intention was.

Outwardly, we are accountable to the shari'ah, and in this realm of existence, *shari'ah* prevails over *haqiqah*. What a number of people or a consensus of society see – provided they are not hallucinating – is what is considered to be true. If everyone agrees on the identity of the killer, that judgement is considered to be valid. As far as *shari'ah* is concerned, the action must be considered murder. The rest is between the killer and Allah. If he killed someone one hundred percent *fi sabili' llah* (in the way of Allah), then even if the people submit him to the sword, he should be happy. He should say, 'The sooner I free myself from these people and go to meet my Lord, the better!'

In the next life *haqiqah* will prevail over shari'ah; the subtle will prevail over the gross. In this world, however, the gross prevails over the subtle, and we start with the gross in order to arrive at the subtle. We start by being correct, by applying the *shari'ah*, by feeding and maintaining ourselves well. If we do not do that, we are mad. If we say we do not care for the world, we are only trying to escape our responsibilities. At the beginning of the journey, we do care. We want to have sufficient clothing and a reasonable diet. This attitude is a healthy one. If from the beginning we do not care for physical needs, we indicate that we cannot attain them, that we have no understanding of them, or that we do not see their use. In having this attitude, we are actually denying Allah's creation. How can we, therefore, understand the meaning of inner kufr (unbelief or covering up) if we are in outer *kufr* from the beginning?

### 10 *And when the pages are laid open,*

*Suhuf* is the plural of *sahifah*, which means 'a scroll, a page,' anything that can be made flat and upon which something is written. It also means 'a newspaper,' because it is flat. *Mashaf* also means 'Qur'an.' These pages refer to pages of news or to the pages of a man's heart in which his intentions are laid open.

There is no point in hiding our intentions. The more we hide them, the more we will eventually have to remove them in order to be able to release ourselves. We use such things as drink, drugs, and other stimulants in order to give ourselves relief. Human nature is concerned with relief; life is nothing but seeking relief and freedom.

Our basic human attribute is inner freedom. Inner freedom can be reached through outer discipline, but outer discipline has to be lived willingly; it cannot be forced. For this reason, Muslims insist on being around people of the right orientation, on having proper companionship. All seekers seek each other, and people who want to know the truth collect together. If a man keeps the company of thieves for forty days, even if he is decent and honest, he will end up by being affected by them because he does not want to be in isolation. *Insan*, the word for 'man, human being,' derives from the verb *anisa*, 'to be companionable, friendly, to like to be together.' Uns, from the same root, means 'intimacy, familiarity.' Man wants to connect; he is a *muwahhid* (a unifier), and he wants to be in *tawhid* whether he realises it or not.

In reality there is neither inward nor outward, only Allah manifesting Himself as inward and as outward. At the moment, we are in confusion because we are in duality and see things only from that perspective. Sayyidna 'Ali says, 'The best of affairs are in the middle.' The best place to be is in the middle. Most people cannot survive at the extremes. The Muslim must combine *shari'ah* and *haqiqah*; we cannot have one without the other. In most of the Muslim world, we are at a loss and are struggling because we are not combining the inward and outward in our daily lives. We talk about *islam*, but we do not live it, and for this reason our youth are at a loss and reject traditional values. We have to be in the middle. In the middle both ends of the horizon are in view and so we are strong.

A vast amount of *shari'ah* with no *haqiqah* is like a giant ship heavily laden with goods but with no sail to catch the wind; it sways and flounders in the sea. *Shari'ah* exists for making distinctions, for differentiation. The business of *shari'ah* is to differentiate among things and let us choose correctly between the alternatives that life presents to us so that we can knowledgeably state what is right and wrong. The distinction must be clear. The nature of *shari'ah* is divisive because it is about *hukm*, which means both justice and wisdom. Justice means that one kind of action is correct while another kind of action is incorrect. From the point of view of *haqiqah*, everything is always in harmonious perfection because everything naturally generates its opposite. If one is balanced in the middle, he has both extremes at his command.

In the same way, *haqiqah* with no *shari'ah* is like a ship with a huge sail but with no goods in it. It will capsize. If a Muslim says, 'I am only concerned with the inward,' he is lying. The true Muslim is the man who is in the middle, who is a *barzakh* (barrier, interval or gap), an intermediary link simultaneously combining both the outward and the inward. According to the *Ahl al-Bayt*, the following ayah is a reference to the Prophet Muhammad (peace be upon him): *Between the two is a barrier which they cannot transgress* (55:20). The Prophet is the *barzakh* between the perfect man, Imam 'Ali, and the perfect woman, Fatimah.

### 11 *And when the heaven has its covering removed,*

*Kashata* means 'to remove, take off ma cover.' The implication is that everything manifested is only an outer covering. From our point of view, the whole creation was created for us; otherwise, it would have no significance. What is of significance is man. Man's existence is only meaningful, however, if he keeps to his purpose, which is to know the cause of his existence. The purpose is to gain knowledge of Allah. The entire creation came by Allah in order for man to know Allah. The apparent heavens which are in constant explosion and expansion are, from the point of view of the Creator, mere fantasies: all the billions of galaxies do not amount to even a grain of sand by His reckoning. When the heaven has its covering removed, or is skinned, we will then see its insignificance. The most significant thing, the sky, is described in the most belittling way to show us the independent wealth of Allah. The heavens are only a skin, a façade, a show, which will eventually be stripped away.

### 12 *And when the fires of hell are lighted,*

Everything in existence was originally created from one dense mass and greatly expanded by burning, after which all the stars and planets and all of creation burst forth over a period of billions of years. That dense beginning is the equivalent of absolute power or *qudrah*. It cannot really be called density because it is beyond density and because one might imagine that Allah Himself was dense; may Allah preserve us from that view. It is a point of power, total and absolute, not related in any way to anything else.

This ayah describes a new situation which is inaccessible to our

conscious understanding because conscious understanding cannot comprehend absolute power. Great power is understandable,
but not absolute power. There is an intermediary link, a *barzakh*,
between absolute and very high power. Absolute zero temperature
cannot be achieved because all the laws of thermodynamics would
be disturbed, but one can get very close to it, and from that limited
point on one can have a subjective understanding or experience of
it.

Similarly, one can get only so close to the knowledge of Reality:
'Not by diligence or striving – a gift from the Generous, the
Compassionate Giver to the slaves' (from the *Fayturiyyah* of Shaykh
Muhammad al-Fayturi). One can only go so close to this knowl-
edge, and passing beyond that point is not a matter of human
endeavour.

This same experience is reproducible by those who follow in the
footsteps of a perfect man and who imitate him as much as they are
outwardly able to. This proximity can also be attained by those who
take on the responsibility of being *salihun* (those who set things
right by their example), who put themselves in the shoes of the
*salihun*, and who bring about *islah* (establishment of peace, happiness and order). They take themselves as far as they can toward that
point by living as though they were in the constant companionship
of the Prophet (peace be upon him). They are in the *maqam* al-ihsan
(the station of excellence). They live in the knowledge that they are
constantly watched: they do not see Allah, but they know that Allah
sees them.

Attaining such a state is the most one can achieve through his
own effort. States beyond this are 'a gift from the Generous, the
Compassionate' and come either in this life or at the moment of
death. We can and must do our best: there is nothing more we can
do. After that we will become like open conduits, and we will be in
harmony with the true meaning of *islam*, the inner meaning of
submission. We will completely and utterly enact our own destiny;
there will be no more resistance between ourselves and the decree.
As far as it is humanly possible, we must be in a state of perfect
submission because that state is the only one in which we can have
an experience of the one and only perfect One. If we are not in that
state of perfect inner abandonment, anything else we speak of will
be merely religiosity.

**13 *And when the Garden is brought near,***

Those who love the akhirah (the next world) already have the key to *jannah* (the Garden) in their heart. Those who love Allah love the *akhirah*, because there will be nothing there but the truth for them. In fact, *jannah* is available to us now. The Qur'an is clear about this; it does not say that it will only happen later, after death, because it describes the people of *jannah* as those who say, 'We remember all this! It is similar to that which we have already experienced!' Thus, we have access to that condition here and now by avoiding what brings us to the opposite state. This way is the only one; there is no other.

We have all experienced trouble; we all know what it is and how it comes about – by fears, expectation, lusts, and so on. But if we are aware of it spontaneously, then we will no longer be troubled. At that point of recognition we will be at the edge of *jannah*, and the key to the Garden will become more and more clearly shaped in our hearts until our hearts are pure; and since the pure heart will be with the maker of the Garden, it will be beyond *jannah* itself. *Jannah* will no longer interest us since we will be with its Maker, with our Maker, Allah.

Our heritage, which we are all seeking, is the Garden. We all love the Garden, the state that the Garden gives us, tranquillity, fullness, abundance, protection, security, and enjoyment of all the good things of life. A visible physical garden on this earth helps us to enter into the mood of contentment, generosity and helpfulness. The Garden of bliss is our real and natural heritage and is to be found by following our hearts. We must be honest about it and recognise that it is there. There is nothing closer to us than truth, and our essence is truth. In our essence is the lover of the Garden, of tranquillity and peace. Our essence is neither life nor death; it is that from which both have come, the Creator. This is the *bisharah* (the good news).

*And when the Garden is brought near* refers to the beginning of self-abandonment. In fact, there is nothing other than the Garden. The Qur'an says that the Garden's width is the expanse of the heavens and the earth, so why are we in misery here? Obviously we are miserable because we are not receptive to the station of self-abandonment. We can receive only that to which we are receptive. When we become receptive to the Ever-Living Eternal, nothing else will exist for us, and we will live fully from moment to moment. When the end of time draws near, we will find it easier to experience full self-abandonment.

**14** *Every self will know what it has brought with it.*

In our own lifetime we may not see this, but our individual ends will come, and as far as we are concerned, our end is the end of the cosmos. We do not care if there are more or less stars up above. The rational man understands that he sees creation according to his interpretation: he is its centre. From a rational point of view, he also knows that his end does not mean the end of the total cosmos. It is quite probable that at our individual death other people will continue their experience of life, and it will not be the end of the outer cosmos, but it will be the end of *our* cosmos, the end of what we experience.

When we remember that the end may come at any minute and we remember that we are suspended in air (one word related to *nafs* is *nafas*, meaning breath), we become more human. The Prophet (may Allah bless him) said, 'People are asleep, and when they die they wake up.' True seekers want to die while being awake m they want to enter a state of total silence. All the practices of the men of Allah from time immemorial lead man, the seeker, to inner death while still alive. If, while we are conscious, aware, and scintillating with life, we can enter a state of self-abandonment, then we will understand what inner death is. If we cannot reach this state, then we will remain in the turmoil of *sa'y*, that is, running between Safa and Marwah in Mecca, or moving ceaselessly around and around. There is nothing intrinsically wrong with that because we are made that way, man is born in *kabad* (trouble, misery). If he recognises his reality, then that *kabad* becomes like a game, and the trouble becomes most useful. The word *kabd*, from the same root, means 'liver,' man's most important organ because it is the purifier of his blood. The liver checks any potential trouble the body may experience from a build-up of toxins.

When any sort of event befalls one, a person should say, '*al-hamdu li'llah.*' Such a person is already in the Garden; he is laughing as does a man of knowledge. Man is only qualified to laugh after he has wept; he is only qualified to live after he has died. Before he was born, he was dead, and the so-called 'I' had no life. Man came from death; thus, in order to know his essence, he has to die inwardly, and he has to be in silence.

Recently, studies have been made of people who have died and were immediately resuscitated. At the point of death, they reported experiencing a rapid review of their entire lives. Everything they had ever done instantly appeared before them. Upon entering death, we take with us what this entity called *nafs* has earned in this life. Everything is as good as it ends, which is why the Qur'an always talks about the *akhirah*. It is for this reason that we want to educate our youngsters to do things which will have a positive effect in the *akhirah*. In a material sense, we like them to invest in something which has a good return. In relationships, we advise them to keep the companionship of people who are good to them and to whom they also are good. In other words, they should invest in something worthwhile.

We all long for the end because we want a better life at the end, and for this better life we are willing to put up with inconveniences now. The Qur'an says that every self knows what it brings with it into death because we ourselves know that what we are taking with us is in our hearts and our psyches. Even now we are preparing ourselves for the end.

It is only when the experience of death occurs to the *nafs* that *every self will know what it has brought with it*. If the sun, the 'I,' is extinguished, and we are brought to a state of extinction which is what *fana'* (annihilation) is, then we will know our nothingness. We will know that whatever we did was out of ignorance, and that, at best, we could have behaved as decent, conscientious human beings. We are only qualified to act if we have surrendered the power to act, if the sun in us has collapsed entirely.

**15 But no! I swear by the stars**

**16 That run their course and hide themselves**

The surah now moves into another phase. *Uqsimu* means, 'I swear by (something).' *La* here is actually a negative article which emphasises and positively affirms what follows it. Here what is affirmed is the evidence of *khunnas* (stars in general). Qur'anic scholars also take *khunnas* to refer to the five planets that are closest to earth. *Jawar* is the plural of *jariya*h, meaning 'vessel, Ark,' and in older usage, 'running streaming.' The verbal root is *jara*, which means 'to flow, run, happen,' and here signifies the stars that run their course.

*Kunnas* is a name that is given to the stars, especially to those planets which occasionally hide themselves in the sun's rays, because they are close to it. The verbal root of *kunnas* is *kanasa*, 'to lie hiding in wait.' The relationship between *khunnas* and *kunnas* comes about because all the planets have a retrograde as well as a direct motion. The implication here is that these stars or planets are hidden in darkness. The planets closest to us are not visible most of the time, but they are there nonetheless. This *ayah* is indirectly telling us to be open-minded and a little more imaginative, since, as we see these planets some of the time, we know that they are there at other times when we cannot see them. They are then in the *ghayb* (the unseen). The *ayah* is saying, 'see how these five planets are not visible most of the time, even though they are your neighbours.'

*17 And the night when it darkens.*

*18 And the morning when it breathes*

Then, when the night comes, with its utter darkness and silence, we do not see anything. Night implies silence and incubation, darkness and hibernation. Then it says, *And when the morning breathes,* because after hibernation we start 'taking in,' and as we do this we inhale. The reference here is to those cycles which go from quiet stillness to life and movement. The juxtaposition of these two ayat shows the duality of existence: one state being inertia, the other motion.

We can also draw a parallel with the earlier reference to the sun and the stars to arrive at the inner meaning of the *ayah* which states, *But no! I swear by the stars.* This refers to those aspects in us, those stars in us, which suddenly appear after being hidden. The luster in us, the generosity, the compassion and selflessness in us which were not obvious before, suddenly appear, like stars burning with the same fire as that of the sun, which is the equivalent of our ruh. The night is like a state of darkness that often overcomes us, and the day is like the time when we are bright and cheerful. The macro-cosm, which is evident in the Qur'an, is reflected in the microcosm, which is our selves.

*19 Surely it is the word of a noble messenger*

*20 The possessor of strength, established in the presence of the Lord of the Throne,*

*21 One [to be] obeyed, and trustworthy*

The reference here is to the words of the noble Messenger, a man of power whose power was from the Possessor of Power, He Who in His almightiness is firmly established on the *'arsh* (throne, founda-tion, support). The Prophet (may Allah bless him) was, however, not obeyed then, and we may ask if he is obeyed even now. What this *ayah* means is that what he says is the absolute truth. He is obeyed by truth, by reality itself. He is united with destiny, with the absolute Decree. He is obeyed by the orchestration of all existence. If we are not in harmony with this orchestra and only listen to our own inner cacophony, we are disobedient.

At the time when these surahs came, the Prophet had only a few followers. The Qur'an says, *A multitude of those of old and a few of those of later times* (56:13–14). The Qur'an always speaks about the few. It speaks about quality not quantity. This is a natural law. From a *shari'ah* point of view, from the creational point of view, this is the truth.

*22 And your companion is not mad.*

*Bi-majnum* really means, 'he is not veiled, he is not talking ob-scurely.' As the Qur'an says, *it is nothing but a reminder and a clear reading-out* (36:69). There are no aspects of his intellect which are hidden. *Majnun* (from *janna*, to cover, veil, hide) in Arabic means 'madman,' but the reason it means 'madman' is because it refers to someone whose intellect is hidden, whose discriminative quality is not evolved but is covered and shaded over and does not express itself outwardly in the form of *'aql* (rationality, intellect). The *ayah* means that he is not hiding things, he is not uncertain. He does not say one thing and mean something else; he is not unclear.

This *ayah* assures us that this Prophet is not mad. We need this reassurance because we have invested in our own system of understanding and when someone tells us that we do not own anything, that we are nothing, that we have come from nowhe
re and will return to it again, and that we must give up everything, we naturally want to declare this person insane.

> *23 And certainly, he saw him on the clear horizon.*

> *24 And he does not withhold grudgingly a knowledge of the Unseen,*

> *25 Nor is it the word of Shaytan, the accursed outcast.*

> *26 So where then are you going?*

An outer meaning of the twenty-third *ayah* is that it refers to the Prophet's having seen the angel Gabriel on Mount Hira. The Prophet saw the truth, saw the message as it came to him, and saw the truth on the horizon, which comes to man from a distance, from the other side of his heart, as is described in *Surat Ya Sin. And there came, from the farthest part of the city, a man (i.e., prophet) running* (36:20). This is because if truth had been near, it could have also been clear from the beginning. The implication is that when the message comes, it must come from far away. The mercy of Reality showed Gabriel to the Prophet in a visible form so that he would not be confused about 'inner voices' and 'inner vision,' which could lead to excesses and abstractions. The Prophet (may Allah bless him) always had a direct, outer sign, in the form of a man, Gabriel, who appeared to him, because he was in a state of *tawhid* (unification).

The word *shaytan* is from the verb *shatana*, which means 'to be obstinate, perverse, to be cast off a path, to be distanced.' *Rajim* means 'stoned, pelted, driven away with stones,' and 'damned, accursed.' Then the surah continues, 'where are you going?' Coming from the womb, going to the tomb, we are caught in this interval. We are simply a vibrating thread between that beginning and that end; there is nowhere to go.

This is the meaning of surrender, of *islam*. It means to surrender to this reality which is in our hearts. We can only do our best, be available every minute, every second, willing to put our faces in the dust from which we have come and to which we return.

If we reach that state, we will be closer to hearing the joy of the song of the Qur'an, and all of it will be clear to us. We can touch it, however, only if we are pure, which means pure of heart, and have no expectations. Our suffering and misery are the result of our own expectations. We believe certain things will happen, and when they do not, we suffer and blame other people. Nobody is to be blamed but ourselves for having had those expectations in the first place. If we come with no expectations, then the whole drama of existence is a beautiful piece of theatre. We enjoy it, do our best, play our part. We cannot experience it in this way except by being pure, so we must start purifying ourselves from the outside-in, the outside being the easier point from which to begin.

*27 This is nothing but a reminder to all the worlds*

*28 To whomever of you wants to go straight.*

*Mustaqim* is 'right, upright, straight.' The root of its verbal form is *qama* and means 'to stand fast or firm.' Many important words are derived from this root. *Al-Qiyamah*, which means 'the Resurrection,' is from the same root. *Al-qa'im*, literally, 'standing firm, upright, certain to come,' is an epithet of the Mahdi, Imam al-Zaman (peace be upon him). It means that he is forever present. *Qum*, also from the same root, means 'stand up, be ready' and is the name of what is now a famous city in Iran. The words related to *qama* imply stability, and if one is stable, one is alert. Alertness does not come when our heads are heavy, dull and low, but rather when we stand up straight and our heads are held high. If our heads are drooping low, our thoughts will not flow well. It is for this reason that when we do *dhikr* (remembrance m here, actual practice thereof in which the Divine Names are invoked) our backs have to be straight and our heads must be held in their highest position.

*29 And you do not will except what Allah wills, the Lord of all the worlds.*

Man cannot wish for anything other than what has been wished for by the Creator. The Creator's law is that man has a choice: *Surely we have shown him the way, he may b e thankful or unthankful* (76:3). If a man is in *shukr* (gratitude) he is content and happy, and if he is happy he is effiient and alive, available, drunk with light. This, then, is the worship of free men who are as near as possible to being absolute, free by being absolute slaves. We cannot have one without the other. The root of freedom lies in servitude.

But whoever is in a state of *kufr* (covering up, denial, ingratitude) covers up and makes excuses for not taking action now. He does not realise that every second is auspicious and every breath a blessing. If we regard each breath as the final one, then all our debts will be settled, we will behave correctly, we will not disbelieve, and we will be generous. We will give only joy to others. If we havce no expectations, we will not talk to people who do not want to listen. We will be like the bird who just sings whether one feeds it or not. That is its nature, it mission; that is its reality.

*Rabb* is that entity which brings every system to its full potential. *Rabb* is 'the Creator, the Lord, the Sustainer.' He gives a being what is due to it in order to cause its growth and full blossoming. When we pray, we surrender to that entity, to that power or force which brings everyone to his full potential, and that full potential is *jiwar al-Rabb* (closeness to the Lord).

Allah says in the Qur'an, *We are nearer to him than his jugular vein* (50:16). Where are we then? Are we in *jiwar* (closeness), or have we separated ourselves from Him? Allah is omnipresent; there is nothing other than Allah. Since this is true, why are we not encompassed and taken over by that Reality? The answer is that we have identified ourselves with this so-called 'I.' The Qur'an is here only to remind us that this so-called 'I' has only come in order to die and that we should give it up quickly and enter into the enjoyment of lordship. Through *tasbih* (glorification of God), man enters into that which encompasses all, and this *tanzih* (worship having no association with a created or anthropomorphic thing) is something which is pure beyond imagination, totally untarnished. Man must bring himself to that state and be sustained therein, and that is the meaning of closeness. One must live outwardly to his utmost according to the *shari'ah*, and be true to his word, because every second counts. In this way, he will reach *haqiqah* (the inner truth).

# Three Surahs

## Commentary by Shaykh Fadhlalla Haeri

*The Decree (Surat al-Qadr)*

*In the Name of Allah, the Beneficent, the Most Merciful*

The Power that created all the creational systems made them according to a measure, the Decree (*qadr*), by which all creational manifestations are brought to their destiny, *qada'*, and final judgement. In this surah we are given a glimpse into an aspect of the meaning of *qada' wa qadr* (denstiny and decree).

*Qada'* means 'fate, destiny, judgement, justice, decree,' and 'that which has passed,' and while *qadr* means 'measure, decree,' it also means 'destiny' because it is according to a measure that things unfold and develop. The judgement, or the final destiny, of any created thing follows according to its measure, its *qadr*, for if it did not, there would be chaos. These measures may fluctuate and interweave within definite bounds, but there must be a measure in order for man to know the limits and to gain knowledge of the world.

*1 Certainly, We sent it down on the Night of the Decree.*

*Laylat al-qadr* is the Night of Power, or the Night of the Decree. The knowledge of what is written descended on the night of power and was made known to the Prophet Muhammad (may Allah bless him). Thus it is the night when he was empowered with knowledge, the night when the hidden tablet was unveiled to him.

*2 And what will make you know what the Night of the Decree is?*

When questions like this arise in the Qur'an, their purpose is to glorify what is being described. In this case, the question glorifies the night on which this event occurred. For each of us there is a possibility of *laylat al-qadr*. Our awakening to our fullest potential occurs on our night of qadr. It occurs when we see the Power behind the power in creation, or the power of the Powerful One, Who is Allah, and we experience the power of inner knowledge. The night of *qadr* occurs according to each person's capacity.

'The Night of the Decree' is that night of revelation when the heart opens, when the tablet within man's heart is unveiled, when the direct recognition that there is only Allah, and that everything which comes into creation comes through that single power, is experienced. This tablet does not contain encyclopedic information: it contains direct knowledge.

It is related that Imam al-Ghazzali was once travelling on a long journey with all his books. A robber suddenly confronted him and the Imam told him to take anything he liked, but to please leave him the mule loaded down with his books. To his great chagrin, however, the robber said, 'But that is precisely what I want,' whereupon he stole them all. Nine or ten years later, Imam al-Ghazzali met the same man again in the street. The robber asked him, 'Do you remember me?' The Imam said he did not. The man then said, `I was the one who rescued you by taking away all your books. I was the cause of your gaining knowledge. When all that information you were carrying was taken from you, you obtained knowledge!'

*3 The Night of the Decree is better than a thousand months.*

The Arabs often use seven or seventy or a thousand, or multiples of those numbers, to indicate a great number. Here *alf* (literally, a thousand) means 'a vast number.' If we suddenly understand something, we realise that the one day in which we were awakened is better than years of ignorance. In a period of ten years we may remember two or three days that were critical, which contained those moments that changed the entire course of our lives and the way we saw things. Those days brought more to us than a thousand months.

Our traditions relate that the Prophet once saw monkey-like figures preaching from his mimbar in Medina, and it is said that by this sign he predicted that for a thousand months after his death, unworthy leaders would misguide the *ummah* (the community of Muslims). One night of opening, the descent of the Qur'an, the revelation of the truth upon the Prophet, more than compensated for the thousand months of misguided leadership. Its truth is eternal; therefore, its light will always overcome darkness.

*4 The angels and the spirit descend in it with the permission of their Lord, with all the commands.*

*Ruh* means 'spirit, soul.' It is related to *rih*, which means 'wind.' *Rahah*, which means 'comfort, contentment,' or 'ease,' also comes from the same root, as does the word *ra'ihah*, which means 'perfume' and *mirwahah*, which means 'fan'. The implication here is that the spirit is like a wind; it is as subtle as a summer breeze. The spirit is blown into the body and later blown out of it. Like the wind, it subtlety is balanced by its forcefulness. It says in the Qur'an, *They ask you about the soul. Say: the soul is one of the commands of my Lord* (*Al-Isra':*85).

On that Night of Power the All-Mighty, All-powerful Lord extends His mercy of knowledge and opens up the skies, and the angelic powers and forces fulfil their merciful duty of bringing forth clearly the message and knowledge of *tawhid* (divine unity) and the command and control of the Lord.

*5 Peace! Until the break of dawn.*

From the knowledge that all creation exists according to a measure and is moving toward a destiny according to that measure, comes the peace of certainty. This inner certainty, which illumines all possible outer manifestations, brings about an equilibrium and balance that renders the awakened being in a state full of harmony and unity. The meaning of that peace, which is the result of knowledge, resides inherently in every heart. For the seed to be unearthed, the heart must be purified and made open. The seeker of the knowledge of Allah spends his days of darkness and nights of vigil awaiting the descent of the opening, and when that occurs it is like the crack of dawn.

*Fajr* means 'dawn, the first light of the morning.' *Fajara*, the root of *fajr*, means 'to crack, to break out, to explode.' The state of the heart of the knower is hidden in the darkness of the night but is illumined inwardly. It is outwardly in darkness yet bright with inner light, outwardly quiet but inwardly active and dynamic in the sea of knowledge. Most spiritual work is done from late at night until the dawn, when outwardly there is the least physical action and therefore a maximum possibility for inner action. The root of everything lies in its opposite. The root of the most beautiful, soft, white, ravishing lily lies in mud, just as the root of maximal inner action lies in outer quietude.

### The Clear Proof

#### (Surat al-Bayyinah)

*In the name of Allah, the Beneficent, the Most Merciful*

**1** *Those who denied [the truth] from among the people of the Book, and the idolworshippers, could not have separated [from the faithful] until the clear evidence came to them:*

In the Qur'an, when there are historical references to specific events, we can take them as applying equally to us in modern times. Those amongst the people who consider themselves to be of the Book who deny and cover up the truth will continue to be in doubt and in that state of denial until the blinding evidence comes to them. Even when it does come, however, they will persist in their denial. People who want to deny will continue to deny, and people who want to doubt will continue to doubt.

**2** *A messenger from Allah reciting pure pages,*

The implication here is that some of the physical, recorded books that had come down before the Prophet Muhammad were not totally intact, but were either altered or else handed down in an incomplete version. This is one of the meanings of mutahharah (pure). The Prophet Muhammad (may Allah bless him), confirmed all the prophets before him; he did not bring anything new. The Qur'an repeatedly relates what happened to earlier prophets such as Moses, Jesus, and others; the same occurrences constantly repeat themselves, with the only changes being in the setting and the social colouration. In essence, man's lower and higher natures are the same at all times.

> 3 *Containing true and sound ordinances.*
>
> 4 *And those who were given the Book were not divided until after the clear evidence came to them.*

*Al-bayyinah* (from *bana*, to be clear, evident) is the evidence of the last Prophet (may Allah bless him), that is, it is his book. *Tafarraqa*, from *faraqa*, means 'to become split up, scattered, divided, and differentiated,' and in this case, it refers to people who were divided in accepting the message of the Prophet Muhammad. When the evidence came to them, confirming what they had in their hands and purifying it from wrong interpretations, some of them accepted it, and some of them did not.

> 5 *And they were not commanded [to do] anything but to serve Allah, being sincere to Him in obedience, upright and keep up the prayer, [purify themselves by] paying the poor-rate, and that is the right religion.*

The order, the command of Allah, the command of Reality, was nothing other than to sincerely worship Allah, the Creator. *Hunafa'* are those who establish the full prayers, uphold the *din*, and perform purification and charity. The command of the Creator is only to adore and worship Allah.

> 6 *Certainly, those who cover up among the people of the Book, and the idolworshippers, will be in the fire of Hell, remaining in it; they are the worst of creatures.*

If we deny the one and only repetitive message which tells us how to be safe, how to conduct ourselves, how to reach our fullest potential in this existence by means of *salat* (prayer) and *zakat* (the paying of poor-rate, thereby purifying oneself), then there is loss and *shirk* (associating other-than-Allah with the Creator). Those who deny the message and the purity of its descent, which has come in the form of evident, revealed books, are already in the state of the Fire, in the state of agitated *jahannam*. This is the bottomless pit wherein there is neither stability nor peace, neither life nor death, but instead, constant agitation and turmoil. Man always seeks stability; this is his nature. The ritual prayer should be performed on firm ground because in our prayers we are seeking the knowledge of Allah, Who is the Permanent, the Everlasting, Ever-Continuous. That which is not stable is not truth; it is only information.

*7 Certainly, those who accept and perform right actions, those are the best of creatures.*

*8 Their reward is with their Lord in gardens of perpetuity, beneath which rivers flow, abiding in them forever; Allah is well-pleased with them, and they are well-pleased with Him. That is for him who fears his Lord.*

On the other hand, those who trust in Reality, who have peace and security within themselves, who have *iman* (trust, faith, belief) that they will come to know, who have trust that what the revealed books contain is the absolute truth emanating from the Absolute Reality, and who translate that trust into correct actions, they are the best of creation. The inward state of trust in Allah's all-encompassing mercy must be translated into action, otherwise it will remain abstract.

*Jaza'uhm* means 'their reward,' and this reward from the Sustainer comes in the form of gardens fed by underground rivers. This implies that they are fed by energies that are not visible. These rivers, or energies, are the higher attributes of man, such as forgiveness, generosity and nobility. The people of trust are forever in that state, because once a person experiences that state, or even catches a glimpse of it, he veers more and more towards it. The Qur'an repeatedly tells us that ultimately the foundation of the Path is patience. That is why we need encouragement, because we are human beings and we measure things by time.

*Allah is well-pleased with them and they are well-pleased with Him.*
They are in a state of *rida* (contentment) and here it means contentment which stems from knowledge, not superficial optimism or
mere positive thinking. *Rida* comes through knowledge and is an
aspect of perfection. At all times that which occurs is perfect, and if
we make no judgements about events we will see perfection in
them. If, however, we have prejudged a situation and are full of opposition, then we will see it only from our own narrow viewpoint.

Looking at a half-empty glass, we do not see the full half and say,
'That is very good! Half of it is full!' Human beings do not like
something only half full; we want all of it to be full. Half of the glass
is empty, however, because half of its contents were drunk. Therefore, we must accept the situation in its perfection. However it
presents itself to us, we must accept it with knowledge, with heart
and head combined. When that acceptance happens, 'Allah is
content with them, and they are content with Him.' Reality is
content with us, and we are content with Reality. When that
happens, everything in existence is content with us, because we are
completely and ecologically in tune.

*That is for him who fears his Lord.* The door to *rida*, the door to
contentment, is *khashyah*, which means 'positive fearfulness.' This
is a fearfulness of transgressing, a fearfulness of taking on a task
which we did not outwardly measure correctly, let alone inwardly,
a task for which we lacked a clear intention when we took it on.
Before we move again, we should ask, Why? When we say, '*Bis-
mi'llah*,' we perform our actions in the Name of Allah, and there is
nothing of us in them. They will succeed or fail and in either case we
say, '*al-hamdu li'llah*,' 'The praise belongs to Allah.' We acted for
Reality's sake, and if we did not succeed that is because Reality did
not want it, even though we did our best.

*Khashyah*, then, is fearful awareness, the first stage before *taqwa*
(safeguarding with fearful awareness). A person with this fear
foresees the likely outcome of following a certain destructive path
and so withholds himself from taking it. *Khashyah* also means
'prevention.' It means to be wary of transgressing, fearful that
transgression will come back upon us. That is why we say
'*astaghfiru'llah*,' and with this phrase we beseech Allah for *ghufran*.
*Ghufran* does not mean 'forgiveness.' There is no such thing. There

is only One, Single, Unified Reality, so who can forgive whom? *Ghufran* means to be protected both from actions emanating from us without the right intention or the right knowledge, and from what we have done in the past that we did not do in the Name of Allah, and which will come back to us. This is *ghufran*, this is the forgiveness that is meant. Forgiveness is not a dialogue between two people, because that is *shirk*, that is duality. What we desire is full realisation of our state of *tawhid;* we desire oneness, with no separation.

### Mankind (Surat al-Nas)

*In the Name of Allah, the Beneficent, the Most Merciful*

The final part of the Qur'an is concerned with taking refuge, while the beginning of the Qur'an is concerned with the recognition that the only path to success is that of glorification, supplication and praise.

The arrangement of the surahs in the Qur'an is a perfect one which was made by the perfect man, the Prophet Muhammad (may Allah bless him). The very fact that he arranged them provides the proof of the Qur'an's unity and completion. The revelation brought to mankind different aspects of the Tablet, or Book of Reality, on different days, in different months, and under different conditions. These diverse aspects, however, all reflected the one and only Light, and only the Prophet knew how they were to be arranged in accordance with the only model which exists.

**1 Say: I take refuge in the Lord of mankind,**

*Nas* means 'people, mankind.' The word comes from the root-word *nasiya*, which means 'to forget,' denoting one aspect of man's nature. The attribute of forgetfulness can, however, be used to full advantage when we forget what is of no use to us and are thus better able to remember what is of priority to us. In this way we will not forget that at any moment we may die.

**2 The King of mankind,**

### 3 The God of mankind,

We take refuge in the Lord, in the Creator of this entity called 'man,' who contains within himself both the higher attributes and the lower attributes. We take refuge in Allah from the lower attributes, from the attributes which cause us loss, which cause us further forgetfulness.

### 4 From the evil whispering of the elusive shaytan,

There is a great deal written about the word waswas, which is the subtle whispering in one's innermost that incites one to evil. In one reference ten meanings are given for *al-waswasah*, denoting ten different attributes of the whisperer. If we overcome them we will understand the *shirk* of *waswas*, and we will be able to truly take refuge from it.

*Waswas* is an onomatopoeic word imitative of the sound of whispering. Whispering is one of the actions which, in our *din* and in our adab (code of courtesy), is very much repudiated, because something worth saying should be shared by saying it out loud.

*Khannas* is an epithet of *shaytan*, and means 'slinking away,' specifically when the Name of Allah is mentioned.

There are sources or rivers which feed the waswas. Just as the Garden has underground rivers which feed it, so too has the *waswas*. One of these rivers is *hirs* (greed or covetousness). That river can be fought, blocked, and dammed by *tawakkul wa qana'* (trustful dependence [on Allah] and contentment).

Another river is amal, which means 'expectation.' This river, too, can be dammed by constant remembrance, *dhikr*. Our hope for things of this world can be stopped by remembering that each breath may be our last. This remembrance will cut the flow of that river which feeds the whisperer who pours distracting suggestions into our ear.

The third river is *shahawat al-dunya*, or 'worldly desires.' These desires can be killed by remembering that the *ni'am* (favours, bounties) will all eventually leave us, and that the *hisab* (account) will have to be made by us. We will have to account for the way in which we spent the bounty and goodness that was given to us. It will be a lengthy account – we are told 50 thousand years – in which every minute detail will be reviewed and examined, and in which even something as seemingly minor as a twitch can be a witness for or against us.

The fourth river, or source, of *waswas* is *tahsil*, meaning 'acquisition.' This river can be stopped by seeing the justice of each person's situation. What a person reaps arises from the justice of his own situation, and we cannot alter it.

The fifth river is *bala'*, 'affliction.' The flow of this can be stemmed by not looking at the affliction in a situation, but rather by seeing the bestowal of the good in it.

The sixth river is *kibr*, or 'pride,' which can be fought by humility. Whenever *kibr* rises up in us, we should immediately call upon the humility within ourselves, so that we break its effect on us.

The seventh river (*tahqir*) is that which entices us to belittle the honourable position of the believers, as well as anything that the believer possesses, anything that is in his domain, and that which is *halal* (permitted) for him and *haram* (forbidden) for others. This river can be stopped by considering the honour of the believers to be great and by respecting it.

The eighth source of *waswas* is the love of *dunya* (this world, together with the desire to be acknowledged and admired by others). This love and desire can be undone by bringing oneself to the state of abasement.

The ninth source of *waswas* which encourages *shaytan* is separation and stinginess (*bukhl*). This can be fought by generosity. There are four types of generosity. *Sakha'* means 'giving according to what the occasion demands;' *jud* means 'giving without being asked;' and *karam* is 'giving whatever has been asked.' These three are attributes of Allah. The fourth is *ithar*, 'giving what one needs oneself,' and this is an attribute which only man can have. Allah cannot have this attribute, for Allah has no need whatsoever of anything. Thus, we can take on this final attribute, which is a great aid for our inner, upward mobility toward that noble state which befits the *khalifah*, or viceregent, of Allah.

## 5 Who whispers in the innermost hearts of mankind,

*Sadr* (plural *sudur*) is the 'chest' or 'breast,' that part of one which faces what confronts one. It is where the battles and dramas take place. It must be remembered that every drama is self-created. Every imaginable human role stirs in the breast of man: the king, the despot, the afflicted, the jealous, the strong, the doubter, and the complainer. We have to take refuge from these, take refuge in the Lord, Whose mercy brings us to the recognition that everything which occurs, visible and invisible, occurs according to a just system, according to perfect laws which govern this passage, this journey through the creation.

## 6 From jinn and mankind.

*Jinnah* is synonymous with *jinn*, and means 'the unseen, hidden forces of power.' *Jannah* (the Garden) is derived from the same root and it refers to the most desirable place to be, a garden, which, in the desert culture of the Arabs of that time where the average temperature was 100 degrees, was a place where there was shade, and where the ground could not be seen for the thick foliage of the trees.
 The ground was 'hidden' by the growth and thus it refers to a hidden state.

# SECTION 6

## Prophets and Imams

*We have not sent thee [Muhammad] but as a mercy to all the worlds.*
(21:107)
*And indeed, within every community have We raised up an apostle
entrusted with this message: 'Worship Allah and shun the powers of
evil!' (16:4)*

*Allah only wishes to remove from you all that might be loathsome, O
people of the House, and to purify you to utmost purity. (33:33)*

# The Transmission of Original Islam

## By Muqaddem Hajj Abdal Hayy al-Amin

*In the Name of Allah, the Universally Merciful, the Specifically Merciful!*

*Has an epoch of time passed over mankind when he was a thing not remembered?*

*Surely, We created man from a sperm-drop, mingled, to test him – we made him hearing, seeing.*

*Certainly We have guided him on a way whether he is thankful or whether he covers up.*

(76:1–3)

There has never been a time on earth when Allah has left mankind without guidance. Even after the death of the last Prophet, Muhammad (peace upon him), Allah has continually been sending guides as pure transmitters of the Prophet's message, keeping the universe filled at a constant level with the Light of Muhammad. Without these guides, the world itself would be dark and cold. One can glimpse the Prophet himself through their living example. They keep the message alive, and by a subtle, inexplicable energy, or radiance, they are able to touch and transform the hearts of people who come to them with trust. By a pure spiritual alchemy, these perfected men transform those in their circle into receptive containers for the deep dimensions of the message, and by so doing, transform them into true transmitters in their turn. This is one of the miracles of Allah, which, by His word, will continue until the end of time.

During the Prophet's lifetime he made many references to certain Companions whose guidance could be trusted, and he made many references to one in particular, Sayyidina 'Ali (may Allah illuminate his face). He also spoke about the special spiritual qualities and destinies of his own family, closely defining them as 'Ali, Fatimah, Hasan and Husayn, saying, 'Love of them is a sign of belief, and enmity towards them is a sign of unbelief. Whoever loves them, loves Allah and His Messenger, and whoever shows enmity towards them shows enmity towards Allah and His Messenger.'

From the death of the Prophet (peace be upon him), the succession of Imams known as the Imamate begins with the man of the vastest spiritual dimension after him, Sayyidina 'Ali. It then continues with his progeny, from father to designated and divinely-sanctioned son within the purified genetic line of the Prophet, until the twelfth Imam, the Mahdi, who disappeared at a young age, and is due to return at the end of time. This is Allah's way of spreading and transmitting guidance within that most beloved of families, confirming what the Prophet himself said about them, and thus carrying on a natural familial heritage, the pure knowledge being carried on via pure receptacles.

This knowledge also spreads out through mankind by way of men that Allah has specially chosen with grace, the awliya' and men of light. Many of them are of the family of the Prophet as well, and are great beacons of knowledge and guides to men in many parts of the world, known today as Sufis. These lights, by their capacity, have guided centuries of men and women to face-to-face knowledge of Allah.

The *nafs* (self or ego) of man, created by Allah 'in haste', as He Himself says in His Book, bloomed again in full force as soon as the Prophet was gone, although there were signs of it about to happen even on his death-bed.

Immediately after the Prophet's death there was both a zeal to protect the original teaching intact, but also as great, if not greater, zeal to overthrow that teaching in favour of political power and a lust for wealth and empire. The question of leadership, both wordly and spiritual, became a burning issue, and in terms of contemporary situations it remains so today. If Allah's guidance had been followed completely, as manifested through His Prophet, there may have been no problem. The fact that now there were over seventy thousand Muslims (some say one hundred and fourteen thousand attended the Farewell Hajj) and that Islam as a religion was spilling beyond containable physical boundaries into distant countries, called for a leader who was best able to combine both the outward and inward teaching as guide and exemplar. But tribal emotions and rivalries, fuelled by a desire for power, led to immediate conflict and compromise. The first steps were taken. They could not be undone. Abu Bakr was elected, in haste, to contain rival factions before the whole thing blew up. Step-by-step a course of action was taken which led, finally, to the Caliph Mucawiyah and his son Yazid, a public profligate, insisting that outward political governance should be separate from spiritual transmission.

During the reign of the first three Caliphs, Sayyidina 'Ali remained more or less in seclusion, although he was always respected by some for his depth of knowledge, and recognised by the second Caliph, 'Umar, as the best one from whom to seek counsel. Sayyidina 'Ali only entered into the passionate arena of governance after the subtle and Spartan teaching of Islam was all but eclipsed by man's wild greed. His nature, ascetic in the pure way of the Prophet, and his attempts to revive the ideals which he himself had absorbed, angered and frustrated many Muslims at this time, so that ultimately he was martyred while praying in the mosque at Kufah.

After him came his two sons, Hasan and Husayn, who in their youth had already been recorded as being remarkable in their comprehension of the truth of the Prophetic message, and obviously were dearly beloved of the Prophet himself, who called them his sons. But the *nafs* was reacting to the spiritual imperative of the Prophet with savage fury and with the emergence of Mu'awiyah and Yazid we are forced to witness one of the most shocking wholesale slaughters ever to have taken place in the history of man, until modern times. A madly inspired vendetta against the family of the Prophet began, and did not end for centuries, vestiges of it continuing even today. The army of Yazid, standing for the lowest in man's nature, in a rage to eradicate the highest, trampled Husayn's body into the mud and from then on not one of the grandsons and even the women within the family line was safe. For centuries even the memory of 'Ali was cursed from the pulpits in the mosques everywhere during the Friday Prayer, by official decree. Politically, the madmen had taken control. It is no wonder that there is such a blackout on the whole story for the majority of Muslims, and such a prejudice against even looking at Sayyidina 'Ali, or the Imams of *Ahl al-Bayt* (the People of the Household).

It is obvious that these inheritors of the transmission within the genetic stream were giants of knowledge and light. When we reach the sixth Imam, Ja'far al-Sadiq, we see a man who personally taught thousands of people, Imam Malik among them. The latter said, `I used to go to Ja'far ibn Muhammad, and he was often smiling, but when the Prophet was mentioned, seriousness and marks of respect showed on his face. Whenever I visited him, I found him in one of three situations, either praying, or fasting, or reading the Qur'an. Whenever he spoke about the Messenger of Allah, he did that while he was in a state of ritual purity and he always spoke the right words. He was from God-fearing people who were not materialistic, but were true worshippers.' Imam al-Shafi'i said, in a poem, 'Members of the House of the Messenger of Allah, your love is an imperative duty that was revealed in the Qur'an. It is a sufficient distinction for you that whoever does not pray for you makes no prayer.'

It is our duty to take from the men whom Allah has most favoured, wherever that may be found. The Prophet (peace be upon him) said, 'Knowledge is the lost riding beast of the believer, so take hold of it wherever you come across it.' This is our position, and this is our Path, the original Islam as expounded by the Prophet who was the first light taken from Allah's Light, when the Lord said to it, 'Be Muhammad!' From him have flowed glorious rivers and channels, from him come and will continue to come great men who are our guides in this world, delivering the message whole, in its totality, soaking us through with its blessing, and washing our hearts with its transformative light. All if Allah wills, within His perfect plan.

*O Mankind! There has come an admonition to you from your Lord, and healing for what is in the breasts, and guidance and mercy for the acceptors. (10:57)*

# Character of the Prophet

## By Zahra Lazarus

According to Islamic belief, Muhammad (may Allah bless him) was chosen by Allah, at the beginning of time to be the Messenger of Allah. In the words of Shaykh Muzaffer Ozak:

> Before creating all these unnumerable creatures, Allah created a light from his Light and said to that light: 'Be Muhammad!' That light became the light of our Master, on him be peace. That light acknowledged its Lord saying: 'There is no god but Allah.' Allah, Exalted is He, responded to this acknowledgement with 'Muhammad is the Messenger of Allah.' This blessed sentence was the lock with which He locked the gate of Hell, the key with which He opened the eight doors of Paradise.

His mission of calling humanity to the worship of one God was absolutely necessary as it was imbued in his nature. Carrying the message of God, the revelation of unity, required that Muhammad (may Allah bless him) challenge the deep-seated beliefs of the most powerful men of his time. The obstacles were indeed formidable, but he never deviated from his mission, fulfilling his potential with urgency and devotion.

In this article we will consider some of the qualities of the Prophet's character which must be followed by those who desire to be raised from ignorance to knowledge and realisation.

**Efficient Perception of Reality**

Muhammad (may Allah bless him) was able to perceive reality clearly. He possessed a keen ability to discern character, and was able to see through established social forms. A good example of this trait is found in a facet of the story of Bilal. Bilal was an uneducated, black, non-Arab slave, owned by a master who tortured him because of his beliefs. On the lowest rung of Meccan society, he had no rights and commanded no respect. Yet Muhammad (may Allah bless him) was able to see through this rough exterior to the beautiful soul of Bilal and paid a high ransom for his freedom.

As Shaykh Muzaffer Ozak recounts:

> The venerable Bilal the Abyssinian (may God be pleased with him) was the Negro slave of Umayya ibn Khalaf, one of the most violent of polytheists. Bilal had a heart of pure light, but Umayya ibn Khalaf was an implacable enemy of the religion of Islam and of the Prophet (on whom be peace). The time came when Bilal was blessed with faith. Umayya ibn Khalaf came to hear of this, so he began taking his slave out into the desert and subjecting him to appalling tortures in the hope of forcing him to apostasize from the religion of Islam... In spite of all this, the only sounds to be heard issuing from the mouth of the venerable Bilal were the names of his Loved Ones: 'O One! O Ahmad!'

When Muhammad (may Allah bless him) heard of Bilal's plight, he sent Abu Bakr to arrange to buy him. Although Bilal was a slave, Muhammad responded to the quality of his heart and the depth of his devotion to God as well as to Islam. He saw through the exterior to the inner essence.

**Acceptance**

A study of Muhammad's life shows him free from unnecessary guilt, shame and anxiety. Life presented him with many extremely stressful situations after he began to receive revelation and share it publicly. He was subjected to persecution, near starvation, attempted assassination and military attack. But he met all these challenges with full acceptance, never succumbing to fear or anxiety.

Muhammad's attitude of acceptance toward the body is clearly demonstrated in a conversation he had with 'Uthman, the most ascetic of his companions. 'Uthman asked permission of Muhammad to make himself a eunuch and to spend the rest of his life as a beggar. Muhammad (may Allah bless him) said: 'Do not do so . . . Hast thou not in me a fair example? And I go into women, and I eat meat, and I fast and I break my fast.'

## Simplicity and Naturalness

Muhammad's actions were described as simple, though simplicity was considered a virtue only when it did not interfere with obeying the commandments of Allah as he perceived them. Whenever he had to choose between two actions, he always adopted the easier, simpler course, as long as there was no sin or breach of Islam involved. If there was any sin involved, however, he was 'the farthest from it of the people.'

In the beginning of Muhammad's prophethood he lived simply, although there was not much opportunity at that time to do otherwise. Food and other supplies were difficult to come by. During the years of the embargo in Mecca, it was hardly possible to gather enough food for his family. But there came a time, after his migration to Medina, when the tides turned. Muhammad (may Allah bless him) became ruler of Medina, and eventually of all Arabia. His religion began to spread at an incredibly quick rate. He won victory after victory, diplomatic as well as material. Much wealth flowed through his hands. There was a great opportunity, at this time, for him to change his simple ways and begin to live a life of wealth and luxury.

But Muhammad (may Allah bless him) maintained his simple and natural lifestyle until his death. He made much of his own clothing. He lived in a simple home. He helped his wives with their housework. He cobbled his own shoes. And he gave away most of what was given to him soon after he received it, dying a relatively poor man.

### Independence, Concentration and Detachment

Muhammad (may Allah bless him) can be described as independent of the culture of his birth. During his lifetime, he rejected one of the main premises of his native culture m idol worship. He was instrumental in the creation of a new life transaction, the *din* of Islam. He centred his life around the mission of carrying the message of One God to a population steeped in idolatry. He was willing to risk everything – his life, his family, his reputation, his wealth – over and over again to carry out his mission as the Messenger of God. It was a task that he knew was given to him by Allah, a task which he felt that he must perform, regardless of whether or not he wanted to.

Muhammad (may Allah bless him) remained unruffled and undisturbed by what normally produces turmoil in others. He was able to maintain presence of mind in the face of extraordinarily stressful situations. His detachment was further exemplified by his ability to concentrate and stay with a task to a degree not usual for ordinary men. When he made a deliberate effort toward some end, there was no earnestness that could compare with his.

In terms of his capacity for autonomy, the Prophet has been described as responsible, self-disciplined and self-governing. His responsible attitude in business led to his being known as *al-Amin*, the trustworthy. His masterful self-discipline was legendary among his followers. His ability to pray for long hours at a time so out-reached the capabilities of other Muslims that he instructed his followers to pray as he said, not as he did. It would have been impossible for others to follow his example even on a purely physical level, to say nothing of their inability to match the inner depth of his prayers.

### Brotherliness or Comradeship

A study of Muhammad (may Allah bless him) reveals a deep feeling of love, sympathy, and concern for his friends as well as for all members of his community. He was often in the position of caring for, protecting, and teaching his brothers. Not only did he make it a point to visit the sick and offer individual assistance whenever and however he could, but he spent countless hours praying for the well-being of his community. Imam 'Ali recalled that Muhammad's last words, on his death bed, were: 'My community, my community.'

Just as Muhammad (may Allah bless him) treated his community with love and care, so did he encourage high standards of brotherhood between members of his community. He taught that no one was a true believer in Islam until he liked for his brother what he loved for himself. He said: 'A believer is like a brick for another believer, the one supporting the other . . .the believers are like one person; if his head aches, the whole body aches with fever and sleeplessness.'

He taught his community ways to build a feeling of brotherhood between themselves. He said: 'Give presents to one another for this will increase your mutual love.' He counselled his people against back-biting and asked them to conceal the faults of their brothers: 'The servant who conceals the faults of others in this world, Allah will also conceal [his faults] on the Day of Resurrection.' He asked his community always to greet each other with the words, *'as-salamu 'alaykum'* (may peace be with you), saying this was another simple way to increase love between them.

### Profound Interpersonal Relations

*'Ali pressed his hand over every part of the long woollen garment [of the Prophet]. 'Dearer than my father and my mother,' he said, 'how excellent art thou, in life and in death.'*

Muhammad (may Allah bless him) maintained a number of profoundly deep relationships with people of an unusually high calibre. Khadijah, Muhammad's first wife had rejected marriage proposals from the wealthiest and noblest members of the Quraysh before her marriage to Muhammad. The marriage lasted twenty-five years and is reported to have been a happy and nurturing one. Her ability to discern that Muhammad was receiving true revelation and her faith in her husband were a great solace and support to him during the early years of Islam.

The story of Zayd, Muhammad's freed man who chose to remain his slave rather than return to live with his real father, is another example of the depth of love and loyalty that the Prophet inspired in those with whom he related. Imam 'Ali was willing to risk his life for him by sleeping in his bed when assassins came to murder him. These are only three of many examples.

## Egalitarianism and Compassion for the Oppressed

Muhammad (may Allah bless him) made it clear from the very beginning that the new religion of Islam did not discriminate on the basis of class, race, education, or any other criteria.

Muhammad (may Allah bless him) made serious efforts to secure the rights of the vulnerable and disadvantaged in his community. He encouraged members of his community to look after widows and poor people. He often spoke of the blessings that would come to one who acted kindly to orphans. It is said that he once met a forlorn looking child who reported to him that his stepfather had died a martyr, his mother had remarried, and his stepfather did not look after him. Whereupon Muhammad (may Allah bless him) adopted the child himself.

Attending to another section of his community, Muhammad (may Allah bless him) introduced a code of ethics dealing with slavery. He declared it most excellent to emancipate slaves, saying Allah would set free from Hell an organ of his (the emancipator's) body for every organ of the freed slave's body. He discouraged all types of slavery and only permitted taking war prisoners when no reasonable way could be found for granting them liberty. For those who kept slaves, he set down some strict guidelines. He asked that the slave be fed with what the master himself ate, that he be clothed with what the master himself wore, and that he should not be burdened beyond capacity. He cautioned that if a master beat a slave, he must expiate his sin by setting the slave free.

The position of women in Arabia was not much better than that of slaves. Muhammad (may Allah bless him) did what he could in his lifetime to help the plight of women. In pre-Islamic Arabia, women were thought of as property and were denied any share of inheritance. The Prophet instituted the practice of making women co-sharers with men in inheritance. He asked his community to treat widows with kindness and generosity. In his own home he was fond of helping with housework whenever he could, and was reported to have treated his wives with great love and respect.

In a similar vein, Muhammad (may Allah bless him) set humanitarian guidelines for the treatment of prisoners. He cautioned that when a prisoner must be killed, he should be killed in a good way, that is, without torture. When possible, it was his preference to set prisoners free. After the Battle of Uhud, he granted pardons to any one of the opposing side who applied to him. After his victory in Mecca, despite his ill treatment for so many years by the Quraysh, he chose to free all prisoners and return to them all their property.

This humanitarian treatment even extended to animals. Muhammad (may Allah bless him) forbade the torture of animals and asked that when they were slaughtered, they be slaughtered without torture, preferably with one's own hand.

He taught his followers that they should act against the abominable. He said: 'He who amongst you should see something abominable should modify it with the help of his hand; and if he has not strength enough to do it, then he should do it with his tongue, and if he has not strength enough to do it, [even] then he should [abhor it] from his heart, and that is the least of faith.'

## Discrimination between Good and Evil and between Means and Ends

A study of Muhammad (may Allah bless him) reveals a strong ethical sense and very little confusion about right and wrong. Even enemies of Islam in Mecca trusted him more than any other man to guard their belongings for them, knowing that he would keep them safe. As a businessman he not only personally practised in an ethical manner, but when he had the authority, he established a number of practices which encouraged honest and humane dealings between his followers. For example, he taught that it was excellent to treat a debtor with mercy, if the debtor's circumstances were dire. On the other hand, if one was able to repay a loan, he encouraged prompt repayment with no delay. He encouraged truthfulness in business transactions and discouraged monopoly, speculative business based on selfish interests, and any transaction where there was not full disclosure.

Muhammad (may Allah bless him) prohibited various activities among his community. A brief look at these demonstrates the strong ethical bent to his nature. He prohibited tale carrying; imposing obligations on those to whom you have done favours; selling under false pretences; slandering innocent women; withholding generosity out of anger; wasting time; back-biting; pride; praising to the point of intoxication; hypocrisy (not doing what you command others to do); ostentation; becoming frustrated with regard to God's mercy; abusing others; committing oppression or acting tyrannically to another; and nursing mutual jealousy, hatred or hostility.

Muhammad (may Allah bless him) was very clear about his end goal: spreading the message of One God to humanity. He never lost sight of this end and used a wide variety of means to help him achieve it. Some of the means at his disposal included preaching, establishing a community in Medina based on the guidance that came to him through revelation, strengthening an army to help defend his community from aggression, and living his life in close harmony with the guidance that he received.

Muhammad (may Allah bless him) taught that every single occurrence has the possibility of good in it because it either represents an opportunity to express gratitude to God for His blessings, or an opportunity to practise patience in the face of adversity.

## Philosophical, Unhostile Sense of Humour

There is a wonderful story of Muhammad (may Allah bless him) which illustrates his humour. He and his army had just captured some of the members of the Quraysh against whom they had been fighting. When the Meccans saw him approaching them, they cowered with fear, thinking they were about to be killed. Muhammad (may Allah bless him) suddenly laughed. At this, the captured members of the Quraysh became very frightened, thinking that he was laughing because he was going to have them tortured. They muttered that they didn't think he was so cruel as to torture captives. At that he said to the captives: 'No, you don't understand. I'm laughing at how I have to chain you and drag you to the truth, and how unwilling you are to accept what is going to be your salvation.' His laughter was not angry or hostile. It was compassionate and philosophical. He was struck by the humour of the fact that he was simply trying to touch these men's lives and bring them a message from Allah, yet they were fighting against him.

## Freshness of Approach and Diplomacy

These qualities are illustrated by the manner in which the Prophet solved the problem of lifting the Black Stone of the Ka'bah to its new resting place. He suggested that the stone be placed on a cloth and that each of the factions who wanted the honour of lifting the stone should hold a corner of the cloth. The Prophet approached the problem creatively and with an open mind. According to biographer Martin Lings, it was believed that 'no voice in all Medina could compare with his for solving a problem or answering a question or settling a dispute.'

> Just as mankind has been created as the most perfect of all creatures, so the venerable Muhammad (may Allah bless him) has been created as the most perfect application of knowledge. It is impossible to give any better example, for none exists, nor will ever exist. Allah has told us so.

> (Shaykh Muzaffer Ozak)

# The Nature of the Imamate

## By Abbas Mubarak

The word of Imam means leader, and it is derived from *amma*, meaning 'being ahead of,' 'in front of.' It is used to describe the twelve men of the *Ahl-al-Bayt* (the People of the Prophet's Household), who by Allah's permission, were sent as *hujaj* (proofs) to the people. It means both the socio-political, as well as spiritual, leader of the Muslim community or *ummah*.

Amongst the Shi'ah, the meaning of the word Imam is based upon Allah's usage. In the Qur'an it appears many times. Allah says in Qur'an:

> *And We made them Imams (leaders) who guided people by Our command. (21:73)*

> *And to make them the Imams, and to make them the Imams, and to make them the heirs. (28:5)*

> *And We made of them Imams to guide by Our command when they were patient . . . (32:24)*

Abraham (peace be upon him) was an Imam. It says in the Qur'an:

*He said: 'Surely, I will make you an Imam of men.' Abraham said: 'And of my offspring?' 'My covenant does not include the unjust,' He said. (2:124).*

Moses (peace be upon him), like Abraham, was also both a prophet and an Imam. It is interesting to note his relationship to his brother Aaron, who was a prophet but not initially an Imam. From a story in the Qur'an, it is seen that Moses had authority over Aaron by his Imamate. Moses ordered Aaron to keep watch over the people in his absence, and when Moses died Aaron, in turn, became the Imam. The Prophet Muhammad (peace be upon him) thus described the relationship between himself and 'Ali as the same as that between Moses and Aaron.

All Muslims know that the Prophet Muhammad (peace be upon him) was sent *as a mercy (rahmah) for all the worlds.* (21:107). They know that he is the last prophet, and that his message is the last message for all the peoples until the end of time. They know that the Book, the Qur'an, is the guide and the criterion (*furqan*) that is valid until the Day of Resurrection. Allah, the infinitely Merciful, has promised that the believers will not be without a guide while they dwell upon the earth.

The Prophet said: 'It seems that Allah has called me to Himself and I must obey His call. I leave two great and precious things among you. The Book of Allah and My household. Be careful how you behave towards them. These two will never be separated from each other until they encounter me at *Kawthar* (in the Garden).'

The Book of Allah and the *Ahl-al-Bayt,* the Prophet's Household, are the two precious gifts which the Prophet (peace be upon him), has left for his followers. Allah says in the Glorious Qur'an:

*And Allah only wishes to remove all impurities from you, O Ahl-al-Bayt, and to purify you completely. (33:33)*

The Ahl-al-Bayt are the purified ones, and from them come the Imams.

The doctine of the Imamate rests upon two fundamental principles. The first is that the Imamate is a prerogative bestowed by Allah upon a chosen person, from the family of the Prophet, who before his death, and with the guidance of Allah, transfers the Imamate to another by an explicit designation. Whether he claims the temporal power or not does not matter, as there is only one man who has legitimate claim to the Imamate. This mechanism of handing over the authority of political-spiritual rule is seen quite clearly in Muhammad's preferential treatment and praise of 'Ali. For example, the Prophet used to say: 'Ali is my brother, my trustee, and successor after me.'

In order to make clear the sound origin of the authority of the Imamate, the first example being that of 'Ali ibn Abi Talib, the following Qur'anic verse is mentioned.

> *Your wali (ruler or friend) can be only Allah and His messenger and those who believe, who establish worship and pay the poor-rate (zakat) while bowing in prayer.* (5:55)

Abu Dharr al-Ghifarri said: 'One day we prayed the noon-time prayers with the Prophet. A person (Gabriel) in need asked people to help him but no one would assist him. Gabriel raised his hands to the sky saying, "O Allah! Be a witness that in the mosque of the Prophet no one would give me anything." 'Ali ibn Abi Talib was in the bowing position in the prayer. He pointed with his finger to the person, who took his ring and left. The Prophet, who had observed this event, raised his head toward heaven and said: "O Allah! My brother Moses said to You, Expand my breast and make easy my tasks, and make my tongue eloquent so that they will comprehend my words, and make my brother, Aaron, my help and vizier. O Allah! I am also Your Prophet – expand my breast and make easy my tasks, and make 'Ali my vizier and helper." ' Abu Dharr then said: 'The words of the Prophet had not as yet finished when the verse (cited above) was revealed.'

It is well known that the Prophet had left the Muslims detailed directions on all forms of worship and behaviour. Is it possible that the Prophet would leave such an important matter as the leadership of the community open to political squabbling? The followers of the *Ahl-al-Bayt* believe that this could not be the case. On the way back from the Hajj pilgrimage, the Prophet received this revelation:

*O Messenger! Make known that which has been revealed to you from your Lord, for if you do it not, you will not have conveyed His message. Allah will protect you from mankind. (5:67)*

There was something that the Prophet had yet to do. He was approaching the end of his life and his deliverance of the message was almost complete. After he received this ayah, the Prophet called the people together. In a Hadith it is related: 'The Prophet, in Ghadir Khumm, invited people towards 'Ali and took his arm and lifted it so high that the spot in the armpit of the Prophet of Allah could be seen. Then this ayah was revealed: "This day have I perfected your religion for you and completed my favour unto you, and have chosen for you as a religion *al-Islam*." Then the Prophet said, "Allah is great, that the religion has become perfected and that Allah's bounty has been completed, His satisfaction attained and the rule (*walayah*) of 'Ali achieved." Then he added, "For whomever I am the authority and guide, 'Ali is also his guide and authority. O Allah. Be friendly with the friends of 'Ali, and the enemy of his enemies. Whoever helps him, help him, and whoever leaves him, leave him." Then Umar, may Allah be pleased with him, said to 'Ali: "May this position be pleasing to you, for now you are my master and the master of all the believers." '

Though 'Umar is reported to have made the above statement to 'Ali, we find that when the Prophet died the Quraysh seized power and claimed that it is better not to have both the spiritual and the political leadership within the same family, that of the Banu Hashim (the Prophet's family). Clearly there was a reaction to 'Ali and the family of the Prophet, which was one of mistrust. Why were the Quraysh afraid of the noble family of the Prophet? There is a revealing dialogue between 'Umar and Ibn 'Abbas indicating the duplicity on the part of the Quraysh. After reciting a poem describing the glory, nobility of descent, and virtues of a certain Arab clan, 'Umar said to Ibn 'Abbas: `I do not know any other clan among the Quraysh to whom these verses can be better applied than the Banu Hashim, because of their kinship and superior claims to the Prophet, but the people did not want to allow the prophethood and caliphate in your family so that you would become arrogant and rejoice at it among the people. The Quraysh, therefore, preferred to choose the leader for themselves and they made the right choice and were guided by Allah in that.'

'O Commander of the Faithful,' said Ibn 'Abbas, 'As for your statement that the Quraysh chose their own leader and were guided in the right choice, it would be correct if the choice of the Quraysh was the same as the choice of Allah. As for your statement that the Quraysh did not like to allow both the prophethood and the caliphate to be with us, it is not surprising, for Allah has described many people who dislike "what Allah has sent down to them and thus render their deeds fruitless." ' At this point 'Umar became angry and said: `I have heard many things about you, but I ignored them because of my regard for you. I am told that you think that we have taken the caliphate away from you through oppression and because of envy.' 'As for oppression, it is evident,' said Ibn 'Abbas, 'and concerning envy, it is obvious: Satan envied Adam, and we are the children of Adam.' 'Umar lost his temper and retorted, 'Alas, O Banu Hashim, your hearts are full of hatred, rancour and false pretensions.' 'Be gentle, O Commander of the Faithful,' said Ibn 'Abbas, 'and do not describe the hearts of those from whom Allah has removed all kinds of uncleanliness and whom He has purified with complete purification. Moreover, the Prophet himself belonged to the Banu Hashim.' 'Let us leave this topic,' said 'Umar. Yet it is precisely what the Quraysh claimed to fear from the leadership of the *Ahl al-Bayt* that they later perpetrated in the most brutal fashion.

Mu'awiyah, who was the major opponent of 'Ali, and later, after his death, of Hasan, said in a letter to Imam Hasan that the interest of the state and the populace must decide the question of leadership. Mu'awiyah did not deny Hasan's exalted position in relation to the Prophet, and his superior place in Islam, but claimed that this was not the criterion for determining the leadership of the community. The qualifications for the position were, according to Mu'awiyah's arguments, personal power and strength, ability in political affairs and administration, expansion of the empire, and the ability to defend the Muslims and rule the subjects effectively. In this way Mu'awayah and later other politically motivated strongmen could justify their position in relation to the people of knowledge, the *Ahl al-Bayt*.

In order to understand the concept and function of the Imamate, it is useful to look at the statements made by the first three Imams.

Each statement contributes to a deepening awareness of the nature of Imamate. After three days of wrangling, the members of the electoral body (the *shura*) still had not come to a decision as to who would succeed 'Umar as caliph. It was then that 'Ali was offered the caliphate if he would agree to rule by the Qur'an and the Sunnah of the Prophet, and comply with the precedents established by the two former caliphs. But 'Ali could not agree to the second rule declaring that in all cases in which he found no positive law of the Qur'an or decision of the Prophet, he would rely only upon his own judgement. At this point 'Ali made a clear distinction between himself and the rest of the companions. The way of life that developed amongst the great companions in Medina after the Prophet's death is clearly shown to diverge from the pure teaching of the *Ahl al-Bayt*.

Hasan, who became Imam after 'Ali, tells Mu'awiyah in a letter that his rights to the leadership of the Muslim Community are based on the nearness of his family to the Prophet. He claims that he is nearest to the Prophet in birth and intimacy. Some years later, responding to the Muslims of Kufah, Imam Husayn the third Imam, explains the concept of *walayah*, meaning that Allah has bestowed upon the family of the Prophet special honour and qualities, making the *Ahl al-Bayt* the ideal rulers, and that it is through their presence on earth that His grace is spread. Husayn also declared that the right of ruling the community is the exclusive right of the family of the Prophet, and that they alone can guide the people in the right path, or in other words, they alone, by virtue of their transmitted knowledge, can combine temporal power and spiritual guidance.

It was stated that the first principle of the Imamate is that the Imams must be clearly designated by their predecessors. The second principle embodied in the doctrine of the Imamate is that an Imam is the divinely inspired possessor of a special body of knowledge which can only be passed on before his death to the following Imam. This special transmitted knowledge includes both the external and the internal meanings of the Qur'an as well as other sciences that nourish mankind. The Prophet indicated the nature of this special rank in knowledge by his statement, 'I am the city of knowledge and 'Ali is its gate.' 'Ali himself said, 'The Prophet fed me knowledge as the pouter pidgeon feeds it to its young,' meaning that is was easily assimilable.

It is clear that the closeness of 'Ali to the Prophet was more than just a physical proximity. The man who proved his valour and courage in innumerable battles in defence of Islam also proved himself to be the most knowledgeable in the sciences of religion.

The position of 'Ali in respect to the first three caliphs was unique. 'Umar used to say, 'If 'Ali were not present 'Umar would be destroyed.' The companions were very aware that the depth of knowledge possessed by 'Ali was greater than the knowledge possessed by any other companion, as was indicated by the Prophet.

'Ali was also the inheritor of the inner sciences of the heart. Most of the Sufi *turuq* (paths) trace their lineage through him directly to the Prophet. He is widely recognised amongst the Sufis as being the spiritual fountainhead of the inner way to knowledge of Allah, and the foremost expounder of the pure and majestic science of divine unity.

He is acknowledged as the founder of the science of Arabic grammar and the recitation of the Qur'an, and he possessed a vast knowledge of many other sciences as well. In his discourses he said: 'The source of life comes from something so small you cannot even see it, but if you could see it, it is like a little double coil, a double spiral.' It is only recently that scientists have constructed a model of the DNA molecule, which manifests itself as a double helix spiral!

This is the man who fathered the blessed Imams of the *Ahl al-Bayt*. Each of these Imams preserved and guarded this special knowledge and made it available to their sincere followers.

Imam Ja'far al–Sadiq related: 'Allah delegated to the Imams spiritual rulership over the whole world, which must always have such a leader and guide. Even if only two men were left upon the face of the earth, one of them would be an Imam, so much would his guidance be needed.'

Thus the Imamate is a covenant between Allah and mankind, and the recognition of the Imam is the completion of faith. The Imams are the proofs (*hujaj*) of Allah on earth, and their words and commands are from Allah. In all their decisions they are inspired by

Allah. They were possessors of the station of infallibility, or freedom from error. This does not mean that they were possessors of super-human qualities. It means that they were in full submission to Allah at all times, thereby completely fulfilling their human potential. They were perfected spiritually, which allowed them to have perfect courtesy towards creation. Their wisdom and judgement flowed from the depth of their submission, which enabled them to act as guides to mankind. Because they were so in tune with the will of Allah, even their so-called mistakes carried a blessing and a teaching for the benefit of the Muslims.

The Imam is the witness for the people and he is a gate to Allah. In the Qu'an Allah says:

*And on the day when the witnesses will stand up (to witness every act done by everyone before Allah).* (40:51)

The Prophet said to 'Ali: `O 'Ali, indeed I see you as if you were compelling some people to the Garden and others to the Fire.' In this way the *Ahl al-Bayt* are like the ark of Noah. He who boards it obtains protection and the Garden. Ibn 'Abbas related: 'The Prophet said, "My *Ahl al-Bayt* are like the ship of Noah; whoever embarks on it will be saved, and whoever turns away from it will be drowned."'

The way to the other Imams is through 'Ali. All knowledge and all permission is through 'Ali. All explanation of the means by which the permission and knowledge is passed on is contained in the relationship between our noble Prophet and 'Ali. 'Ali in turn passed the permission on to Hassan, who passed it on to Husayn, and so on. There were twelve Imams, the last of which is al-Mahdi. He has not died but is in hiding – he is in the unseen, *ghayb*, just as Jesus (peace be upon him) is in the *ghayb* and ready to return at any moment. It is a feature of the leaders of the Shi'ahs, those who are the great scholars or *'ulama*, that they are constantly aware of the Madhi, the he may return to the *mulk*, the sensory world, at any time. Though the people call Khomeini the Imam, he is not the Imam. If you were to ask him, he would say that he is the vice-Imam. He is standing in for the absent Imam.

The Prophet said about the Mahdi: 'If there were to remain in the life of the world but one day, Allah would prolong that day until He sends in it a man from my community and my household. His name will be the same as my name. He will fill the earth with equity and justice as it was filled with oppression and tyranny.'

The Imamate is that portion of Shi'ism which connects the follower to the divine guidance carried by the Prophet. The Prophet has told the Muslims to bless his family along with him. He who has no love for the family of the Prophet while professing love for Muhammad (may Allah bless him) has lost the way.

The Prophet said: 'There is a piece of flesh in the body that if it is healthy then the body is healthy, and if it is diseased, then the body is diseased. That piece of flesh is the heart.' The physical heart is a pumping station. It pumps blood throughout the body, nourishing it. Through its constant rhythm, all other bodily functions are harmonised. But we also say that there is more than just the physical heart. The Prophet indicates the existence of a spiritual heart as well.

The spiritual heart (*qalb*) is the place of manifestation of love. Without love, the heart is spiritually dead. Without love, all spiritual practices are useless. The Sufis say: 'Two *ra'akat* (cycles of prayer) performed with love are worth a thousand without love.'

The spiritual heart of the Muslim community is the *Ahl al-Bayt*. They are the inheritors and the followers of the way of love. They are Allah's gift of love to His creation. Through them, Allah's mercy has spread throughout the community. By denying them, the Muslims have been plunged into turmoil.

# Eternal Karbala

This article is dedicated by the writer, Umm Hussain, a Scottish Muslim, to the memory of Imam Muhammad Baqir al-Sadr who remained true to the teachings of his Master Imam Husayn and following in his beloved footsteps gave up his life in the struggle for truth. May his sacrifice inspire the living to ceaselessly strive against the powers of evil whenever and wherever they arise.

The battle of Imam Husayn and Yazid is the relentless battle between the higher and lower *nafs* waged daily in the hearts of men, the eternal Karbala of the self. As we enter the month of Muharram Muslims the world over remember the martyrdom of Imam Husayn and keep the Ashura, the anniversary of his death, as a day of solemn mourning. But what is the use of the wailing and the beating of breasts if the memory of Imam Husayn is buried in emotionalism conveniently separate from our lives in a world where daily the heirs of Imam Husayn struggle against modern Yazids? If his death is to have any meaning for us today we must ask ourselves, who was this man? Why did he die? What did he teach us?

Contemporary documentation is clear on the following facts: on the 10th of Muharram 61 A.H. (9th October, 680 A.D.) at Karbala, Iraq, Husayn, beloved grandson of the Prophet Muhammad, second son of 'Ali ibn 'Ali Talib and Fatimah Zahrah, was slaughtered along with many of his family and close followers by the armies of Yazid b. Mu'awiyah, self-styled Caliph of Islam. The reason for

Imam Husayn's death was his refusal to acknowledge and pay homage to Yazid, a notorious debauchee who openly flaunted the laws of Islam, as the leader of the Muslim world.

The issue at stake was not an isolated conflict between two men of differing ambitions and viewpoints but the resolution of that key question which is still a matter of contention today – what manner of man has the right to rule the Muslim world – the spiritual heir of the Prophet or one of worldly strength and power? Are men to be led by the light of Muhammad or by brute force? Can there be a split between the secular and spiritual in light of the knowledge of divine unity (*tawhid*) which permeates the teachings of the Prophet? Can a man place himself at the mercy of a temporal ruler if his only allegiance is to Allah? This split was unacceptable to Sayyidina 'Ali and to his sons, Hasan and Husayn.

When the Prophet addressed the people at *Ghadir al-Khumm* on the return journey from his last pilgrimage, it is recorded that he said: 'I leave behind amidst you two great things, the Book of Allah and my *Ahl al-Bayt* (the Prophet's family). Should you be attached to these two, never will you go astray from me for verily these two will never part company until they both meet me at the Spring of *Kawthar* (Paradise).' Then he continued: 'The Lord Allah Almighty is my Master and I am the master of every true believer.' And taking the hand of Hazrat 'Ali in his, he raised him high over the vast assembly and declared: 'He is the master of all those whose master I have been. O Allah, love those who love 'Ali and hate those who hate him.'

The love of the Prophet for Hazrat 'Ali is illustrated by many Hadiths (traditions); chief among are the following:

'I and 'Ali are of one and the same Divine Light.'
'I am the City of Knowledge and 'Ali is its Gate.'
'O 'Ali! You are my brother in this world and the next.'
'O 'Ali! You are to me as Aaron was to Moses, save that there is no apostleship after me.'

Yet three times Hazrat 'Ali was passed over and the caliphate moved to Abu Bakr, then 'Umar, then 'Uthman. On each occasion Hazrat 'Ali decided against fighting for the caliphate despite his firm conviction that he was the rightful successor to the Prophet.

His dedication to the continuation of unified Islam was such that he could not instigate any internal conflict which might destroy the young and vulnerable Muslim community. Rather he elected to retire from public life, helping the caliphs whenever necessary in the interests of the people, and refusing to lead any rebellions against them. The favouritism shown by 'Uthman to his relatives, the Bani Umayyad, and to certain of the wealthier families connected with them had caused much hatred against him. Finally a violent mob beseiged his house. Although Hazrat 'Ali sympathised with the complaints against 'Uthman he had played a key mediatory role. He even placed his sons, Imam Hasan and Imam Husayn, outside 'Uthman's house to protect him. The mob, however, overpowered them and gaining entry to the house murdered 'Uthman. When Hazrat 'Ali heard the news, he rushed to the scene of the murder. It is said that he was so angry with Imams Hasan and Husayn for their failure to defend the caliph that he struck them.

The people begged Hazrat 'Ali to accept the caliphate. To this he reluctantly agreed, fully aware that his enemies would then accuse him of complicity in the murder of 'Uthman. As he expected, Mu'awiyah b. Abu Sufyan, Governor of Syria, used his relative's murder as an excuse to question the validity of Hazrat 'Ali's appointment and demanded vengeance on 'Uthman's murderers. Mu'awiyah, a strong and capable administrator, had been appointed as Governor of Syria by 'Umar, his position endorsed by 'Uthman. The son of the Prophet's old opponent Abu Sufyan, he had forged a considerable power base for himself in Syria and now cherished ambitions to seize the caliphate for himself and his family. He also feared that once Hazrat 'Ali had consolidated his own position, the latter would try to remove the Syrian governorship from his hands. The forces of Hazrat 'Ali and Mu'awiyah met at the indecisive Battle of Siffin but before a more final confrontation could take place Hazrat Ali was murdered in the mosque at Kufah on 21 Ramadan 40 AH (25th January 661 CE)

Imam Hasan, the eldest son of Hazrat 'Ali, was proclaimed caliph by 40,000 people in Kufah after his father's murder. Mu'awiyah immediately denounced his appointment. Through bribery and his extensive espionage network, he worked to undermine Imam Hasan's position. Then with an army of 60,000 men, Mu'awiyah began a slow march against the caliph. He had no desire for a swift confrontation as it was not in his interests to defeat Imam Hasan in battle or kill him at this juncture, as the latter's death would simply mean the emergence of another contender from the *Ahl al-Bayt*. His scheme was rather to induce Imam Hasan to abdicate in his favour, thereby giving some legal validity to an otherwise tenuous claim. In a letter written to Mu'awiyah at this time, Imam Hasan argues his family's claim to the caliphate on the grounds of the *Ahl al-Bayt's* position as the spiritual heirs of the Prophet from whom the authority of the caliphate sprung. In his reply, Mu'awiyah did not deny the Prophet's Family's exalted position in Islam but rather defended his claim on the premise that practical experience rather than spirituality was the necessary qualification for the leadership of the community and that the caliph should be a man whose political and military strength enabled him to preside over the expansion of the Muslim empire.

The vacillating Iraqis who had been the first to acclaim Imam Hasan proved easily amenable to Mu'awiyah's bribes and the caliph's position was soon threatened from within. In the ensuing confusion Imam Hasan decided that, in order to avoid further bloodshed, he should abdicate in favour of Mu'awiyah upon the latter's acceptance of the following treaty:

1. That Mu'awiyah should rule strictly according to the Holy Qur'an and the Sunnah of the Prophet.
2. That Mu'awiyah should not appoint or nominate anyone to the caliphate after him but that the choice should be left to the Muslim people.
3. That the people will be left in peace, wherever they are in the land of Allah.
4. That the persecution of the Shi'as, the followers of 'Ali, should immediately be stopped, their lives, properties and families guaranteed safe conduct and peace.
5. That no harm should be done secretly or openly against Imam Hasan, his brother Husayn or any of the *Ahl al-Bayt*.

Imam Hasan's sole concern was the continuation of pure Islam. He realised that battle with Mu'awiyah would probably end in defeat and the slaughter of many of the strong Shi'as. For this reason he gave up a position which was only meaningful to him if it enabled him to guide people towards Allah. His sacrifice was

patience and forebearance in adversity, his achievement to preserve the Shi'ah movement as a living entity, albeit undercover,
until a time when strengthened and expanded it might rise again.

The Imam retired to Medina to lead a life of prayer and teaching.
However, Muwawiyah's plan to secure the succession of the
caliphacy for his son Yazid required that Imam Hasan predecease
him. He therefore bribed one of the Imam's wives, Ju'dah bint al
'Ash'ath, to poison him in 40 AH (CE 669). Whereupon the Shi'as
of Kufah acclaimed his brother Imam Husayn as his successor and
invited him to lead them against Mu'awiyah. Imam Husayn, hon-
ouring his brother's treaty with Mu'awiyah, refused to accept their
offer and told them to stay at peace so long as Mu'awiyah ruled.

Insofar as the struggle (*jihad*) of Imam Hasan lay in the path of
restraint, so the destiny of his brother Imam Husayn was played out
against the field of action. Two sides of the same coin, the two
brothers shared the blessings of close proximity to their grandfather, the Prophet, during the early years of their childhood. Many
stories are told of the loving companionship bestowed upon the
boys by Muhammad who called them, 'Chief among the Youths of
Paradise.' The Prophet is reported to have said, 'Husayn is of me
and I am of Husayn.' Shaykh-i-Saduq reports from Huzayf-i-
Yamani, `I saw the Holy Prophet holding the hand of Husayn and
saying , "O people! Know this Husayn son of 'Ali and Fatimah,
know that by the One (Allah) in whose hand is my soul, that he
(Husayn) is of heaven, and his friends will be the inmates of
heaven." '

Here was a man raised in the very cradle of Islam; his life
dedicated from birth to Allah, knowing nothing but the path of
service. Various Hadiths (traditions) corroborate that the Prophet
and the Ahl al-Bayt, including Imam Husayn himself, were aware
of his future martyrdom. His whole life was but a preparation for
the appointed time when it was incumbent upon him to make the
supreme sacrifice of the lives of himself, his family and friends.
With the death of Mu'awiyah this time had arrived.

On Mu'awiyah's death his son Yazid was proclaimed caliph
thanks to the former's strong military control of the Muslim world
and the carefully placed bribes by which he attempted to secure
Yazid'a succession. The so-called 'Commander of the Faithful' was

a notorious reprobate whose public wine-drinking and licentious behaviour has never been denied by any historian. Despite the acknowledgement that he received from the tribes of the Muslim empire, Yazid was aware that his title was not secure until he had received homage from the four most respected men of Islam, who were all sons of the Companions of the Prophet. These were Imam Husayn, Abdullah b. al-Zubayr, Abdullah b. 'Umar and Abd al-Rahman b. Abu Bakr. Despite many attempts Mu'awiyah had been unable either with bribes or coercion to secure their support to his son's succession. As soon as his father was dead Yazid sent a messenger to al-Walid b. 'Utbah, the Governor of Medina, commanding him to extract homage from these four men, particularly Imam Husayn, who should be killed if he refused. The Governor duly summoned Imam Husayn in the middle of the night. Realizing that this urgent summons must mean Mu'awiyah was dead, the Imam took a contingent of his supporters with him to the Governor's palace, as a protective measure. When the Governor asked him for homage, Imam Husayn replied that for an act of homage to be valid it must be made in public, therefore the people should be summoned to the mosque the next day, and he would ask their counsel as to whether he should pay homage to Yazid. Marwan b. al-Hakam, an old enemy of Islam who had been expelled from Medina previously by the Prophet, advised Walid to murder Imam Husayn on the spot rather than let him leave the palace without having taken the oath of allegiance. Walid, who was sympathetic to Imam Husayn, would not do this and Imam Husayn left him in safety. Two days later, accompanied by most of his family and close supporters, he escaped to Mecca by night.

Once in Mecca Imam Husayn was inundated by requests from Shi'ah groups to take up an active role as their leader and overthrow the tyrannical rule of Yazid. Chief among the petitioners were the Shi'as of Kufah who had also been the first to acclaim the caliphate of Imam Hasan. Although Kufah was a Shi'ah stronghold peopled by many loyal and sincere men, both Hazrat 'Ali and Imam Hasan had found to their cost that when times were difficult the promises of the majority had come to naught. Hence Imam Husayn sent them word that he was sending his cousin Muslim b. 'Aqil to ascertain the state of affairs in Kufah. If he reported favourably, the Imam would come to them. However, they must be aware that he had no taste for temporal power and that his sole function was to interpret the Holy Qur'an and to lead a life of justice and honesty dedicated to the service of Allah. The role of the Imam is fully described by Imam Husayn in his letter to the Shi'ahs of Basrah:

> Allah chose Muhammad from among his people, honoured him with His Prophethood and selected him for His message. After he warned the people and conveyed His message to them, Allah took him back unto Himself. We, being his family, his close associates endowed with the quality of guardianship, his trustees and viceregents, and his heirs and legatees are the most deserving among all the people to succeed him. But people preferred themselves over us for this. We became contented, disliking dissension and anxious to preserve the peace and well-being (of the community), though we were fully aware that we were more entitled to this (leadership) than those who had taken it for themselves ... I have sent my messenger to you and I call you to the Book of Allah, and the Sunnah of His Prophet, the Sunnah which has become obliterated by innovations. If you listen to me and obey my instructions I will guide you to the right path. May the Peace and Mercy of Allah be upon you.

Could the man who wrote this letter have acknowledged the rule of one who openly mocked the message of the Prophet? The very purity of his being rendered martyrdom inevitable. Even the conniving Mu'awiyah who paid at least lip service to the laws of Islam was preferable to the flagrant atheism of Yazid against which all true believers were bound to fight, until they or he be destroyed.

The inhabitants of Kufah received Muslim b. 'Aqil with enthusiasm. Nearly 18,000 people pledged their allegiance to Imam Husayn at the hand of Muslim. The latter was so impressed by this reception that he wrote to Imam Husayn encouraging him to come to Kufah and take up the leadership of the people. Meanwhile Yazid, hearing of the support of the Kufans for Imam Husayn, sent Ibn Ziyad, the ruthless Governor of Basrah, with authority to take over the governorship of Kufah from the weak Nu'man b. Bashir. Ibn Ziyad was given instructions to crush the Shi'ah movement as quickly and as brutally as possible. Within a few days of the new Governor's arrival, the leaders of the town had been bribed to desert the cause of Imam Husayn and the people threatened with instant death and confiscation of property should they even be suspected of being supporters of the Imam. So the Kufans deserted their Imam, despite their promises, as they had done his father and brother at their time of need. It must be remembered that although many of those who swore allegiance to Imam Husayn through Muslim were sincere spiritual seekers, the majority would have been politically motivated. The enmity between the area we now call Iraq and Syria was such that the people of Kufah would not have welcomed the rule of either Mu'awiyah or Yazid backed by Syrian troops.

The hapless Muslim tried to organise an immediate revolt, but he found no support and had to wander homeless and hungry through a town in which a few days previously he had been feted. He was soon arrested and beheaded by Ibn Ziyad together with Hani b. 'Urwah, the man in whose house he had stayed in Kufah. The bodies of the martyrs were dragged through the streets of the city and left to hang for many days at the gates of the city as a warning to all Shi'as. Realising that his arrest was imminent, Muslim has despatched his two young sons in the direction of Mecca to warm Imam Husayn of the situation in Kufah. Tired and hungry the two lads made their way through the desert. Finally they took shelter with a kind woman, only to meet their death at the hands of her husband for the sake of the blood money on their heads.

The very day Muslim was beheaded, Imam Husayn left Mecca for Kufah accompanied by a small band of close friends and family. He had intended to stay in Mecca for the pilgrimage but decided to leave when he heard that Yazid had sent soldiers disguised as pilgrims to murder him as he performed the Hajj. Imam Husayn could not risk the desecration of the Holy Ka'abah. Stunned by his decision to leave him on the very eve of the pilgrimage, the people of Mecca came to ask him the reason for this surprising move. To which Imam Husayn replied, 'This year's Hajj I have to perform at Karbala.' When asked what animals would be sacrificed, Imam Husayn replied, 'In this Hajj I have to offer the sacrifices not of animals but of my own family.' Imam Husayn brought his half-brother 'Abbas, his eighteen-year old son 'Ali al-Akbar, his nephews Qasim, Aun and Muhammad, and others, and showing them to the people declared, 'These are my sacrifices.'

As Imam Husayn and his party travelled towards Kufah, Ibn Ziyad was enforcing the most stringent restrictions on the Kufans. He blockaded all roads leading to Kufah from the Hijaz and set up strong military surveillance of all border areas. At Tha'libiya Imam Husayn received word of the murder of Muslim and Hani b. 'Urwah. Then at Zubala he heard that his messenger, Qays b. Mushir al-Saydawi, who had been carrying a letter to the Kufans informing them of the Imam's imminent arrival, had been captured and killed. Qays had been thrown from the rooftop of Ibn Ziyad's palace in Kufah when he refused to curse Imam Husayn to save his own life. On hearing of this faithful follower's death, Imam Husayn is reported to have quoted a verse from the Qur'an: *Among the believers are men who have been true to their covenant with Allah. Some of them have completed their vow (sacrificed their lives) and some others are waiting (to die) but they have never changed (their intent) in the last (Qur'an 33: 23).* O Allah make Paradise an abode for us (the survivors) and for them (the murdered), and unite us all in a resting place under your mercy, and make your reward our only object of desire and our treasure.' He then warned his followers that they were marching towards certain death and that any who had joined him in search of worldly gain should leave him. Many who had joined him as he traveled did leave at this juncture.

As Imam Husayn drew closer to Kufah, he learnt of the strong military presence at al-Qadisiya and changed his route. The enemy, however, soon realised his change of plan and sent a contingent of 1,000 soldiers under the command of Hurr b. Yazid al-Tamimi al-Yarbu'i to intercept Imam Husayn. By the time Hurr's troops reached Imam Husayn they had run out of water and were dying of thirst in the savage desert sun. Imam Husayn, on hearing their plaintive cries for water, ordered that all his camp's reserves be distributed to the enemy force; he himself served the Umayyad soldiers with the precious supplies of water. Hurr, an honourable man, had no wish to harm the grandson of the Prophet, and although he and his forces marched close by the Imam's, keeping them under close surveillance, he used no force against him. Such was his respect for Imam Husayn that he prayed behind him at the hours of prayer. As they marched Hurr received a message from Ibn Ziyad ordering him to prevent Imam Husayn from making camp except in the open desert away from water. When Imam Husayn's men heard this, one of his companions suggested that they attack Hurr's small contingent before reinforcements arrived, but the Imam refused on the grounds that he would not instigate any hostilities. On the 2nd Muharram 61 A.H. (2nd October 680)

Imam Husayn reached the plain of Karbala and ordered they pitch camp there.

He summoned the owners of the plain and purchased the area from them. He then gifted it back to the local people, informing them that on the tenth of the month they would see the headless corpses of himself and his followers lying on the ground. He begged them to take the bodies and give them proper burial. He also entrusted to them the responsibility of acting as hosts to the many pilgrims who would in future years visit their tombs.

With every step he took Imam Husayn seemed to be conscious of his tryst with destiny. Before he reached Karbala four leading Shi'as of Kufah managed to reach him to warn that certain death awaited him there. Their guide Tirimmah b. 'Adi al-Ta'i offered to lead him to safety in the mountains from where, reinforced by twenty thousand warriors from the local tribes, he would be able to mount an attack on his enemies. He refused to do this although to continue as he was doing meant certain death.

On the 3rd of Muharram 'Umar b. Sa'd arrived with an army of 4,000 men with instructions from Ibn Ziyad to blockade the road to the river cutting off the Imam's water supplies. By the 7th of Muharram the little band was without water; women and babies gasping in the desert sands. Ibn Sa'd, although reluctant to shed the blood of Imam Husayn, still refused to give the women and children anything to drink. Ibn Ziyad, impatient with Ibn Sa'd's inaction, sent him a message by Shimr ordering him to attack Imam Husayn immediately or hand over the command of the army to Shimr. It was this very same Shimr who, when imprisoned in Kufah by Hazrat 'Ali, had begged Imam Husayn to intercede on his behalf. When Imam Husayn made the appeal, Hazrat 'Ali asked him if he realised that this very man would be his murderer and the torturer of his family.

Ibn Sa'ad, afraid of losing his command, proceeded to march on the camp. Imam Husayn sent his half-brother 'Abbas and a handful of men to ask the commander for a night's respite. This was granted. Thus on the eve of the 10th day of Muharram Husayn assembled his family and supporters and spoke to them accordingly:

'I give praise to Allah who has honoured us with the Prophet, has taught us the Qur'an and favoured us with His religion I know of no worthier companions than mine. May Allah reward you will all the best of His regard. I believe tomorrow our end will come . . . I ask you all to leave me alone and to go away to safety. I free you from your allegiance to me and I do not hold you back. Night will provide you with a cover, use it as a steed.'

Soon only a few remained in the camp. They spend the night reading the Qur'an and in prayer and supplication preparing for their assured end. On the morning of the Ashura Imam Husayn drew up his army of 72 men, who ranged in age from the seventy year old Muslim b. Aswaja to Qasim the fourteen-year old son of Imam Hasan. Dressed in the cloak of the Prophet, perfumed with musk, the Qur'an raised in his hand, the Imam rode alongside his men addressing them thus:

'O Allah you are my only Trust in every calamity, you are my only hope in every hardship, you are the only promise in the anxiety and distress in which hearts become weak and action becomes slight, in which one is deserted and forsaken by one's own friends, and in which the enemies take malicious pleasure and rejoice at one's misfortunes. O Allah I submit myself to You, my complaint is to You alone against my enemies and to You alone is my desire and request. Who else other than You can relieve me from grief. You alone are the custodian of every blessing and the Master of every excellence and the last resort for every desire.

The enemy, on hearing his words, retorted with vile insults. Still Imam Husayn would not let his companions fire a single arrow. For according to the old Arab custom, it was prohibited to fight in the month of Muharram in addition to three other months in the lunar calendar. Hence the Imam would not allow his men to act as the aggressors. As the heat of the day grew, Imam Husayn came forward again and again to remind them in the name of Allah and his Messenger of the heinous crime they were about to commit, of his own relationship to the Prophet and the merits of his family. Each time their only retort was that he must pay homage to Yazid.

A few, however, in the enemy camp had not been indifferent to the words of Imam Husayn for on the morning of the Ashura thirty nobles of Kufah, who were with Ibn Sa'd, had come over to Imam Husayn's side electing to die with him rather than face eternal damnation. Hur, the commander who had obstructed the Imam's way as he neared Karbala, had also been brooding over the situation and finally chose to join Imam Husayn bringing with him his son, brother and a slave. Throwing himself at the feet of the Imam, he begged to be allowed to give his life for him in redemption of the crime he had committed by waylaying Imam Husayn's path. To this Imam Hussain gladly agreed and Hur was one of the first to die in the battle.

As afternoon approached the fighting became fiercer and soon only the Imam's family remained alive. Then one by one they to gave up their lives. First was 'Ali al-Akbar, the son of Imam Husayn, who was said to look so like the Prophet that when he went into battle the enemy forces were temporarily stunned, believing that the Prophet himself had risen again to aid his beloved grandson. Yet they stopped only for a moment and the boy was attacked from all sides and fell with a lance pierced through his breast. He died before his father's eyes even as Imam Husayn prayed to Allah that this sacrifice of his dearest son would be acceptable in His eyes. Qasim, the son of Imam Hasan, begged his uncle that he too might join the fight presenting him with a closed letter that had been written by his father with instructions that he should open it only when the worst calamity befell him. The note instructed Qasim that when a time came that his uncle Husayn was beseiged by his enemies on all sides and when every true lover of Allah and the Holy Prophet laid down his life defending the cause of truth, Qasim must sacrifice his life on behalf of his father. Imam Husayn remembered it had been his brother's wish to marry one of his daughters to Qasim. He therefore celebrated the wedding of his nephew to his daughter Fatimah-Kubra. The wedding ceremony completed, Qasim departed to the battle fray and after killing five famous warriors from the enemy forces fell from his horse and his uncle watched helplessly as the cavalry trampled his body to death. Even Aun and Muhammad, the ten and nine-year old sons of Zaynab, the sister of Imam Husayn, on their mother's instructions entered the battle ground giving up their young lives with the other martyrs of their family. 'Abbas, the half brother of Imam Husayn, his steadfast comfort and support throughout all these events, was cut down after a valiant dash to the river to obtain water for the thirsty children. Imam Husayn, answering the call of his sister, Zaynab, went to the women's tent where he found his six-month son, 'Ali al-

Asghar, whose mother's milk had run dry, dying of thirst. Taking the baby in his arms he went towards the enemy forces begging them to bring water for it. Fearing that this piteous sight would cause his soldiers to mutiny, Ibn Sa'd ordered one of his men, Hurmula, to fire on the Imam. The arrow pierced through Imam Husayn's arm cutting the infant through the neck. The baby died in his father's arms.

Wounded, exhausted from thirst, his body smattered with the blood of his baby son, Imam Husayn returned to the women's tents to bid them a last farewell and warn them of the trials and tribulations that would befall them after his death. To Zaynab, his beloved sister and close companion since childhood, he entrusted the care of the women and children, particularly his young daughter, Sakinah, who was known for her strong attachment to her father. He told Zaynab to bear with fortitude and patience that which Allah had ordained for his family. 'Ali Zayn al-'Abidin, his only surviving son, was lying helpless on his sick bed unable to join the battle. Imam Husayn went to his bedside to appoint him as his successor, entrusting him to carry on the Light of Muhammad to mankind. The young man, who was too weak to stand unaided, struggled b to his feet, begging his father that he might be with him in the final fight. Imam Husayn restrained him, reminding him of his sacred duties and of the blessed progeny that were destined to be his issue – the future Imams of the *Ahl al-Bayt*.

All through that day, Imam Husayn had gathered the dead bodies of his companions and brought them to his tent, laying them carefully side by side to await burial. It was to this solemn task he returned during the last few minutes of his life. And there, by the side of his tent, a group of enemy soldiers led by Shimr found him. Attacking Imam Husayn from every side, they hacked his body to the ground. All the while, the women and children watched horror-struck. Abdullah, the youngest son of Imam Hasan, threw himself across the path of the soldiers trying to protect his uncle with his own body, and was thus martyred. Finally, Sinan b.Anas b. 'Amr severed the head from the body of the mutilated Imam.

The mortal life of Iman Husayn had ended but his memory lives on eternally. By his sacrifice, he had revitalised Islam, saving it from corruption and decay. Men had fallen into easeful sloth when the

great light of Muhammad had been closely followed by the darkness of Mu'awiyah and Yazid. The shock of Karbala forced many to
reconsider the meaning of true Islam and to question the extent of
their commitment to Allah. The martyrs of Karbala had left for
posterity the highest example of living Islam. The majority of
Muslims who followed them might remain subservient to corrupt
rulers and fall short of this ideal, but a standard of behaviour had
been set. None could deny that the way of Imam Husayn was the
way of Muhammad, the perfect man.

Tyrants might come and go; indeed, Yazid lived on to order the
pillage of Mecca and Medina, but never again did a caliph of either
the Umayyad or 'Abbasid Houses attempt to extract an oath of
allegiance from the *Ah al-Bayt*. The defeat of the body was the
victory of the spirit for the light of Karbala guides us still.

# SECTION 7

## Inner Reality / Outer Practices

*True pity does not consist in turning your faces towards the east
and the west – but truly pious is he who believes in Allah, and
the Last Day, and the Angels, and the Scriptures, and the
Prophets, and spends his substance – however much he may
cherish it – upon his near of kin, and the orphans,
and the needy, and the wayfarer, and the beggars, and for the
freeing of human beings from bondage, and is constant in prayer,
and renders the purifying does (**zakt**); and truly pious are they
who keep their promises whenever they promise; and are patient
in misfortune and hardship and time of peril: it is they who have
proved themselves true,
and it is they, they who are conscious of Allah. (2: 177)*

# The Inner Meaning of Faith

## Talk by Shaykh Fadhlalla Haeri at the University of Texas at Austin, December 3, 1981.

In every aspect of this life we are balanced between two opposites – on the one hand, to a gross physical experience, on the other, to an attribute which is more subtle. We all fluctuate from one extreme to another, for example from the feeling of love to hate, from being awake to being asleep. Life, then, hangs on these opposites. From life we are heading only towards death, whether we like it or not. The only true statement we can make at all times is that we are dying. If we are sane, we do not like to say this because the echo of Reality, the eternal on-goingness is within us. Reality is forever. It will go on *ad infinitum*, in different forms or phases. It may be in the form of absolute and utter peace – another attribute of reality. We take refuge from one extreme to another – from cold to heat and from poverty to wealth. We veer from the one extreme we have experienced to its opposite. This going back and forth between the extremes is the norm. It is a fact of life. As long as we are alive we are hanging on air, inhaling it when exhaling it.

The seeker is not satisfied with the *status quo*. He is searching for an inward answer. He asks why he is born if only to die at the end, and what is the meaning of death? Is there another realm of consciousness, or is it only sleep and wakefulness? How is it that we cannot remember the womb, and what is the meaning of the tomb? Such are the important questions that the heart of the true seeker asks. People of heart question their direction in this existence. This point of inner questioning usually comes about with a jolt, after one has seen the futility of one's life encompassing only the narrow circle of family, country, wife, job, etc. With this understanding comes the conclusion that happiness and fulfilment do not really arise from someone or something outside, but from within oneself. This is where the question of *iman* (faith or trust) begins to play its role, otherwise it would just be another useless dogma in a super-stitious world. When faith begins to occur, it is a cybernetic process – the more it is true faith the more it grows, and its reward or result is more experiential faith.

The Sufi understands the meaning of faith as trust in the total ecological balance of Reality – in absolute ecology and not just the particular local ecology which is directly relevant to him. From the Sufi point of view the whole world is one. One individual in any spot can influence the entire world, though it may not be measurable. It is part of the balance of the mercy of Reality that we are limited in our sensitivity. If there was no limit, the limitless would be meaningless. If there is no constraint, then there is not the possibility of freedom from it. You cannot begin to taste life unless you know death. The more you awaken to the fact that every breath is taking you one breath closer to death, the more your zest for life is heightened. Once the individual realizes the totality and oneness of this ecology, then he sees that everything in existence is interlinked and interdependent with both visible and invisible forces and powers governing the universe.

Once this is understood, the seeker can begin to pursue self-knowledge. The answer itself springs from where the question came. There is no outside as such, for the individual contains the totality within himself. It is for this reason that the Sufi says, 'You are the microcosm and the macrocosm'. The two are unified within the individual if his individuality is real and wholesome. When the inward is correct, the outward is bound to reflect it. If the outward is put right, the result is bound to affect the inward. One opposite leads to the other. The more we understand a quality the more we are qualified to understand its opposite.To achieve this end we need to experience the realm of opposites.

Having realised the ecological balance between the outward and the inward, the seeker recognises the benign nature of Reality. He also sees that sickness is a blessing. It is only a period of rest for the body, at the end of which the world will still be there and death will still be drawing closer. If you love and respect yourself enough to reflect upon the situation, you will see that you have no control over what happens in this existence. You are like every other created being in this existence, containing and emitting fears and anxieties, love and hate, good and bad, etc., and yet the shape or style of these attributes may differ slightly. The base or essence is the same. We all know the meaning of inner fire, and the meaning of the inner garden, in which we dwell if we are singing for no discernible reason. If there is a reason, then it is only a mood, and a mood passes. If, however, you dwell upon what is genetically encoded in every created being and surrender to it, then you will begin to see the beauty of the symphony. You will even see the beauty of the truth behind the most obnoxious act that man can commit – war. From a point of view of knowledge you begin to see action and reaction. Greed in the rich north resulting in poverty in the poor south is bound to cause friction. When you begin to see the meaning behind it, you can go closer to the cause of it, rather than spending a lifetime being an activist against effects. Prevention is the cure, and this cure comes about when awareness, pure and simple, of the overall situation takes place.

Trust grows inwardly as the ignorance that caused confusion is dispelled. This, in turn, nourishes further the source of knowledge within one, so that the outward actions will not cause harm to oneself or to others. Since charity starts at home, rest assured that those who are causing others outward harm are already causing themselves greater inward harm. The spring fills the holes that are closest to it. Actions are the result of the flow of the spring from intentions, through thoughts and then into grossified actions. This process is a chain reaction and there is no separation or gap between the various stages. It is the hypocrite who says one thing and means another, portraying the imbalance of his inward and outward situation. There is only one power behind the entire creation:

*Allah is the light in the heavens and the earth.*

The more you meditate inwardly and the less your mental agitations, the more you can dive towards inward and outward unity – towards a universal, ecological oneness.

Faith is the trust in one's own ability, as time passes, to come to know. This is the inward security of the man of faith. It is not blind faith, for that is useless dogma. *Iman* implies trust that the Cause behind the entire creation is a merciful and beneficient one, and that what we perceive as death cannot be an end. There must be a balance or relationship between what is in the heart and Reality. The fact that we do not want to die is a mere echo of the One never-ending (*al-Baqi*). In a Hadith Qudsi, Reality (Allah) describes the situation as:

> *The Heavens and Earth do not contain me, but the heart of a mu'min [one who has iman] contains me.*

Knowledge has its root within the heart of wholesome individuals, otherwise it is not permanent. Information, on the other hand, is acquirable. It is not inherent within the heart of man. The knowledge we are seeking is of a permanent kind, that is not bound by time and will not end with death. *Iman* ends in the Absolute. *Iman* will bring one to the source of knowledge. It is the gateway to knowing Allah, to experiencing the mercy and reality of Allah. We can only experience life because we will experience death, and the former is dependent on the latter. The latter is only meaningful because of the former. The two are caused by One.

The word Sufi stems from *Saffa* – purity. The Sufi is in pure awareness, not awareness of some thing. If you are aware of something, then there must be two, not One. Becoming aware is the beginning of awakening, of being subtle. Pure awareness is for its own sake, by its own reality. The *mu'min* believes that the entire existence is based on a Divine pattern that only unfolds to the extent of one's ability to move with the unfolding. The science of the inward implies an opposite direction to the knowledge of the outward. Each has its discipline and courtesy. Mixing the two is ignorance. The pursuit of self-knowledge is something that can only start when you begin, not by the discussion of beginning. The key to this pursuit is in the hands of the individual. The reward of this trust is itself, and it is immediate. Action and reaction are immediate when you are talking about something which is so subtle:

*Allah is fast in the account*

Action and reaction are equal and opposite, and one brings about the other. The more subtle you become inwardly, the more the rewards of that awareness are instantaneous. For example, we all suffer from anger because, basically, we are all seeking peace, inward and outward. We are all seekers of peace and yet we are in action, a state of disturbance. If we try to curb the anger within us, we end up with another effect of it, such as an ulcer or a skin rash. We become angry when we realise that our desires have not been achieved. The maximum anger is suicide. It is against Reality. If man kills himself, he has killed humanity, for there is only basically one humanity. That is why from the Sufi point of view, if you have killed yourself you have killed the entire creation. If you disrupt the balance within, you must also have disrupted the balance without, for the separation is only a subtle one. The Sufi follows the rules which says: 'Tell me what the man eats and where he lives and I will tell you who he is.' You cannot pretend to be tidy in the office and yet be untidy at home, for sooner or later your characteristic and habit will show itself in its true light. The extent of anger rising within one is a direct reflection of expectation. You would not be angry if you had no expectations, because you would be free inwardly. Nowadays in the world, we all pretend to be outwardly free. This is the proof of our inward slavery. If we are inwardly attached, or full of expectations and desires, we try to make up for it outwardly. The more one of inner faith moves towards awareness without expectations or desires, the more one finds inward knowledge taking root. The more a person is aware instantaneously of anger, the more chance there is for this anger to subside automatically. The more you are aware inwardly, the more you are connected inwardly.

*Those who have faith remember Allah a great deal, sing his praise morning and noon, for it is Allah Who blesses you.*

The Sufi lives trust. The Sufi's intentions, actions and life reflect and echo it. If not, then one is only pretending or attempting to live the pure life. The application of the Sufi science of the knowledge of Self (*nafs*) is its own reward. The more you progress along the path, the more you are in greater self-awareness. The result of applying this science of knowledge is recognising the oneness of Truth from which one is never separate.

You cannot tune in to the Rahman (the Merciful One) unless you recognise and suffer Satan, for this life and its taste hinges on duality. From unhappiness we veer towards happiness by avoiding what caused us unhappiness. From illness we go to well-being, and from ignorance to knowledge. Each of us writes his own biography. When occasionally we suffer, it is nobody's fault. It is simply ignorance – *jahal* (darkness) – resulting from expectations. Once you can see the situation in its reality you have become a great deal more subtle and can move swiftly along that same path as the system feeds upon itself. This path is easier if you keep the company of other sincere seekers, other Sufis who are regaining their inner purity. The more you are inwardly in *iman*, the more you outwardly associate with people of the same orientation. Such people trust that everything is in perfect harmony and balance. When you then observe the condition of the whole world, you will see the wisdom of it outwardly, and the beauty and meaning of it inwardly m inward beauty, outward majesty.

Faith (*iman*) is the door to Reality, and the correct path is the key to that door. The source of this knowledge is within you, and if you do not move along the path of recognising the Cause within you, then you are frittering life away, and the meaning of faith is lost. The purpose of this existence is to recognise the way out of inner bondage. For inner freedom we have to apply outer discipline. You cannot enjoy the spontaneous taste of inner freedom unless you have been under the tyranny of your own vulgar expectations and desires. You must have suffered and now be willing to harness the *nafs*.

Along the path of Sufi self-knowledge, faith is its own reward. It is the reward of the path of the eternal sing, the book of knowledge, that is imprinted in every gene, giving us all the same potential which can be realised according to the degree of our individual inner abandonment. The more you are attached to something, the more you are as good as that to which you are attached. The faith we have tried to describe here is a positive, liveable, usable, and dynamic force that brings about its own reward. Life is a great blessing from Allah. There is only Allah. Total trust in Reality can only result in a closer understanding of the nature of that Reality from which no one is ever separate. Diversity only appears by the grace of that One Cause. May Allah guide us along the path of submission and surrender, and drown us in the ocean of eternal Oneness. *Amin.*

# Tapping the Inner Springs of Faith

## By Shaykh Fadhlalla Haeri

From the moment of his birth, man seeks harmony, wishing to neutralise all his agitations, be they of a physical nature such as hunger and the need for shelter or the desires for emotional fulfillment of love, understanding and companionship. Man's cry for that state of intellectual balance and fullment is as continuous and dynamic as life itself, ever changing in its shape and magnitude. He longs for those moments of balanced equilibrium when his intellectual, mental and physical demands are met and nourished by the generosity of Nature. Momentarily, he is tranquil and at peace. Among the attributes of Allah are Peace and the Peacegiver.

To adore Allah is to worship Him and if that worship is positive and accompanied by knowledge, it results in knowledge of the laws emanating from Allah. Praying to know these laws will bring about knowledge of the boundaries; recognition and respect which will bring safe conduct; correct behaviour from which beginnings, spontaneous contentment and ultimately joy will be attained.

Seeking that contentment and joy is inherent in man. So everybody is following his nature (*fitrah*). But the tool with which to tap that inner fountain is genuine adoration and prayer. There are many levels of prayer. The anguished cry of the mother bemoaning the death of her child whom she misguidedly thought was hers, or the man wanting to know the reason for his failures and confusion in life, are lower forms of prayer. A very high state is the seeker's burning desire to know what Allah wants for what Allah wants will prevail. If the Decree of Allah is known, the seeker can easily follow the Decree, walking steadfastedly along his allotted path in the spirit of faith and certainty. Such was the state of the great prophets and saints. What the ordinary man sees as their afictions they regarded as their natural and prescribed role which they knowingly and joyfully undertook.

At the dawn of civilisation primitive man saw prayer only as a method of appeasement, making gods of the sun and the moon, the wind and the rain, thus attempting to pacify by sacrifices those very elements whose helpless slave he was. With the prophets came the message of one Lord and His Teachings, which if followed would enable His creatures to live their lives in submission to the Decree and in harmony with His Laws.

Then with Muhammad, the Seal of the Prophets, came the revelation of the Holy Qu containing many *ayat* emphasising the value of prayer:

*And your Lord said, Call on Me, I will respond to you. (40:60)*

*Say, O my servants who have transgressed against yourselves, despair not of Allah's Mercy: Truly Allah forgives all sins and really, He is the Forgiving, the Merciful. (39:54)*

*And when my servants ask you about Me, then I am near to them. I answer the call of anyone who calls on Me, so let them respond to Me, and believe in Me, that they may attain perfection. (2:186)*

The significance of prayer to the Muslims is echoed in many Hadiths and in the teachings of the Imams of the Household of the Prophet.

The Holy Prophet teaches us: 'Prayer is the salvation of the true believers, the pillar of faith and the light of heaven and earth.'

The Commander of the Faithful, 'Ali ibn Abi Talib, said: 'The best devotion is to abstain from what is prohibited: and prayer turneth away a decree, even though ordained; it is the key of Mercy, the instrument of the satisfaction of needs and the shield against every calamity.'

The Imam Muhammad al-Baqir declared: 'Whoever prays shall never want.' He once said to one of his pupils, Mir: `O Mir, pray and do not say: whatever is ordained shall come to pass. Truly there is a rank of nearness to Allah, which cannot be attained save by entreaty; and really one who shuts up his mouth and asks nothing of Allah, shall receive nothing from Him.' To the question, 'what was the best devotional act?' he replied: 'There is nothing more agreeable to Allah than prayer and supplication, for Allah loves those who pray to Him; and there is nothing more hateful to Him than one who proudly abstains from devotion and prayer.'

Prayer according to the teachings of those Perfect Beings should be regarded as a means by which the supplicant may learn to move in harmony with the Divine Decree. During prayer man is away from creation and closer to the all encompassing Mercy of the Beloved Creator. In this state he may enjoy the delights of witnessing and in the spirit of submission, not expectation, marvel at the justice of the Decree. The perfect man is the perfect actor; pny with what is written for him, wanting to please no one but his Lord and Sustainer, the writer of all scripts and the Power behind all acts.

Thus Sayiddina 'Ali, at the moment his murderer struck him, could cry out, 'I have won!' for he had met his Destiny. He played his role without fear or hesitancy, calling upon Allah his heart, obeying the call as a true slave in submission acting out in the world the role of the perfect Companion to the Prophet, the perfect father and husband to his family, the perfect ghter for truth and justice, the perfect man of awareness and light, caring only for the life hereafter and recognising the worthlessness and shortness of this transitory existence; knowing iis heart with absolute certainty that beyond the experience of death lies the abode of eternal bliss.

The inevitability of his death is the only certainty man has in this existence. Without knowledge of Allah, he is condemned to live in fear of that dreaded day. The gift of prayer brings us closer to Allah and to that knowledge of Reality which means freedom from our enslavement to the now in the recognition of our everlastingness.

The man of submission should echo in his heart the prayer recited by Imam 'Ali Zyn al-'Abidin when he heard of anyone's death or whenever death was mentioned:

'O Lord, bless Muhammad and his family and save us from extended hopes, and shorten them for us because of our good deeds, done sincerely; so that we may not expect [even] the completion of one hour after another, nor the accomplishment of one day after another, nor the connection of one breath with another, nor the succession of one step to another.'

'And save us from their delusion, and give us security from their mischief. And fix Death before our eyes, permanently [as a fixture] and let not our remembrance of it be intermittent.'

'And let our service consist of good actions, whereby we may desire to return unto Thee soon; and because of which we may long to join Thee quickly.'

'So much so that Death may become our associate, from whom we may derive comfort; and our favourite for whom we may long, and our next of kin to whom we may love to be nigh. And when Thou sendest it down upon us, and bringest it to us, then let us be fortunate with it as a visitor, and familiar with it as a sojourner.' And do not render us unfortunate in entertaining it and do not disgrace us with its visit. And let it be one of the gates to Thy forgiveness, and one of the keys to Thy mercy.'

'Let us die guided (righteous), not misled; obedient, not unwilling; repentant, not sinning, and not persisting in sin, O Surety for the reward of the righteous and Reformer of the actions of the corrupt.'

# Qalaba –
# The Turning of the Heart

## Discourse of Shaykh Fadhlalla Haeri

'Only by the dhikr of Allah is the heart made tranquil.' Dhikr is remembrance, recalling what is already present. That which is ever-present is not perpetually and spontaneously recognised and known by man, because he has been deflected by forgetfulness (ghaah). Remembrance is not meaningful unless there is its opposite, forgetfulness. It is part of the play of duality. The deeper one is in ghaah, the greater is the chance that one will return to dhikr. The night becomes darkest before the break of dawn. These are the immutable laws of reality and have nothing to do with man.

The physical laws of creation enable us to maintain the platform of the body, which is an intricately balanced and magnificent form. These laws are discernible. But it is the subtler laws that are to be discovered and contemplated for they actually govern, and are the essences or the attributes from which actions come. The subtler the law, the more powerful it is because it is closer to the ultimate subtle point from which everything arose. It is closer to that ultimate ocean of stillness which is like the moment of creation, or the non-creational state of absoluteness from which this apparent motion, which is 'in time', has taken place.

Man has been given a guidebook to discover the subtle laws governing the creation. This book, the Qur'an, is written in Arabic, which is a language whose words are interlinked through their roots. If one looks at the Arabic roots of the Qur'anic terms, one will come to see the many aspects of the word. One realises that the full meanings of the words are lost when a translation is made. The translating function takes an aspect of a total garden-like consciousness or culture out of its context, and at best the Arabic translates into a poetic rendering, with an incomplete orchestration of meanings.

We shall now explore a key term in the Qur'an, *qalb*, by drawing out from a dictionary its various meanings. Immediately we shall see the difficulty of trying to render Qur'anic concepts into English. To facilitate reaching the core meanings of the word, we will return back to the Qur'an. It will reveal the meanings of its own words, because the entire message of Truth is in it.

Literally, *qalb* means heart. It is a *mudghah*, a physiological unit, a lump of flesh, an organ. The Prophet (peace be upon him) describes it as an organ in the breast of man which if it is well, the entire being is well; and if it is not, the entire being is not. By the Prophet's indication the qalb is not just a physical organ but something like an electro-magnetic energy field with its centre at the heart. It is a subtler force superimposed on what we call the physical heart.

From the dictionary we find the verb *qalaba* to mean: to turn around, turn about, turn upward, upturn; to turn, turn over; to turn face up or face down; to turn inside out or outside in; to turn upside down; to tip, to tilt over, topple over; to invert, reverse; to overturn, upset, topple; to capsize; to roll over; to subvert, overthrow; to change, alter, turn, transform, convert, transmute; to transpose; to exchange.

If we were to think of man as being a holograph or anything like that model—though man is far more complex than any model he can think of, for in fact, he is the model—we could see the meaning of some of these terms.

Man attempts to understand his nature by the facilities and faculties that are available to him. All of these are inherently limited—every system has its limitation. He tries to draw a model from existence in order to better understand his reality. All things in the creation are a model of its Creator. The best model to be constructed by man, within the limitations of systems and models of self-representation, is that of a holograph. It reflects and functions like the original model and yet it is not the original. It does not contain all the dimensions of the original.

Man appears to have the characteristics of the unlimited. He attempts to imitate the characteristics of the Unlimited, the Omnipotent and the Omnipresent, yet he is not It. He seems to contain the attributed meanings, but he is not them. He seems to have contained and inherited attributes of his Creator, but he is not the root of them because he is like a hologram. This description or model is limited, because we are only able to analyse it by means of the limited faculty of analysis.

The fact that we can talk about the limited, and describe it within limits and bounds must, out of necessity, imply that this limited situation exists within an unlimited situation. The analytical approach does not bring us any closer to understanding the entire nature of the Creator. A great deal, however, may be understood by discussing the manifestations that have arisen from the Creator.

If your heart is fixed on a situation, you are likely to reflect that situation. If it is set on something, you are likely to attain it, given all the physical possibilities. Wherever your heart turns, it is towards a discernible thing. Its function however, its genetic code is to be ever-turning, never to be fixed upon anything. It is the scanner of objects which gives it the nature of reflectiveness. Its reality, though, is beyond that. The nature of radar and what makes it function operation is based on wavebands. What makes a heart a heart, a *qalb* a *qalb*, is an entity which is unique, which is *Ahad*, which is not related to anything that the *qalb* reflects and discerns.

We can make a holograph of anything, but its origin is not the thing. A heart cay situation, any mental image or thought, but what gives it the power to have that nature of turning, non-attachment and freedom is none of these and it is over and above that, and there is nothing like it. In other words, what is trying to be expressed isfferer from the heart's reflection is you and I. And that suffering is part of our endowment. There is no way out of it.

Translating what we have been saying into an existential recipe, if we allow the *qalb* to be a turning *qalb*, then existentially we will be secure. Allah owns the heart. We will suffer harm from it if we do not allow it to be its nature.

By selecting some examples from the Qur'an itself, we can deepen our understanding of various uses of the verb *qalaba*. For example:

*And to Him you will turn.* (29:21)

*We turned them about to the right and to the left.* (18:18)

*Allah turns over the night and the day.* (24:44)

*A day their faces will have turned.* (33:66)

Their faces were turned towards ss, at the reckoning, there will be no possibility for man to be distracted, their faces will have invariably turned to another state. The people who do not believe in the reality which Allah describes, 'fear the day in which the hearts and sights will have turned [suddenly],' realising that what they perceived as real, is no longer.

We have given from a dictionary the entries under the verb *qalaba*. Now, let us see what there is listed for the noun *qalb*. It says: reversal, inversion; overturn, upheaval; conversion, transformation, transmutation; transposition, metathesis; perversion, change, alteration; overthrow (of government); heart; middle, centre; core, gist, essence; marrow, medulla, pith; the best or choicest part; mind, soul, spirit.

As man moves on in his search for happiness, progressing towards a balance between his desires and their satisfaction, discriminatingly filtering what comes to him from the outside, he is bound to reach the conclusion that there is no end to the attempt of trying to match the individual, the microcosm, with the macrocosm of the world. Man will not be successful in b alancing the opposites because as soon as he controls one factor, another factor appears.

Man has imposed upon himself conditions that have nothing to do with the thing itself, originally. In other words, happiness is one's own nature, but unhappiness has been superimposed upon it by placing conditions upon happiness. We say, 'I will not be content unless I have this or that.' Because these conditions differ from one person to another and are constantly changing, they cannot be the causes of the inner states of happiness. As a child, you may impose the condition upon yourself that to be happy you have to have a bicycle. But when you are a man this same condition is out of place and silly. The conditions are variable and therefore, unacceptable, because we want to reach the common denominator, the fundamental condition.

I have chosen to plunge into the meanings of the word *qalb* because it is the key concept in turning what one's life to a realization that what one is pursuing, what one has invested in: an ambience, a profession, a friendship or a bank account, can only bring about bring about a superficial and perishing situation. That which man is really seeking is happiness: moments of happiness when the mind is brought to a standstill.

Mind, in Arabic, does not exist, and there is no specific translation for it. What is used is the word *'aql*. Ultimately, you use your *'aql* by your heart, as the Qur'an describes it. Your faculty of reason is in the heart, not in the head. The head is, according to the Qur'anic tradition, a convenient measuring device.

I would like now to mention a few *ayat* in which the noun *qalb* appears. We are talking about that which is the core. The Qur'an repeats several times that knowledge and ultimate happiness or ultimate winning lie in the seeker's coming to Allah with a sound heart. The *ayat* of the Qur'an which contain the word *qalb* are more than one hundred. *Qalb* and those words related to it through its root are mentioned in more than two hundred *ayat*.

*And he came with a repentent heart.* (50:33)

*(Munib is from anaba which is to repent, return or turn back.)*

*Most surely there is a reminder in this for yhim who has a heart.* (50:37)

This does not mean that there are people who do not have hearts, butt that their hearts have been blinded or covered.

*Do not obey and follow he whose heart We have made to be in ghaah (detected from the source).* (18:28)

The diseased heart is described in many different ways in the Qur'an:

*So he who in his heart is sick would be greedy.* (33:32)

Greed is one attribute of a sick heart. A man of heart will not have greed because he has trust.

Guidance also comes from the same faculty, the heart:

*And whoever believes in Allah, He guides his heart.* (64:11)

And if one does not believe:

*Thus does Allah set a seal over the hearts of the disbelievers.* (7:101)

He who denies this one and only infinite situation from which the infinite has come, has his heart enclosed:

*Thus do We make it to enter into the hearts of the guilty.* (15:12)

Concerning those who heed the warnings, Allah says:

*They have hearts with which to understand.* (22:46)

When the *qalb* functions properly then:

*He sends down peace into the hearts of the believers.* (48:4)

Another attribute of disconnectedness, of not being in *tawhid*, is expressed by:

*They say with their tongues what is not in their hearts.* (48:11)

This is also a definition of hypocrisy. *Munafiq* (hypocrite) is rooted in the verb *nafaqa*. *Nafaq*, which is from the same three-letter root, is a tunnel. The one who tunnels, his *nafs* is hard to catch. As soon as it goes into one hole, it comes out of another, and therefore, does not have the opportunity to turn.

The hearts of the *munafiqun* are as hard as stone, but Allah says, even from stone, waters may spring forth.

The heart of the *munafiq* is described in various ways:

*We put upon their hearts covers.* (6:25)

*Their hearts are full of foolishness.* (21:3)

*Rust is upon their hearts.* (83:14)

*Allah turned away their hearts* (61:5)

*Zagha* is to turn aside; to depart, deviate (from); to swerve, to turn away (from), turn one's back (on); to wander, stray, roam (eyes); to cause something to deviate.

Elsewhere in the Qur'an Allah says:

*Allah has not made for any man two hearts within him.* (33:4)

If one continually seeks material security, one will end up destitute of the other values. Two arrows cannot be shot from the same bow at the same time. You can shoot one after the other, but often we stop after the first. First, we want a proper material situation: environment,friendship, wife, in order that we may satisfy the gross and immediate needs, the human parts; then we may move into the divine domain of this journey.

You will find the great masters following in the footsteps of the Prophets and their followers, the Imams, because what is real, is real forever and does not change with time. What may change is the outer manifestation. You may have different colours or forms of dress, but a dress is a dress. A house is a house, a room is a room, a filled stomach is a filled stomach which may have been filled for days or weeks with one, two or five hundred varieties of food. What matters is the ultimate state of the situations.

If we look at the lives of the Prophets and their followers, we will find one thing in common and that is revolution, that is *qalb*. They had turned against what they considered to be futile. Each one of them, in his own way, at a certain time in his life, discovered the same thing.

The five great Prophets, Noah, Abraham, Moses, Jesus and Muhammad (peace be upon them) and many of the others whom we do not know enough about, transformed the history of mankind. It was not necessarily that they renounced the house in which they were raised or their mothers or wives, it was that they recognised what they considered to be essential for them to reach the state which would give them full security and fullment, unconditioned by these relationships and the values which they represented. They simply turned away from the relationships which were keeping them from their goal.

If your heart has turned away from something, eventually your face also will turn away. This existence is one unified field. Eventually, the body's electromagnetic field will physicalise into a movement of muscles and limbs away from what is futile. When Moses came to the land of Pharoah and found the people taken in by despotism aided by magic, he could not accept it. He a advocated instead the worship of the one and only Reality. He then moved away from oppression, taking his people with him. The Prophet Jesus (peace be upon him) came to revive what Moses had brought, and he also turned away, revolting against the dominant values.

Man wants longevity and has invested in cultural habits and traditions which oppose the imposition of the prophetic message. The message is bound to be opposed. In fact, the first opposition to every spiritual seeker occurs at the nearest place to him–his mother, or his wife. The opposition begins at home, at the closest quarters, because it has begun at the closest possible part of him, which is his heart.

Revolution is an essential meaning of *qalb*. If, however, we do not leave the state of foolishness and indiscrimination, we will equate revolution with an outer havoc not based upon an inner reality. If the revolution is a real one, it will not cause outer havoc. The revolutions of the Prophets and the *awliya* (the friends of Allah) were the most peaceful revolutions. Muhammad (peace be upon him) did not wage war, he only defended himself as a last resort.

If there is a turning away from that which has not been conducive to that state of complete bliss and fulfilment, by first recognising that we have been looking in the wrong direction, then there will be no revolution and no turning of the heart. Once there is a turning of the heart, the most devastating peaceful revolution has been brought about. Once you have recognised that your happiness is not dependent upon the dominant *kufr* system of behaviour, your turning away from it is the biggest threat to the system, far greater than reacting against it because you have deed the entire situation. You have demonstrated that your happiness does not lie with an increased rate of interest in the bank.

The situation of the awakening heart is that, by the shaking, by the turning, by the afflictions, by the fact that it has not yet reached a point of tranquillity and stability, it will stimulate an awakening. That awakening is the 'turning away from'.

The definition of the path is *sirat al-ladhina an 'amta 'alayhim*, the path of those who have received the *ni'ma*, the blessedness; *ghayri l-maghdubi 'alayhim wa la dallin*, and of those who are not alienated. It follows that alienation is a proof that the heart has not focused on what matters and is distracted.

The nature of existence is in fact the nature of the *qalb*. Everything in this existence depends on the *qalb*. The health of a child in the womb depends on its turning. The nature of any health, physical, mental, economic, or otherwise, is based on its turning around. If you want to be mentally healthy and alert, able to think beyond what you are trying to solve, you must go beyond it and be willing to face any change. Heart attacks occur because the heart becomes fixed in a specific direction. It can only be attacked if it is positioned or visible. If it is *qalb*, constantly turning, how can it be attacked? Where can it be seized or afflicted? Why should the heart be disappointed?

If someone has a heart which is willing to turn, and you were to come up to him saying, 'I am sorry, but all that you had owned is destroyed,' he would recognise or remember the day when he had nothing and put himself in that state. He would say, 'There was a time when there was nothing, a time when I did not even exist. So what is all this fuss about?' The attainment of this state is not a foolish technique of saving one's physical heart from a heart attack, but is a reality that recognises a time when there was no problem. Someone with a turning heart remembers his afflictions, how they disappeared; and he remembers the only member of this existence inferred and deduced by experience, which is God.

Man will move towards this goal faster when the environment in which he surrounds himself becomes more spiritually conducive. In order to do that, he must attempt to leave all other distractions behind. As a group, those seeking the dynamic state of the heart do not inflict their boring biographies upon each other.

Within this environment of the world, the teaching of truth becomes real. Unless you physically see your attachment to your children, wife or country being genuinely, directly and subjectively confronted, this teaching remains a superstitious religiosity. It is a useless prescription or menu which is without the benefit of the nutriments that would be taken from the meal itself.

Man is born in order to learn to reach the state of tranquillity. By getting closer to the state of tranquillity without the aid of outside stimulants, man obtains more and more access to that medical cupboard within himself, directly and instantly. By closing his eyes, and having no thoughts, he will be able to enter into an unending ocean of non-description. This is the heritage of man. It is diving into the state of pre-creation, which all men will taste at the moment of death. This is the message of the Qur'an, and all the Prophets of true religions, and of all men who have attained various degrees of awakening. Their messages have been nothing other than a reflection of the truth.

We often hear that all paths lead to the same end, but are we on a path? If you are not specifically on a path which you are certain has been trodden, and which you know within your heart gets you to the desired goal, it is of no use. It will lead you to continue discussing the fact that all paths, all religions are the same. So what? What about you and I? Have you been in the workshop that will teach you how to manufacture the key to your inner bliss, which is the key to the garden? This life is the workshop in which we clumsily fool around with the toys of day to day living, until the time when we know exactly where to put the key, and how to turn it. Then instantly you are able to return to that ocean of non-description, revived beyond revival.

This is the message of the Qur'an. It can only be absorbed if the courtesy of the Qur'an is taken on, which is the courtesy of that culture and that language. The Arabic language, along with Aramaic, Sanskrit and several other ancient languages, many of which have already disappeared, are able to communicate beyond the humanly communicable. A point is reached at which man is at the edge of an inner silence, beyond reason. Reason is only given its nourishment and meaning because it is based upon that 'beyond'.

The Qur'an describes the Prophet Muhammad (may Allah bless him) as *rahmatan lil-'alamin*, as a mercy for all the worlds, visible and invisible, for all time. It is part of the mercy of the Ever-Merciful Creator Who created only out of love. If man does not begin upon that foundation, whether he builds cities or civilisations, his actions will not be nourished by the inner fountain which keeps his heart throbbing. His efforts will be cast aside, unused – a reminder of his inadequacies.

The sincere men of knowledge gather together simply to sing the one and only song which they have learned from the beyond and before time. When other lesser songs stop, the heart sings what it has known from before time, which is the message of the Qur'an. The rest of their actions function as an outer containment in order to corner them into a final point of abandonment. From abandonment comes the awakening, the safe conduct in this world. And from it, eventually, man ends up reaching his full spiritual evolution. He is promised by Allah that it will take place.

Just as it appears that man is evolving along this thing called time, biologically, so he appears to be evolving spiritually. The Qur'an promises that the earth will be inherited by the men of knowledge. A time will come when everyone who is walking on this earth will be like a saint. What we witness of upheavals and so on, are of no significance. If we want to find their significance, we will find their meaning in our hearts.

# Discourse on Du'a

## By Shaykh Fadhlalla Haeri

The root of the word *du'a* is *da'a*, which means to call. You can only call if there is inherently within you, an energy which will bring about an answer. From where the question comes, the answer will come. The caller is calling upon one entity. He is able to call because he has an energy within him, in the form of life which is the source of desire. What you are calling upon is rooted in what enables you to call. With experience, a person realises that you can only call on what you know is realisable. It is the development of the faculty of the intellect or reason.

In Arabic the world is *'aql*, which means tethering. *'Aql* is the faculty of reason which can be developed if there is a tethering, if there is an *'iqal*. It is part of the nomadic culture to make the camel sit down, otherwise, you cannot subdue him, you cannot put things on his back. The *'iqal* is that rope which they put around the front legs of the camel.

If a person moves in this direction, he will realise that he cannot make a supplication, he cannot ask for anything unless it is realisable. A foolish man will ask for the impossible. It is romanticism, drunkenness, or poison. A point is reached in which the supplication becomes so personal, so subjective, so inward, that all it can do is elevate, open and light up the inner recesses of one's heart. That is the ultimate *du'a*. A *du'a* is not made to improve the outer unless it continues into the improvement of the inner. If an ordinary person makes a since re supplication for a better house, his intention will then be to acquire a better house. That intention in time will nd a way of becoming grossied, manifesting outwardly in his acquiring the knowledge to earn a house. If the expectation is not incongruous with the laws that govern existence, then it is realisable by the person. By his expectation, he will uncover for himself the means to the acquisition of what he has been asking for. On this the Qur'an is very clear. There must be a means for these things to occur. Mary, the mother of Jesus, had to shake the palm. The dates would not drop without that. We must do something for our provision (*rizq*) to come to us. It is maximum efficiency when you know precisely how to do it and when to do it.

Expectations move from the gross to the subtle. There is nothing wrong with that. If you want a companion and you have an idea as to what sort of a companion you want, you will start searching for that person until you nd a match. This is the promise of nature. We are brought up in this life to be fulfilled, yet we are already fulfilled. We have created in ourselves unfullfilment. We go on and on trying to fill the potholes that we dig in our own hearts.

Supplication begins grossly and ends up in silence before the dawn prayer at the end of night.

We all want the right environment in which we can function well. We all want safety in order to reflect and examine cause and effect in our little laboratories in this life. We all want outer protection in order to move inwardly to discover the meaning behind what is manifested. *Du'a* begins with the outside demand. We want an ambience in which the temperature does not fluctuate too violently. The more you satisfy the grosser needs of a human being, the more he may move towards the subtler elements, until a point is reached at which language stops, and there occurs the awakening of the recognition that there is no two. That is the ultimate fulfillment. He is then encouraged to return to life with the full confidence that his so-called self is only a secondary existence.

We are all biologically animals in time, but you can have real enjoyment, which is nothing other than service, waiting for the next opportunity to do something useful for others. If fulfillment is not our real nature, why are we seeking it? If happiness is not our reality, why do we want it? If peace is not our real nature, why do we seek it? If interrelationships and the knowledge of interrelationships is not already implanted within our subgenetic levels of heritage, why do we seek to understand creation in the small and large? These are all inherent within us. They must be, otherwise we would not unify with them.

A man who seeks Allah makes demands upon nature. He says, 'I want a better situation so that I may contemplate and nd out.' But often he stops at that. Once the house is obtained, it becomes the object of worship. You often nd that people are free before they acquire possessions but once they have a little piece of the world they become fixated upon it.

The heritage of Ja'fari Islam is founded on *du'a* because it unifies us in wanting to improve our basic motives. It lifts us higher and higher. One recognises the limitations that are imposed intrinsically. Once those limitations are recognised, there are no disappointments. There is only an appointment for us to exist over a period of time. It is up to us to make full use of our appointment. It is an interview into which we must enter, leaving behind those things that are created by us and given importance by us. They differ from one man to another and from one day to another.

Man is caught in the time flux, yet rooted in the timeless. That is why we reflect the love of timelessness, but in a perverted way. We seek foods that give us longer life, not knowing that the cause and the source of life is beyond time, so the question of length of time is irrelevant.

This is what real supplication does. It helps the gross, the ordinary, the illiterate man get a better plough, a piece of land, or a wife. It also helps the man of deeper intellect reach the point beyond which there is no point. That is the *sirat al-mustaqim* (the straight path). It is a line, which if looked at from its point of beginning, becomes an infinite number of points superimposed upon each other but experienced as one point, which is the Reality. It is a point beyond which there is no other point. And that point is man. Man is the point of it. He is the proof of it. He contains the meaning of his own cause and effect.

Allah (may He be glorified) says: 'The heavens and earth do not contain Me, but the heart of a believer contains Me.' He also says in a sacred Hadith :'I was an unknown treasure and I wanted to be known, so I created.' That is how duality occurs. The confusion of the two begins and ends in the fusion within the One.

# Ramadan

*O you who believe, prescribed for you is the Fast, even as it was prescribed for those before you, that haply you will have taqwa.*
(2:183)

'A great month, a blessed month, a month containing a night which is better than a thousand months has approached you people. Allah hntary practice. If someone draws near to Allah during it with some good act he will be like one who fulfils an obligatory duty in another month, and he who fulfils an obligatory duty in it will be like one who fulfils seventy obligatory duties in another month. It is the month of endurance, and the reward of endurance is paradise. It is the month of sharing with others, and a month in which the believer's provision is increased. If someone gives one who has been fasting something with which to break his fast, it will provide forgiveness for his wrong actions and save him from the Fire, and he will have a reward equal to the fasting man's reward without his reward being diminished in any way...Allah gives this reward to anyone who gives one who has been fasting some milk mixed with water, or a date, or a drink of water with which to break his fast, and anyone who gives a full meal to one who has been fasting will be given a drink by Allah and will not thirst until he enters Paradise. It is a month whose beginning is mercy, whose middle is forgiveness, and whose end is freedom from the Fire. If anyone makes things easy for his slave during it, Allah will forgive him and free him from the Fire.'

From a discourse given by the Prophet (peace and blessings be upon him) on the last day of Shaban. Reported by Salman al-Farsi (*Mishkat al-Masabih*).

# The Virtues of Fasting

## By Shaykh Abu 'Ali-Fattaah

This article is a translation by Shaykh Abu 'Ali Fattaah of *Mahajjatu l-Bayda*, a classical treatise by Muhsin Fayd al-Kashani. In this text the author presents Al-Ghazali's *Ihya Ulum al-Din*, deleting the un-authenticated Hadiths and adding Hadiths of the *Ahl al-Bayt* as well as his own commentary to further illuminate the *Ihya*.

Glory be to Allah who has given so much grace to His slaves by driving from them the plots and arts of Satan, returning their hopes and causing their ideas to fail, when He made fasting a bastion and a shield for his close ones. He opened for them the doors of the Garden showing them that Satan's way to their hearts is through hidden desires, and that by crushing them the self becomes tranquil and its power becomes clear about how to cut its enemy off with immense strength.

Blessings and much peace upon Muhammad, the leader of Truth, the one who made the way of behaviour easy; and upon his sacred household; his followers, those who possess weighty intellects.

Now then, surely fasting is a quarter of faith, according to the sayings of the Prophet (may Allah bless him): 'Fasting is half of patience'; and: 'Patience is half of *iman*.' Fasting is half of patience and therefore its reward goes beyond the law of estimation and accounting. Also, fasting has been distinguished by a special relationship to Allah, apart from all the other pillars of Islam, by what Allah says in a sacred Hadith: 'Every good deed will receive ten times its like, up to seven hundred fold, except fasting; it is for Me and I reward by it.' And Allah has said:

> Say O my servants who believe! Be careful of [your duty to] your Lord; for those who do good in this world is good, and Allah's earth is spacious; only the patient will be paid back their reward in full without measure. (39:10)

Allah says in a sacred Hadith: 'When he leaves his desires and his food and drink for Me, then the fasting is for Me and I will reward by it.'

And the Prophet (may Allah bless him) said: 'There is a door to the Garden called *rayyan* ['Sated with drink' so named because the fasters are thirsty during the fast.]. Nobody will enter through it except those who have fasted.' It is promised that they will meet Allah as a result of their fasting.

He said (may Allah bless him): 'For everything there is a door and the door of worship is fasting.'

And I [Kashani] say: 'Islam is based on five things, prayer, Hajj, *zakat*, fasting and *wilayat*.'

The Prophet of Allah (may Allah bless him) said: 'Fasting is a shelter from the Fire.' Also He said: 'He who is fasting is in worship even though he is asleep on his bed; unless he backbites a Muslim.' And he said: 'Allah says, "Fasting is for Me and I reward by it. For he who fasts there are two joys: when he breaks his fast and when he meets his Lord, the Mighty and Glorious. By He Who holds the soul of Muhammad in His hand, the changed smell of the mouth of the one who fasts is sweeter to Allah than the smell of musk." '

The Prophet (may Allah bless him) said to his companions: 'Shall I inform you of something which if it is done will keep Satan away from you as far as the east is from the west?' They said, 'Yes, please tell us, Oh Prophet of Allah.' He said: 'Fasting, it will blacken his face; charity, it will break his back; love of Allah and assisting in good deeds, it will break his ways [of approaching]; and asking for forgiveness, it will break his strength. For everything there is a way of purication and for the body it is fasting.'

And he also said: 'Allah and all His angels are praying on behalf of those who fast.' And he said: 'Gabriel informed me from his Lord that He said "I have not ordered My angels to pray on behalf of any of My creatures unless I have answered them."'

Imam Ja'far al-Sadiq said: 'Allah says, *Seek help in patience and prayer*...(2:45).' The Imam then said: 'By patience He means fasting.' And the Imam said: 'When there occurs a severe accident to a man he should fast. Surely Allah, the Highest, has said, "Seek help in patience and prayer."'

The Imam said: 'He who has fasted for Allah, the Glorious and Mighty, and is in the discomfort of heat and struck by thirst, will have his face wiped and be given the good news by a thousand angels whom Allah has entrusted to him until he breaks his fast; at that point Allah will say: "How sweet is your odour and your soul. Oh angels witness that I have forgiven him."'

Imam al-Kathim said: 'Rest before noon for Allah, the Glorious and Mighty, feeds the one who fasts and gives him drink while he sleeps.'

Imam Ja'far al-Sadiq said: 'The sleep of the one who is fasting is a worship and his silence is a glorification; his action is accepted and his supplication is answered.'

The greatest of all fasting in reward is the fasting of the month of Ramadan. The Prophet said: 'He who fasts the month of Ramadan outtops his hearing, sight and tongue from being against mankind, Allah will accept his fasting and will forgive him all past sins and all sins to come, and will give him the reward of those who are patient.'

Imam Ja'far al-Sadiq said: 'The Prophet (may Allah bless him) was asked about the Night of Power. He stood up to speak and after thanking and glorifying Allah said: "As for now, you have asked me about the Night of Power. I did not keep it away from you because I did not have the knowledge of it. Know, Oh people, that whoever witnesses Ramadan and he is well, fasts its days and worships part of its nights, keeps to his prayers, attends its Fridays and meets the *'Id* Feast, he has reached the Night of Power and has won by Allah the great gifts of his Lord." He has won by Allah the great gifts, which are not the same as the normal gifts of human beings.'

Also Imam Ja'far al-Sadiq said: 'Allah made fasting obligatory in order that the wealthy and the poor [in the worldy sense] be made equal. That is because the rich do not taste the hunger that would cause them to be kind to the poor. Whenever the wealthy want something they can achieve it. So Allah desired to make equality within His creation, the wealthy tasting of hunger and pain so that they could have sympathy for the weak and compassion for the hungry.'

And it was said: It is enought that fasting is a means of elevating the lowest level of the human being to the highest level which is that of imitating the spiritual angels. Surely, that is enough of a virtue and a glorious deed.

Imam al-Ghazali says: Indeed, fasting is for Allah and contains greater glory and honour for Him: although all forms of worship are for Him. The analogy is that He honoured the house [the Ka'bah] accordinghe glory and honour of fasting. One of them is that the fast is abstention and stopping [cutting-off]. It is a secret without a be witnessed by the creation, the witnessing of fasting is not known except to Allah, because it is an action of the inward by pure selfless patience.

Secondly, it is vanquishing the enemy of Allah. Surely, the means of Satan, the curse be upon him, are desires strengthened by eating and drinking. And thus the Prophet (may Allah bless him) said: 'Satan flows in the son of Adam in the same way as his blood. Constrict his passage by hunger.' For as fasting is specically to curb Satan, to block his ways and tighten the passages whereby he enters your heart, it helps to give victory to Allah. And Allah's victory for His slave is dependent upon him giving victory to Allah. For Allah says:

*If you help Allah, Allah will help you and make your feet firm. (47:7).*

The beginning is the slave's exertion and effort, and the reward is guidance from Allah. And therefore, He said,

*And those who make jihad for Us We will show them Our ways. (29:69)*

Also in *Surat al-Ra'd,* Allah says:

*Allah will not change the condition of a people unless they change that which is in themselves. (13:11)*

As for change, it can only occur by the breaking of desires. They are the breeding ground of devils where they roam and feed. As long as it is fertile, they will not stop their coming and going. And as long as they are alive, the Majesty of Allah will not be revealed to the slave. The Prophet (may Allah bless him) says: 'If it were not for the devils (*shaytans*) roaming around, surrounding the heart of the son of Adam, he would have seen the world of the unseen.' Therefore, from this point of view fasting has b ecome a door of worship and a means of shelter. Since its virtue is to this extent so great, it is necessary to explain its conditions, and mention its foundations, courtesies and practices, hidden and known.

**Concerning the Secrets of Fasting and its Inner Conditions**

Know that for fasting there are three degrees: the fasting of the common people, that of the élite and that of the élite of the élite. As for the fasting of the common people, it is depriving the stomach and the private parts of achieving their desires. The fasting of the élite is depriving the hearing, sight, tongue, hands, legs and all the other faculties from committing sins and errors.

I [Kashani] say: I will give you an indication by what was related from Imam Ja'far al-Sadiq: 'When you fast, let your ears, eyes, hair and skin fast.' He enumerated many things other than these and said: 'Do not let your day of fasting be the same as your day of breaking the fast.' In another narration he added: 'And I give you another tradition. Give up any aspect of showing off and hurting whoever is serving you. You must bring upon yourself the dignity of fasting, for the Prophet (peace be upon him) heard a woman cursing her servant girl while she was fasting. He called for food and said to her, "Eat." She said "I am fasting." He then said, "How can you be fasting while you have cursed your servant. Fasting is not from food and drink alone."'

Imam al-Ghazali says: As for the fasting of the élite of the élite, it is the fasting of the heart from all low ambitions and worldly thoughts; and it is depriving them entirely from anything other than Allah. According to this fast, breaking the fast occurs from any thoughts other than Allah and the last day, and from thoughts of this world, unless the world is wanted for the sake of the *din* – for the provision of the next life not for this world. This is true to such an extent that the masters of the hearts say: 'He who made any effort so that during his day he concerns himself about what he is going to break his fast with, a sin is written upon him.' Because that is a proof of their lack of trust in the overflowing generosity of Allah, and their uncertainty about His promised provision. This is the station of the Prophets, the righteous and the close ones. There is no point in examining it in detail through speech, what matters is conrming it in action. It is to be completely directed and concerned with Allah, abandoning other than Allah, enfolded in the meaning of the ayah:

*Say Allah and then leave them sporting in their vain discourses. (6:91)*

Kashani says: Accom Ja'far al-Sadiq, 'The Prophet (may Allah bless him) said: "Fasting is protection." ' This means it is a screen from the evils ention to restrain yourself from desires and to sever the determination of the plots of Satan by putting yourself in the station of he who is sick, desiring neither food nor drink, anticipating at any moment to be cured from the illnesses of wrong actions. Purify your innermost from any impurity, distraction or darkness which cuts you off from the meaning of allegiance to the face of Allah, the Highest.

Fasting kills the elements of the lower self and the natural desires. From it comes a purity of the heart, limbs and faculties, a well-being of the inward and outward, a gratitude for blessings, a beneficience towards the poor, an increase in supplication to Allah, humility and weeping. It is the rope of taking refuge in Allah, the cause for breaking all desires. It reduces the accounts and multiplies the good deeds. The benefits in it cannot be counted. It is enough that we make the person with discernment aware and that he or she may find success in its use.

Imam al-Ghazali says: As for the fasting of the élite it is the fasting of the righteous ones. It is restraining the limbs and faculties from the commission of offenses and it is achieved by six things.

The first is that one lowers his eyes in modesty and restrains himself from extending his sight to all that is blameworthy and detestable (*makruh*), as well as all that distracts the heart from the remembrance of Allah. The Prophet (may Allah bless him) said: 'Looking is a poisoned arrow from the arrows of Satan. Whoever leaves it in fear of Allah, Allah will bring him faith (*iman*), the sweetness of which he finds in his heart.' The Prophet also said, 'Five things will break the fast: lying, speaking behind people's backs, creating mischief between two people, swearing falsely and looking with lust.'

The second is that he protects his tongue from talking nonsense, lies, slander, mischievous gossip, vulgarity, curtness, discord, argument and hypocrisy. He enforces silence upon his tongue and makes it constantly occupied with the rememberance of Allah and the recitation of the Qura'an. This called the fasting of the tongue. The Prophet (may Allah bless him) said: 'Fasting is a protection, so if anyone of you is fasting he is not to behave in an unbecoming way nor ignorantly. If a man fights or curses you, you should say, "I am fasting."'

It has been related that two women who were fasting during the time of the Prophet found hunger and thirst to be very difficult for them at the end of the day, to the point that they felt they would perish. So they sent the Prophet a request for permission to break their fast. In return he sent to them a bowl and asked them to vomit into it what they had eaten. One of them vomited until it half filled up with blood and thick lumps of meat. The other woman vomited the same thing until the whole bowl was filled. The people were very surprised by this. The Prophet (may Allah bless him) said: 'These women have fasted from what Allah has permitted them and broken their fast upon what He has forbidden to them. They would sit next to each other and slander people and this is why they have eaten of the flesh of man.'

And I [Kashani] say: From our sources (the *Ahl al-Bayt*) it is reported that the Prophet said: 'He who slanders a Muslim nullifies his fast and breaks his *wudu* (ritual state of purity). If he dies while he is in that state, he has died having made permissible to himself what Allah has forbidden.'

In *al-Kafi* it is related that Imam Ja'far al-Sadiq said: 'Lying will break the fast.' A person who was there with him asked, 'Then how can anyone of us manage a fast?' The Imam said, 'It is not as you think. It is when the lie is against Allah, His Prophet and the Imams.'

Imam al-Ghazali continues by saying: The third is that he refrains from listening to what is despicable, for whatever one is forbidden to say is also forbidden to be heard. And thus, Allah has equated one who listens to a lie with one who eats what is forbidden. And He (Allah) says:

*They are listeners to lies, devourers of the forbidden...(5:42)*

Keeping silent in the presence of slander is forbidden (*haram*). Thus the Prophet, may Allah bless him and his family and grant them peace, said: 'He who backbites and he who listens are partners in the sin.'

The fourth is that he restrains his limbs and faculties, from his hands to his feet, from the despicable. Also he must restrain his stomach at the breaking of the fast from that which is doubtful. The fast has no meaning when there is an abstention from permitted (*halal*) food only to be followed by a breaking of the fast with that which is forbidden (*haram*). He who fasts like this is like the one who builds a palace while he destroys a country.

The fifth is that he does not take too much of the *halal* food at the time of breaking the fast, thereby filling himself up. There is no vessel more distasteful to Allah than a stomach full of *halal* food. How can the faster benefit from fasting, overwhelm the enemy of Allah and break his desires, if he makes up what he missed during the day at the time of breaking his fast. He may even increase in the types of food to the point that it becomes a habit that foods are stored for Ramadan, foods which would never be eaten during the other months. It is known that the goal of the fast is the emptying [of the stomach] and the breaking of the desires so that the self becomes strong in *taqwa* [fearfully guarding the limits of Allah]. When you push your stomach all day long until the night prayer, its desires are stirred and its expectations are made strong. If you then feed it, filling it up with all the delicious foods, you have only increased its future desires. In fact, you may develop new desires that would not have been developed if they had been left to their past habits.

The heart of fasting and its secret is to weaken the powers which Satan uses to lead one to evil. That cannot be achieved except by reduction, which is to eat a meal in the evening that would be eaten every evening, as though one had not fasted. When the one who fasts collects what he would have eaten during the day to be eaten at night, he obtains no benefit from his fast. In fact, it is part of the courtesy [of fasting] that he does not sleep much during the day, thereby tasting hunger and thirst, so he becomes aware of his weakness and thus puries his heart. Every night he continues this, keeping a bit of that weakness, performing his *tahajjud* prayers and night vigil in the hope that Satan will not swarm his heart, so that he can look into the *malakut* (the realm of the unseen). The Night of Power itself is a night in which aspects of the *malakut* are unveiled. The intent is as Allah says: 'Surely We have sent it down on the Night of Power.' Whoever puts between his heart and his chest layers of food will be veiled from Allah, while he who has emptied his stomach would have the veil raised until he is free of concerns for other than Allah. That is the entire affair! The beginning of it all is by reducing the intake of food.

The sixth is that his heart, after breaking the fast, stands unsettled between fear and hope, because one does not know whether his fast has been accepted, and therefore, whether he is one of the close ones, or whether his fast has been returned to him and he is one of those who are outcast. Let him be in that state after every form of worship that he completes.

It is related that Hasan al-Basri passed by some people on the day of the *'id* and they were laughing. He said: 'Allah the Glorious and Mighty has made the month of Ramadan a way for His creatures to race to His obedience. Some people raced ahead gaining the reward while others stay behind disappointed and unsuccessful. It is the wonder of wonders that there should be someone who would laugh and play on the day in which those who have sped have gained victory, while those who are in vanity and futility have been unsuccessful. By Allah, if the veil were lifted, the man of *ihsan*, (excellence – referring to one who raced ahead) would be occupying himself with his ihsan and the man of evil would be ridding himself of him busy from play while the regret of return bars the other one from the door of laughter.

I [Kashani] say: This tradition is Hasan and Imam 'Ali ibn al-Husayn (peace be upon them).

Imam Ghazali says: And these are the inner meanings of fasting.

I [Kashani] ask about one who limits himself to stopping the desires of his stomach and his sexuality while leaving the inner meanings. The scholars say his fasting is correct but then what does this mean?

You should know that the scholars of the outer establish the conditions of fasting by outward indications which are indications we have mentioned regarding the inner conditions of fasting, like backbiting and its like. But the scholars of the outward are not expected to burden the people who are forgetful and active in this world with more than what is easy.

As for the men of knowledge of the hereafter (*akhira*), what they mean by the correctness of fasting is its acceptability; and the acceptability of a fast is whether or not it has enabled one to reach one's objective. They understand the objective of fasting to be the taking on, as much as possible, of a character which contains one of the characteristics of Allah: the Self-Sustainer; and which resembles the angels in their having no desires. The angels are not contaminated with desires. By his, he sinks to the lowest level and enters the category of wild beasts. And every time he manages to curb his desires, he rises to the highest of the high and attains the same level as the angels, and the angels are close to Allah. Whoever follows their example by taking on a character similar to them will be close to Allah, for he who looks like those who are close is close, and that closeness has nothing to do with physical position, it has to do with characteristics. If this is the secret of fasting with those concerned with the heart and the innermost, what is the point of postponing the meals of the day only to eat them all at the time of breaking the fast while diving into desires all day long? Consider the words of the Prophet (may Allah bless him): 'How many a man there is who fasts while there is nothing for him in his fasting except hunger and thirst.' Concerning this Abu Darda has said: 'How much better is the sleep and the breaking of the fast of the wise ones – they will not be cheated like the fools in their fasting and keeping vigil. A little bit of inner certainty and piety is preferable by far than mountains of worship performed by the arrogant.' And it is for that reason that the men of knowledge say: 'How many people who are fasting are actually breaking their fast, and how many who are breaking their fasting are actually fasting?'

The one who is breaking his fast but is actually fasting is he who keeps all his faculties free from any errors and sins, while eating and drinking. The one who is fasting but has broken his fast is he who feels the hunger and thirst of the fast but allows all his senses and faculties to be rampant. He who understands the meaning of fasting and its secret knows that the likeness of one who refrains from eating and sexual intercourse, then breaks his fast by committing many errors, is as the one who wipes all his limbs properly during ablution (*wudu*), with all the courtesies, supplications and properties, but leaves out the most important action, that of performing the *ghusl* of *janabah* (ritual purification from sexual impurity). His prayers will be returned to him because he is ignorant. The likeness of one who is not fasting from food but is fasting by all his faculties from any wrong actions is as the one who has wiped all his limbs according to what is necessary for him and then limited himself to doing the obligatory. His prayers are correct and acceptable according to what is obligatory even though he may have left out the recommended. And the likeness of one who combines both fasting from food and the faculties is as the one who has combined the obligatory with what is recommended – that is the complete way.

The Prophet has said: 'Fasting is a trust upon you so let everyone of you keep his trust.' The Most High says:

*Allah orders you to return the trusts to their lawful owners. (4:58)*

When the Prophet (peace be upon him) recited this *ayah* he put his hands upon his ears and upon his eyes and said: 'Hearing is a trust and seeing is a trust.' If they were not parts of the trust of fasting, he would not have said: 'Let him only say I am fasting,' meaning: I have kept my tongue protected; how am I going to let it loose by answering you? So it has been made clear from what we have revealed that for every type of worship there is an outer and an inner – there is a shell and there is an inner core. Within the shells there are degrees and for every degree there are layers. It is up to you to choose whether to be content with the shell or go deeply into the heart of the core.

## The Voluntary Aspects of Fasting

I [Kashani] say: It is related from Imam 'Ali (peace be upon him) that the Prophet (may Allah bless him) said: 'Whoever fasts a day voluntarily, Allah, the Mighty, the glorious, causes him to enter the Garden.'

Abu Ja'far [Immam al-Baqir] said: 'He who has sealed a day by fasting will enter the Garden.'

The Prophet (may Allah bless him) said: 'He who fasts one day for Allah's sake it is as though he had fasted one year.' He also said, 'There is no one fasting in the presence of people who are eating but that all his faculties are glorifying Him and the prayers of the angels are upon him, blessing him, asking forgiveness for him.'

It is related that 'Ali (peace be upon him) said: 'No one is more despised by Allah, the Mighty and Glorious, than a man who is told that the Prophet did such and such and then says, "Allah will not expect me to exert more effort in prayer and fasting." '

Imam al-Sadiq said: 'The Prophet (may Allah bless him) fasted until it was said that he did not break his fast. Then he broke his fast until it was said that he does not fast. Then he fasted the fast of David, one day fasting and the next day not. He departed from this world fasting three days in every month. The Prophet said: "These days are equivalent to fasting permanently. They will take away from you the doubts and uncertainties in your chest." The Imam was then asked, 'Which were these days?' To this he replied: 'The first Thursday in the month, the first Wednesday after the first ten days of it, and the last Thursday in the month.' And then, 'How did fasting on these days come about?' He said: 'When theree was a punishment to be sent to the peoples before us, it was on these days that it was sent down. The Prophet fasted on them out of fear.'

Al-Fadil ibn Yasar relates that Imam al-Sadiq said: 'Whany one of yousts three days in the moth, he should not enter into dispute nor should he rush to swearing himself to anything, and if one has been wronged let him bear it.'

The Commander of the Faithful ['Ali] said: 'Fasting the month of patience [Ramadan] and three days of every month will take away all the uncertainties in the breast. Fasting three days of every month is the continuous fast. Surely Allah, the Mighty and Glorious says:

*And he who brings a virtuous deed will be given ten times its like. (6:160)*

Imam al-Sadiq said: 'When there are two Thursdays close to the beginning of the month, fasting the first one is better. And when there are two Thursdays both close to the end of the month, fasting the last one is better.'

In another narration Imam Ja'far al-Sadiq was asked about two Thursdays being within the last ten days of the month, and he reportedly said: 'Fast the first, you may not reach the second.'

'Ays bin al-Qasim asked Imam al-Sadiq: 'If someone does not fast the three days of every month because it is distressing for him, does he have to pay a penalty for missing that day of fasting?' He said, 'A portion (*mudd*) of food for every day.'

Ibrahim ibn Muthinna came to the Imam and said: 'It is very difficult for me to fast three days every month. Can I give in charity a dirham (*sadaqah*) for every day?' The Imam said, 'A dirham in charity is better in your case than fasting a day.'

Someone asked one of the Imams: 'When fasting three days of every month, can I delay it from summer to winter? I find that much easier for me.' The Imam told him, 'Yes, keep to that.' Also there is a tradition which says that all of the traditions confirm that fasting three days every month is what has been the norm.

And among the other recommended fasts that are certain there is the fast of the month of Rajab and Sha'ban, or what you are able to fast of them. Rajab is the month of Imam 'Ali (peace be upon him) and Sha'ban is the month of the Prophet (may Allah bless him), in the same way that Ramadan is the month of Allah, the Most Mighty and Glorious. And for fasting these two months, Rajab and Sha'ban, there has been a great deal of encouragement and promise of reward.

Abu Hamid al-Ghazali says: When the times of grace and virtue appear, for the sake of perfection, it is important that a person understands the meaning of fasting. Its objective is to purify the heart and to give up to Allah one's anxieties. He who is an expert in the intricacies of his heart, will look at his states. It may be important for him to continue fasting, or it may be important for him to continue breaking his fast, or it may be important for him to mix fasting and breaking the fast. If he understands that the meaning and the boundaries of his passage towards the next life are confirmed by means of watching his heart, he will be aware of what is the right condition of his heart, which does not mean that he has to continue in one continuous state. Thus, it is related that the Prophet (may Allah bless him) used to fast until it was said that he never broke his fast, and he used to break his fast until it was said that he never fasted. He used to sleep until it was said he never arose, and he used to be up until it was said that he did not sleep. This was according to what was revealed to him by the light of prophecy about the execution of the perfect use of the times. And praise belongs to Allah.

# Hajj – A Personal Account

## By 'Abbas Mubarak

*The months of the pilgrimage are well known; so whoever determines to perform pilgrimage therein there shall be no immodest speech, nor abusing, nor altercation in the pilgrimage. And whatever good you do, Allah knows it. And make provision for yourselves, the best provision being to keep one's duty. And keep your duty to Me, O men of understanding. (2:197)*

### Introduction

Amongst the many tasks that the Muslim must full is the Hajj. It is the most distant of the obligations. The prayer is performed daily; the declaration of faith is on the tongue constantly; *zakat* and Ramadan occur yearly, always to be planned for or looked forward to; but Hajj occurs usually only once in a life-time – if it occurs at all.

Though Hajj is one of the pillars of Islam, it is not obligatory upon everyone. According to Shaykh al-Tusi, one of the great Shi'ah scholars, the one upon whom the Hajj is obligatory is he who is 'free [i.e., he is not a slave], mature [i.e., he has reached the age in which Islam is obligatory upon him], responsible for himself [i.e., he is sane] and has the capability to do it.' Speaking of the capability he says, 'the means to perform the Hajj is having the provisions, the transportation, the livelihood to return to when the Hajj is over [i.e., a skill or trade to enable one to earn a living], and a freedom from the swarm of obstacles in the way; such as, the permission of an authority [to travel through a country to make the Hajj] or the threat of an enemy.'

When one looks at a world map one sees that the Hijaz, the land in which Mecca is placed, is very far away. Only a hundred years ago travelling to the Ka'bah would have entailed years of planning and months of travelling. But today, with adequate finances, one can take a jet from New York to Jeddah. Within twelve hours the pilgrim is in Saudi Arabia only hours away from the home of Abraham. There is something almost comical about flying through the air in an air-conditioned cabin, being served kosher roast beef, watching movies and being waited on by women, with the thought of the Hajj foremost in your mind – it all being part of 'the most difficult journey.'

We were informed that we were approaching Jeddah. 'In an hour we will be landing,' continued the captain's dull voice, 'those who are performing Hajj can, if they wish, put on their *ihram*' (the clothing of the pilgrim).

This produced a little wonder in me. These people who had put on their *ihram* had, I thought, begun their Hajj. When was I going to begin? It now became apparent to me that it was important to know the 'game plan' of the Hajj. For though there are literally millions of people running the course with you, there are different methods of doing the Hajj.

I had heard so much about the Saudi government and its treatment of the pilgrims. I had also heard of the ignorance of the pilgrims and their terrible behaviour. At the airport, going through customs, when four young boys who were insolent, indolent and rude crudely examined our passports, I could see that we would have to deal with a barrier of officialdom distracted madly by the world, self-righteous, and all too willing to inflict punishment according to a code of conduct scarcely understood by them. I had yet to witness the behaviour of the hajjis (pilgrims).

Our first move was to attach ourselves to a group, an Iranian group. We had heard of their good organisation, and of course we knew that they practise the glorious din of Muhammad as taught by the beloved Ahl al-Bayt. After hours of difficulty in making the necessary arrangements, we were accepted by an Iranian group from Najafabad and Isfahan. We would be travelling by bus with them to Mecca.

First arriving at the airport in Jeddah at 1 p.m., we got to the Hajj terminal tents at 4 p.m. and were now leaving for Mecca at 4 a.m. The waiting had an excitement, shared by all the hajjis. There was a constant influx of new pilgrims, fresh from their respective countries. At the same time there was the periodic massive loading of a group of pilgrims into their waiting buses. As I walked through the terminal I saw pilgrims from many different countries. The Iranians were the most numerous; they seemed to be everywhere: 150,000 Muslims from Iran were coming to Hajj this year. Each country had their own dress and distinctive markings. People were strewn everywhere on straw mats and blankets, sleeping or resting, exhausted from their long flights.

Finally, at fajr (dawn), we boarded a bus. It was a school bus painted white with blue trim, and it had a curious feature; the roof was cut off. According to Ja'fari fiqh (law), the men were to ride in open buses or on the roofs of buses when performing the 'Umrah (lesser pilgrimage) of the Hajj. Our first stop was Jahfa where we were to put on our ihram for 'Umrah. There are ve stops at which the pilgrim may put on his ihram whether he is beginning Hajj or 'Umrah. The station or stop to which you go is determined by the direction from which you approach Mecca. Jahfa was the closest station to Jeddah, and we arrived there in the middle of a red-tawn desert plain two hours after sunrise.

There are three types of Hajj in Islam: tamattu' (sequence), ifrad (singularity), and qiran (conjunction). In the Hajj of ifrad, the pilgrim dedicates himself for the Hajj alone, and when he completes it, he performs the 'Umrah. In the Hajj of qiran, the pilgrim dedicates himself for both the Hajj and the 'Umrah combined, and there is no space of time between the performance of the 'Umrah and the Hajj. The third type of Hajj, Hajj tamattu', is generally performed by most of the pilgrims who come from long distances to Mecca. In Ja'fari fiqh it says: 'This hajj is called Hajj tamattu' because the hajji (pilgrim) enjoys a period of ease between the 'Umrah which is to be performed first and the Hajj. This Hajj is composed of two obligations which are 'Umrah of tamattu' and 'Hajj of Tamattu'.'

The Hajj that I was going to perform was the most common one, the Hajj of tamattu'. The first thing I had to perform was the 'Umrah, and it began here in the middle of the desert, in Jahfa. There were three obligations I had to fulfil in performing the act of putting on the ihram. The first was the actual donning of the two pieces of unsewn white cloth, each two yards long, which make up the ihram garment. The second was making the intention which is 'I am performing this 'Umrah of tamattu' in order to come close to Allah.' Uncertain but determined, I entered the humble mosque in my ihram repeating the intention over and over to myself. I made two raka'at (cycles of prayer) and then began to repeat the formula which is the third obligation over and over: Labayk Allahuma labayk; labayk la sharika laka labayk; inna al-hamdu wa ni'matu laka wa al-mulk; la sharika lak (I am at Your service O Allah, at Your service; I am at Your service, no associate with You; truly the praise and the blessing and the Kingdom are Yours; there is no associate with You).

As we left to board the buses, there were still people there making du'ah (prayers of supplication), and more coming in singing 'Labayk Allahuma labayk...' Wrapped in our towels, the wind unfurling our ihrams, we raced through the desert, our hearts already in Mecca eager to greet the Ka'bah. Again and again 'Labayk Allahuma labayk' arose from everyone in the bus.

## Entering Mecca

And We made the House a refuge for men and a sanctuary, [saying]. Take the place of Abraham for a place of prayer. And We enjoined Abraham and Ishmael, [saying]: Purify My House for those who visit it and those who abide in it for devotion and those who bow down [and] those *who prostrate themselves.*

(2:125)

*And when Abraham said: My Lord, make this city secure, and save me and my sons from worshipping idols.*

*My Lord, surely they have led many men astray. So whoever follows me, he is surely of me; and whoever disobeys me, Thou surely art Forgiving, Merciful.*

*Our Lord, I have settled a part of my offspring in a valley unproductive of fruit near Thy Sacred House, our Lord, that they may keep up prayer; so make the hearts of some people yearn towards them, and provide them with fruits; haply they may be grateful.*

(14:35–37)

As indicated in the Qur'an, Mecca is a difcult place to live in. Virtually nothing grows on the hills and mountainsides surrounding Mecca. In a small valley of this desolate mountain region sits Mecca, and at the bottom of Mecca is placed the Ka'bah.

Once in Mecca, we quickly arrived at our hostel, a three-story building with a roof, which was used for morning and evening meals. Here we were to live for the entirety of our stay in Mecca, about seventeen days, ten days before the Hajj and seven days after it. Through the Iranian caravan our stay in Mecca was made comfortable. With three good meals a day, a clean room and toilet facilities we could maintain our strength to visit the House of Allah daily, offering supplications and worshipping.

### 'Umrah

After lunch and a short nap, I set out for the Ka'bah to complete my *'Umrah.* Most of the people in our group were waiting for night to fall because of the heat. It turned out that between *'asr* (midafternoon) and *maghrib* (sunset) was a good time to go, because the heat had abated somewhat while the pilgrims were still indoors. It is important to try to do the obligatory acts of *'Umrah* and Hajj at times when there are fewer people.

Surrounding the *Masjid al-Haram* (the mosque encompassing the

Ka'bah) is a souk or open market. Passing quickly through it, I discovered the mosque. It is huge, built completely of marble. I followed the other pilgrims with my slippers in hand through one of the many doors. There was an unspeakable excitement when I caught a glimpse of the Ka'bah between the many columns inside the mosque. I felt I was coming home to a familiar place. The Ka'bah was my heart, an empty house, built to contain only the love of Allah. At the Ka'bah, placed at the centre of a large marble-tiled central courtyard, were hundreds maybe thousands of people, men and women with or without ihram, walking counter clockwise around its high walls.

> *And when We assigned to Abraham the place of the House, saying: Associate naught with Me, and purify My House for those who make circuits and stand to pray and bow and prostrate themselves.*
>
> *And proclaim to men the Pilgrimage: they will come to you on foot and on every fast mount, coming from every remote path:*
>
> *Then let them accomplish their needful acts of cleansing, and let them full their vows and go round the Ancient House.*
>
> (22:26–27,29)

I stood in this immense courtyard of the mosque, my eyes moving from the worshippers to the Ka'bah and back again to the activity of the *tawaf* (circumambulation of the Ka'bah). I could not move for the activity and majesty of the scene. A young Saudi guard came to me and asked me to move back out of the way. Somehow I communicated to him that I had come from the U.S.A. to perform Hajj. He then greeted me warmly and shook my hand. I felt I had been welcomed by the Ka'bah and with firmly set purpose plunged into the swell of people whose intent I shared. I became one of the unit – a owing mass of worshippers. All the discomforts and discourtesies at which I later came to take offense were nothing to me as I heaved and flowed around the house. Each time I passed the black stone I saluted the House of Allah, continuing to call with my heart, and carefully marking in my memory the number of times I had gone around the house. While I was doing the *tawaf* I thought of Muhammad (may Allah bless him and his family) and how he would have behaved as he circumambulated the Ka'bah. I tried to maintain a loving and kind courtesy towards the madly intent units of the heaving sea of humanity.

After the seventh turn around the house, I allowed myself to drift on past the black stone and the *maqam* (station) of Abraham, until the pressure of the crowd thinned out. I was then able to make my way to the *maqam* of Abraham. Behind it I found a place to do two *raka'at*. Having finished them, I completed the third obligatory part of my *'Umrah*. The first was the putting on of the *ihram*; the second was the performance of the *tawaf*. In both the performance of my *tawaf* and the two *raka'at* behind the *maqam* of Abraham I tried to maintain a middle course, in that I did not allow myself to get overly caught up in their performance, and thereby cause discomfort to others. I performed the *raka'at* solemnly, but quickly and proceeded to the *sa'i*, the next obligation.

After asking a few questions I found out where the beginning of the *sa'i* was. Leaving your position behind the *maqam* of Abraham, the hill of Safa is to your right as you move away from the Ka'bah. I climbed the gently sloping hill of Safa and put my feet upon the rock of the original hill, most of which had been covered with tiles. The *sa'i* is the re-enactment of the trial of Hagar, Abraham's Egyptian wife. Having been left in the desert, at the very spot where the *sa'i* is performed, with her baby Ishmael, she ran frantically back and forth between Safa and Marwah (two hills) looking for water. We could say that *sa'i* is the re-enactment of our own striving for gain in the world. Back and forth we run anxiously striving for what eludes us. *Sa'i* consists of walking seven times between Safa and Marwah causing you to end up at Marwah. I strove between the hills trying to re-enact the trial of Hagar and attain its meaning.

At the end, having reached Marwah for the last time, you must perform the last of the obligatory actions, the cutting of a bit of the hair or nail.

That night I stayed until after *'isha* (the night prayer) at the House of Allah, vowing to return for the dawn prayer. When I got home I took off my *ihram*, putting it away until I could use it for the Hajj.

At two in the morning, well ahead of the call to prayer for *fajr*, I left my bed for the House of Allah; I was caught, intoxicated by the Ka'bah. I made the night prayers and read Qur'an until *fajr* was prayed. When it was over I returned to my hostel and rest.

In Mecca there is nothing to do but to go to the Haram. So every day one plans when to go, trying one's best to avoid both the crowds and the heat. I would go there just to read the Qur'an, offer *salat* and walk around the inside of the mosque doing *dhikr: La ilaha illa'llah* or *al-hamdu lillahi wa shukru lillah*. Frequently, I would visit the well of Zamzam. It is in the inner courtyard at the outer parameter between the black stone and the station of Abraham. Going down the steps to it one is wafted by a cool and moist wave of air. It is the welcoming of the waters of Zamzam which has healing and revivifying qualities. The Saudi government has modernised the well to such an extent that getting water there is like standing at a water fountain in any modern office building in New York City.

## The Hajj

Finally, the time came to start the Hajj. It was the eighth of Dhul Hijja, *yawmul-tarawiy*, the day that the Ka'bah is washed and that the pilgrims may start out for the plain of 'Arafat.

There was not very much to take with me as I boarded one of the open-topped buses. I had my *ihram* on and a small bag with a few necessities. Three days we would be camped outside Mecca.

For about an hour we drove east of Mecca. There was quite a bit of traffic but it was not too difficult. Through a tunnel and small valleys, the bus soon emerged on to a large plain which was 'Arafat. It was covered with tents – a city of tents. Along one of the avenues the bus stopped. We hopped out and the group leader and his men, who were paid to care for and feed the pilgrims in the group, put down mats and set up the kitchen facility and water dispensers. Within a few hours everything was ready. I put down a blanket and established a little place for myself. The whole group was under one tent.

Shortly after we beached, so to speak, I walked out to familiarise myself with the neighbourhood. The streets were roaring with vehicles and bustling with people. One large street was reserved for pedestrians and lining its sides were shops under tin roofs selling food, drink or clothing. Wherever I went to perform acts of worship (*'ibadat*), whether in Mecca, Mina, or 'Arafat there was the business of selling and buying being carried on.

> *It is no sin for you that you seek the bounty of your Lord. So when you press on from 'Arafat, remember Allah near the holy place* [Muzdalifah], *and remember Him as He has guided you, though before that you were of the erring ones.*
>
> (2:198)

We spent the night, seventy men under one tent. All through the night men would rise to pray or take care of their needs. It was restless but sweet in its singleness of purpose. In the morning we prayed in congregation for the first time as a group. To perform the Hajj one had to be here, on the plain of 'Arafat, during the afternoon on the ninth of Dhul Hijja until the sun set. We were early in our appointment with Allah.

Desiring to take advantage of the coolness of the morning, I set out directly after breakfast to climb Jabal ul-Rahmah. There was a small path with steps leading steeply up the mountain. It was swarming with pilgrims desiring to climb. At first I felt there was no room, but in time I found I could climb up and miraculously I found a spot, a rock upon which to settle with the intention of making a supplication (*du'ah*). The act of asking Allah, which had seemed so small an act while I was at home in the U.S.A. working and participating in an active life, had become the only significant act, requiring my full attention; an act which at this point in time and place was of very high value. I made the best of the moment given to me, made my supplication and left the mountain.

The performance of Hajj while at 'Arafat is a special type of *'ibada*. It is unlike the prayer in that it is not so much of an action. You only have to be somewhere at a particular time, that is all! There I sat or lay, sweating in the great heat, trying to make the best of what was supposed to be a great moment in my life. One's performance of service to Allah is completely immersed in the life situation and without a prescribed outward act. I became highly impatient; I knew I was at the moment in which something tremendous should happen, but there was nothing but sweat and inaction. Finally, I was drawn to the only recourse I had which was recitation of the Qur'an and supplication to Allah. Only Allah knows the ramifications of being at 'Arafat during Hajj.

By *'asr* (mid-afternoon) the streets were full of people and vehicles bound for Muzdalifah where everyone had to spend the night before entering Mina. Our group hung back until *maghrib* (sunset) before we boarded our buses. We made our way slowly towards Mina where we were supposed to be on the tenth, but into which we could not go until the sun of the next day arose.

After four hours of slow movement through traffic, exhausted, we pulled off the side of the road. All along the road buses, cars and trucks were parked, or one might say stranded for the night. This was Muzdalifah, the vagabonds' heaven. If anyone has experienced the life of a wanderer along the highways of America toting only a sleeping bag, in the hopes of a long ride and a bed to sleep in, then this place was the essence of that experience, its meaning. For here one is surrounded by stranded travellers, sleeping by the side of the road, homeless, comfortless and weary; but with the intention of worshipping their Creator.

It is here at this comfortless station that the *hajji* picks up ammunition to fight Shaytan when he is in Mina. At about one in the morning I searched along the ground, sifting through the roadside dirt mounds for the small stones that I would later throw at the Jamarat (the stone pillars that represent Shaytan). I collected seventy and stored them away for use in Mina.

At the breaking of dawn, Muzdalifah came alive with pilgrims bound for Mina. We hopped back into the bus. To go five miles it took us three hours. Mina is a very small outcrop of the city of Mecca, but at the time of Hajj it swells to accommodate millions of *hajjis*.

Arriving in Mina marked the second day of Hajj and the *'Id al-Adha*. For most of the *hajjis* this day is especially busy. Apart from the stoning of the largest of the *Jamarat, al-'Aqabah*, and the slaughtering, the Sunni Muslims had to return to Mecca to perform a *tawaf* around the Ka'bah, then return to Mina. I thank our Imams for the beauty of the Ja'fari fiqh. According to our imam, Imam Khomeini, whose exposition of the law we were following, we could return to Mecca on the twelfth and do our obligatory *tawaf* anytime after that. No words can express the hardship suffered in large crowds. So while millions of pilgrims trooped off to Mecca on the tenth of Dhul Hijja, I stayed in Mina waiting for the best time to stone the big Shaytan, *al'-Aqabah*.

Because of the tremendous heat, I waited until afternoon to go to the Jamarat. I and my American friends went at a time when there were the minimum number of people stoning. Despite the danger of being hit by a stray stone, there was no problem getting close enough to hit the pillar of Shaytan. The next thing to do was slaughter an animal, but because it was late we decided to postpone that until the next day. One has three days in which to make the sacrifice.

Among the many advantages we had by being a part of the well organised Iranian group was that it had an *'alim* (learned man) who could explain to the people the details of the Hajj and solve any problems in fiqh that might arise. Also he was accepted by all as fit for leading the prayer and leading the group in the proclamation of the intention to perform a certain part of the Hajj. For instance, at 'Arafat, directly after *dhuhr* (the midday prayers), we repeated after him words that stated our intention to remain at the plain of 'Arafat until sunset in order to come closer to Allah. This act was repeated before every obligatory action that we had to perform. I was not familiar with this practice, but I found it of immense help. It served to cut through the distraction of the heat and the crowds, and bring meaning to each task.

After the animal has been slaughtered, there is only the shaving of the head, or for those who have done Hajj before and do not wish to shave their heads, there is the cutting of a little bit of the hair or beard or the pruning of a nail.

With the shaving of the head finished, I could now take off my *ihram*. I was very glad to change clothing. The clean clothes that I put on took on a greater than usual significance; it was another step in the process of purification.

I had only one more thing to do this day and that was to stone the Shaytans. On the second day of a *hajji's* stay in Mina he has to stone first *Jamarat al-Awal* then *Jamarat al-Wasat*, then, and it is the most difcult, *Jamarat al-'Aqabah*. It is done by walking up to each one in turn and tossing seven small stones at the pillar that represents Shaytan. For me this was the most difficult obligation in Hajj to perform. The people, the *hajjis*, were mad in their approach to this symbolic act.

Again on the third day all three of the Shaytans had to be stoned. At the last Shaytan, *al-'Aqabah*, I clearly saw the workings of Shaytan. Because *al-'Aqabah* is against a wall there is much less space to throw your stones. As a result, the people are crowded together, each one fiercely battling to get close enough to the Shaytan in order to hit it. There is a veritable battle going on. Stones fly everywhere, people push and shove in fear, wild with the intent to perform their obligation, completely oblivious of other peoples' presence.

*Every one of them, that day, will have concern enough to make him indifferent to others.* (80:37)

Everyone was only concerned for himself. I caught a glimpse of a man who had climbed up onto the platform of the pillar. He was a dark silhouette against a light background. He was drunk with passion. In this mass hysteria he had become so excited that he had climbed up and was shovelling the heap of thrown stones that lay at the base of the pillar and was showering the Shaytan. He was a worshipper of Shaytan. May we take refuge with Allah from the accursed Shaytan. People threw shoes, boxes, anything. The ground was almost a foot deep with sandals and debris. At a certain point I lost my sandals and I had to struggle to get them back.

I left al-'Aqbah thinking of the Last Day and I was in confusion. I seriously questioned the Hajj. What I had seen was, I was convinced, not part of Islam. Soon I realised that I was questioning Allah's wisdom. He is the Most Wise. Everything in the Hajj has to be a sign upon which to reflect.

It was now time to travel to Mecca which was only a few miles away. I would soon be seeing the Ka'bah again.

Returning to Mecca, I waited until the next day at about *'asr* time to go to the mosque and perform the *tawaf* of Hajj, the two *raka'at* behind the station of Abraham and the running (*sa'i*) between Saffa and Marwah. This time the *tawaf* was very difficult for me to do. I kept seeing the behaviour of the people as vulgarities arising from ignorance. In the midst of a swarm of people, and so close to the House of God, I had to make the effort to see the perfection of God's creation and His Wisdom spreading over it.

There was now only one more act to perform, and that was *tawaf al-Nisa* along with two *raka'at* behind the station of Abraham. There was no question of doing it that evening, I was exhausted. The next night, when the heat of the day had ebbed, I would finish my Hajj.

## The Trip to Medina

Even after finishing the Hajj we stayed in Mecca another week. Finally, the time came to go to Medina, the city of the Prophet. In America, thinking of the Hajj, I had considered Medina the goal. I thought that it was the place of the ultimate experience. There I could be close to the Prophet, the man who had the ultimate experience of Allah's gifts.

We travelled all night and most of the next day; by noon we had reached Medina.

Our hostel was very close to the Prophet's Mosque. Within ten minutes you could be at his door. On the way was al-Baqi, the huge graveyard that held the graves of many of the family of the Prophet, as well as many of the great Companions. In the tradition of the Wahhabis, the graveyard had been destroyed in a futile attempt to extinguish the Muslim's love for these great beings. Every grave was now only a dirt mound, barely distinguishable from the ground next to it. At the front entrance, where the gate is always closed, stood the lovers of the family of the Prophet.

If you go up to the gate or off to either side you can see the graves of the five *ma'sums* (infallible ones) that are buried there. They are Fatimah, Imam Hasan al-Mujtaba, Imam Zayn al-'Abidin, Imam Muhammad al-Baqir, and Imam Ja'far al-Sadiq (peace be upon them). Five of the great beings of the Prophet's family act as a reminder of the perfection of the Prophet and his message.

Finally, I arrived at the Prophet's mosque. People were leaving the mosque having finished the *'isha* prayer when I slipped in. Immediately I noticed a place for me to sit, directly in front of the Prophet's tomb. I had almost an hour in this spot before I was forced to leave by the guards. Within that short sitting I had greeted the Prophet. In front of me there had been a small group of men greeting each other in love and respect. They talked, some wept, others joined them; then they left. The mosque had emptied out.

After I had greeted the Prophet and read some of the Qur'an I reflected that I had finally reached what I had been waiting for. But now that I was here I realised it was Mecca, it was the Ka'bah that was the great source of light for the Muslims, and that the Prophet, may Allah bless him and his family, was an extension of that light. When I left the mosque I felt that I had finished what I had come for. I could have returned to America then, but as it was we stayed another ten days.

Within those ten days I became closer to the Iranian group that I was with. It was an extraordinary honour to be with these people.

When we left them, they gave us the most affectionate of send-offs. They were as if part of my family; each one personally greeted and sincerely kissed me, passing me on to the next man waiting to wish me well. I have nothing but love and admiration for them.

Upon reaching home, my life was turned outside-in and inside-out from the experience of the Hajj. It is Allah's plot to perfect us and make us ready for the next world. The Hajj, enjoined upon us by Allah, serves to catapult us from lethargy and forgetfulness into necessary action.

*Most surely man is in a state of loss, unless he be of those who attain to faith, and do good works, and enjoin upon one another the truth, and enjoin upon one another patience in adversity.*

(103:2–3)

# SECTION 8

## On the Path

*In the Name of Allah, the Beneficent, the Most Merciful*
*Have We expanded for you your breast?*
*And alleviated for you your burden,*
*Which had so heavily weighed down your back?*
*And raised up for you your remembrance?*
*For certainly with every difculty there is ease,*
*Certainly, with every difficulty there is ease.*
*So when you are freed, remain steadfast, expend!*
*And make your Lord your exclusive object [of longing]!*

(The Expansion)

*Hadith:* 'I was a hidden treasure, and I desired to be known, so I created [the world].'

——— ⋆ ———

*Hadith:* 'And when I love him [My slave] I am the Hearing with which he hears and the Sight with which he sees and the Hand with which he grasps and the Foot on which he walks.'

# The Path of the People

## By Shaykh Ahmad ibn Muhammad ibn 'Ajiba al-Hasani

Translated from *Al-Futuhat al-Ilahiyya fi Sharh al-Mabahith al-Asliyya*

The knowledge which the Sufis seek is of the highest order. It is without doubt the most noble and the most excellent knowledge. The one who brought it is the Messenger (may Allah bless him). He is the best of creation. The sound intellect appreciates perfections, and there is no doubt that Sufism exists only to realise perfections by knowledge, deeds and state. It is the science of perfecting beliefs, purifying souls, and improving behaviour. With regard to its confirmation by recorded knowledge, there is no doubt that the Book and the Sunnah and the consensus of the imams praise its features, such as turning to Allah, fearful awareness, straightness, sincerity, truthfulness, tranquillity, doing without, scrupulousness, reliance upon Allah, acceptance, surrender, love, watching, witnessing, and so on.

The true Sufis are the most eager followers of the Sustainer of men. Therefore, they are the most loved by Allah of all creation, for Allah the Exalted says in the Qur'an:

*Say: If you love Allah, follow me, and Allah will love you.* (3:31)

And the Prophet, may Allah bless him and grant him peace, said: 'Not one of you is one who trusts until I am more beloved to you than his wealth, his children and all people.' The proof of love is to follow.

The path of the people [the Sufis] is auspicious and blessed for everyone who travels it with sincerity, love, gravity and struggle. It is said that its fruits are giving up the self easily, soundness of the breast, and excellent behaviour. Al-Junayd, may Allah be pleased with him, said: 'Our knowledge is chained to the Book and to the Sunnah.' The one who does not listen to the traditions, does not sit with the jurisprudents, and does not take his courtesy from those who have courtesy, will destroy those who follow them. Sahl ibn'Abdullah said: 'Our foundation is built upon six matters: the Book of Allah, the Sunnah of the Messenger (upon whom be blessings and peace), eating what is permitted, preventing all harm, avoiding all wrong action, turning to Allah, and fulfilling the rights.' Abu 'Uthman al-Hayri (may Allah be pleased with him) said: 'He who places a command of the Sunnah over himself by speech and action speaks wisdom. The one who commands himself by desire in speech and action speaks with innovation.'

Abu Ishaq al-Shatibi has explained this in *Al-'Uddah*: All that the notable Sufis practise originates in the *shari'ah* (religious law). The Sunnah is a proof against them, and their work is not a proof against the Sunnah. The Sunnah is free from faults and the one who follows it is free. No leader is denifitely free, unless he has a proof from the *shari'ah*. The Sufis are just like others. They are free from neither faults nor forgetfulness, nor great and small disobediences, nor permitted and reprehensible innovation; all these faults are possible for Sufis. The scholars say that everything the Sufis say may be either accepted or rejected, except what comes from the Prophet (may Allah bless him and grant him peace).

Al-Qushayri has made the best decision. He said: 'Is the *wali* (friend of Allah) immune? If you mean necessarily, as is the case with the Prophets, then no. But if you mean that he is protected so that he does not persist in wrong action, even though he has committed errors, lapses and major faults, then yes, he is protected.' In the same way that it is possible for others to be disobedient and commit innovation, it is also possible for the *awliya* (friends of Allah) to do so. Our duty is to limit ourselves to following the one who makes no mistakes, not to follow those who make mistakes, if a problem arises in following the latter. What is presented by the leaders of the religion must be weighed by the Book and the Sunnah. If it is in accord with these, we accept it, if not, we leave it. We do not follow the Sus except after we have weighed their action and their speech according to the Sunnah. And this is the counsel of the Shaykhs of the Sufis.

Everything that comes from the man of ecstasy and taste, of knowledge and states and unveilings, must be weighed by the Book and the Sunnah. If there is proof in the Book and the Sunnah for it, that is fine; if not, it is not valid. Because of the high regard in which they are held, one must look at what they have compiled and the actions which distinguish them from others. If you find their actions not according to the *shari'ah*, then stop following them, even if they are among those who are being followed. Do not stop in order to go against them or to reject them, but because you did not understand the basis of what they did in the *shari'ah* as you have understood how other matters are based on the *shari'ah*. Therefore, it is our duty with respect to their point of view about the path of discipline not to act blindly according to what they have established. We must, on the other hand, follow their traces, guided by their lights, contrary to the one who decides to imitate them in what is not proper in their school. The proofs of the *shari'ah*, the law, praise the one who guards himself and purifies his religion and preserves his dignity.

People are divided into three types: the scholar, the worshipper, and the realised Sufi. All have taken their portion from the inheritance of the Prophet. The scholar has inherited his sayings with the condition that he should be sincere and truthful. Otherwise, he is turned away from the inheritance completely, because deeds without sincerity are like bodies without spirit. The worshipper has inherited his actions: fasting, praying at night and outward struggle. The Prophet (may Allah bless him) stood up at night until his heels split. He used to fast much, and also break his fast. The realised Sufi has inherited everything. In the beginning he takes from outward knowledge what is necessary for him. He plunges to its depth and then moves to action in the most perfect state. He has also inherited the behaviour which the Prophet (may Allah bless him) used to apply to his inward self: doing without, scrupulousness, fear and hope, patience, forbearance, generosity, courage, contentment, humility, reliance upon Allah, Sahl, may Allah be pleased with him, said : 'The Sufi is the one who has clarified his cloudiness and is filled with reflection and is isolated with Allah, without humans. Gold and mud are the same to him.'

Allah the Exalted gave to the Prophet (may Allah bless him) certain things which no one shares with him. He was very strong. Whoever examines his worship finds that no one could stand where he stood. Whoever looks at his inward behaviour finds that no one could equal him. Whoever looks at his gnosis finds that no one could reach him, or even come near him. His station was one that cannot be reached and cannot be known. Look at what Shaykh Ibn al-Mashish said: 'In him realities ascended and the knowledges of Adam descended. Creation is incapable beside him. Understanding is a trifle compared to him. No one from among us can reach him, neither those before him nor those after him.' Neither scholars, nor worshippers, nor Sufis can have more than a drop of his knowledge, action and behaviour. May Allah increase al-Busayri who said in his *Burdah*:

They all petition the Messenger of Allah
For a ladleful from the ocean or a sip from the torrential rain.
They stand with due respect to their limits in comparison with him.

I say that there is no doubt that the Sufis have shunned wrong actions. This means that they have put them behind their backs and have purified their hearts from them. The means whereby wrong actions and faults are purified is the purification of the source and of the head. The source of wrong actions and faults is mixing with the ignorant The one who mixes with the mob and thinks that he will be safe from wrong action thinks the impossible. He is like the one who mixes dry wood with fire and thinks that he will be safe from getting burned. As to the head of wrong actions and faults, it is the love of this world which dwells in the heart, as tradition states: 'The love of this world is the fountainhead of every wrong .'

The realised Sufis have perceived something other than bodies, which they call the spiritual world. I say that the degrees of existence are three: the kingdom of forms, the kingdom of unseen forms, and the kingdom of power. Existence has three approaches.

One point of view is the timeless, original existence which has never come into the world of shapes and forms, and it is called the world of the command, the world of the unseen, which is also called the kingdom of power. Another is a derivative existence of light which overflows from the ocean of the kingdom of power. It consists of everything that enters the world of forms and shapes, whether subtle or dense. This world is called the world of witnessing, or the world of dominion. It is what we call the kingdom of unseen forms. The third is an illusory existence which is the place of the actions of the Lord and the reflection of the names of Majesty and Beauty. This is the kingdom of forms. One of the Sufis said: 'The worlds are four: the world of witnessing, the world of the unseen, the world of unseen forms, and the kingdom of power. The first is made up of sensory densities. The second is made up of the subtleties of the unseen, like jinn, angels and spirits. All of these are also in the kingdom of unseen forms, the third world, the function of which is to gather these things to their origin and to realise witnessing. The fourth world is the kingdom of power, which is the original vastness. It is subtle and timeless before its appearance in these other degrees.' The travellers travel from the kingdom of forms, which is dark, sensory and illusory, to the kingdom of unseen forms, which is made of light; then they rise to the kingdom of power, which is original and timeless. If the branches are gathered with the trunk, everything becomes the kingdom of power.

This is the spiritual world indicated by saying that they have perceived something other than bodies. The phrase means that the world of bodies is the world of the kingdom of form, and that the world of spirits is the kingdom of unseen forms. They are in fact one, because we have only one existence. But the glance differs according to realisation. As long as the slave is imprisoned by the sensory walls, shut in the form of his self, he dwells in this corporeal world, that is, the kingdom of form. The fields of the kingdom of the unseen forms are not open to him. He makes no distinction between spirituality and humanity, nor between the sensory and the inner meaning. If Allah the Exalted opens his inner eye, and and his self and his money and his kind, he sees the light of the kingdom of the unseen forms overflowing from the ocean of the kingdom of power. That witnessing will veil him from the darkness of the sensory and from seeing the cosmos, by witnessing the One Who made the cosmos. The origin of the cosmos is light, but the appearance of wisdom is the veil. The one who sees the cosmos and does not see light in it or before it or with it, misses the lights and is veiled from the suns of realisation. If he joins the light to its origin, everything becomes one light, and this is the light of the kingdom of power. So know that the kingdom of forms, unseen forms, and power are in one place, as are the corporeal and spiritual worlds. The people behind the veil see nothing except bodies. The people of realisation, and these are the people of the station of excellence, see nothing but the world of spirits, despite the fact that the place is one. Since their veil has thinned and become subtle, they have perceived something in addition to the world of bodies, and this is the world of spirits. It can also be called the world of meanings.

Know that the self and the intellect and the spirit and the secret each have limits of understanding and grasping. The witnessing of the lights of the kingdom of unseen forms and the secrets of the kingdom of power are beyond the grasp of intellects. The intellect functions before and after the spiritual world, so there is no way that it can grasp that world. We have already heard what Ibn al-Farid said:

Beyond recorded knowledge there is another knowledge
Too fine to be grasped
By the soundest of intellects.

The sun of gnosis cannot be trapped by intellect or proof, but it is grasped by selling the self for the spirit and leaving that to which the self is accustomed and what intellects can comprehend. If you arrive at this, you will grasp the lights of the kingdom of unseen forms united with the ocean of the kingdom of power. Nothing will veil you from Allah: not the earth and not the sky, neither the Throne nor the Footstool, neither the planets nor the angels. You will become the caliph of Allah on His earth and the dot on the circumference of His cosmos. And Allah has immense generosity.

These meanings are not always openly stated in the words of Allah, but sometimes are indicated. For example, the phrase of Allah the Exalted: *When the earth shakes with the Earthquake* (99:1), means the earth of the self, *and it yields up its burdens* (99:2), means it yields its contents of knowledge, wisdom and secrets. Man says in amazement to the self: 'What is the matter with it today that it is showing its secrets and its gifts?' The people of the outward do not agree with this interpretation, but it is tasted by the people of the inward. These matters are unveilings which shine on spirits and secrets. At first they are hints, then gleams, then appearances; then light remains until one is fixed and firm. When they rise to the station of fixity, they have arrived at a station which is such that if the veil were removed their certainty would not increase. The degrees of unveiling have no end. When the Sufis perceive that reality is within them, it having been unveiled, and they know that they have arrived and are firm in it, another veil is lifted and all the veils are removed from their hearts, and they have clarity from their Lord.

The heart and the spirit are like a talisman which is written, folded, wrapped up and then stamped. One cannot see what is inside it except by breaking the seal and the wrapping. This seal that Allah the Exalted has created by His wisdom and His justice as a veil on the hearts to the secrets of the unseen is the world of nature. The desires of the self and its habits are mixed up with ited has mentioned:

> Fair in the eyes of men is the love of things they covet: women and sons, hoards of gold and silver, horses, branded, and cattle and well tilled lands. Such are the possessions of this world's life, but nearness to Allah is the best of goals (3:14.)

So the self is busy providing food and drink, clothing, dwelling, marriage and so on. It is veiled by this from its origin and from witnessing the lights of its Lord, except for the one whom Allah has made happy with His friendship, and for whom it has previously been decreed.

When the Sufis recognise these obstacles which prevent them from arriving at their Lord, and when they have discriminated among these barriers and nets which immobilise them, they draw swords from their elevated yearning, with which they are determined to cut off those attachments and reject those desires. When they have connected their yearning to Allah, and have oriented themselves to Him completely, those attachments are severed and the veils are lifted. They realise that the greatest obstacle is to be busy with the burden of appearance and the belly. If Allah wants someone to remain veiled, He allows his heart to be filled with the desire for clothing and food. This is what has veiled most people. The one who finds that what covers him is enough clothing, and that what stops his hunger is enough food, the heart of this one is gathered to Allah if he is oriented with yearning towards Allah. The worth of he who is concerned with what enters his body is measured in what leaves it. In the tradition we find: 'The one who shuns beautiful clothes is given the robe of nobility on the Day of Rising.' The Prophet (may Allah bless him) also said: 'Satan runs within the son of Adam like blood. So narrow his paths by hunger.' The purpose of all this is to turn away from occupations which veil one from Allah, whether they be clothing or food.

I say that the veil hidden in the selves is love of desires and its fountain is love of other-than-Allah. It can be connected to the outward, like love of wealth, beautiful clothes, good food, good riding beasts, good wives, or it can be connected to the inward, like love of election, seeking nobility, love of praise, love of leadership and exhibition. The consequences of these are jealousy, pride, hatred, dishonesty, anger, impatience, meanness, flattery, and so on. Everyone who fights himself in order to strip from himself these ugly attributes and to put on their opposites, like humility, obscurity, soundness of heart, generosity, forbearance, patience, acceptance and surrender, finds the veil removed from himself, and then he wears the robe of purity and fulfilment. He is of the near ones who drink from the spring of the blessed garden the drink which is sealed. The water is pure for the one who is pure, but not for the one who is not pure. The one who drinks the glass of the love of the Lord, puried of desire, drinks a pure drink from the spring of the blessed garden. He who mixes his love with the love of his desires, drinks with the mob and makes no step toward the Majestic King.

The Prophet (may Allah bless him) indicated the struggle with the self and its purification by saying: 'The Muslim is the one from whose hand the Muslims are safe. The believer is the one whom people make a trustee over their wealth. The one who has emigrated is he who has emigrated from what Allah has forbidden, and the warrior is the one who fights his self and his desires.' The Prophet (may Allah bless him) also said: 'The fierce one is not the one who is fierce in a match, but the one who controls himself when angry.' Regarding this, it has been said:

The courageous one is not he who defends his catch
On the day of battle when the fire of war glows,

It is he who lowers his eyes and keeps his foot from the forbidden;
He is the heroic horseman.

Shaykh Abu al-'Abbas al-Mursi said concerning the self: 'It is the self that you cannot conquer, but Allah surrounds it.' And in the *Hikam* [the *Bezels of Wisdom* by Muhi al-Din ibn al-'Arabi]: 'If He wants to take you to Him, He will cover your description with His description, and your attributes with His attributes. He brings you to Him by what is from Him to you, not by what is from you to Him.'

The people, with respect to arrival at Allah, have looked at the root of the spirit and its purity like a polished mirror. Everything that faces it is imprinted upon it, past and future. When it is connected with this body, the sensory forms of creation are imprinted upon it. Therefore, it is veiled from its root. There are two obstacles. The first is lack of nearness to the Presence and occupation with forgetfulness. When the spirit left nearness to Allah and did not expend itself to the utmost in going toward Him, it became dark and veiled from its root. Had it been ceaselessly occupied with the remembrance of Allah and annihilated completely from other-than-Him, its mirror would have been polished once more.

The second obstacle to the spirit is the rust that is imprinted on it. There is a Prophetic saying: 'Hearts rust the same way that iron rusts.' This rust is the forms of the cosmos which are imprinted on the heart so that it becomes connected with them by belief and occupation. The *Hikam* contains these questions: 'How can a heart be enlightened when the forms of beings are imprinted on its mirror? How can it travel to Allah when it is chained by its desires? How can it enter the presence of Allah when it has not purified itself from the impurities of its forgetfulness? How can it hope to understand the finest secrets when it has not returned to Allah from its mistakes?' According to another Prophetic tradition: 'For everything there is a polish. The polish of the heart is invocation (*dhikr*) of Allah.' It must be an invocation from a heart unified and yearning, otherwise it is ineffective.

Do you not see that the Day of the Contract was a day upon which all spirits knew the Real? But when they became connected to the sensory mode, the darkness of forgetfulness, desire and habits arose in them. They became used to the sensory world, accepted it, and were veiled from the secret. Not Him by invocation or reection. Otherwise, the secret will disappear like a mirage.

Empty your heart of otherness and you will fill it with realisation and secrets. The Prophet (may Allah bless him) said: 'There will always be a group of my community who follow the truth until the order of Allah comes.' This group consists of gnostics of Allah, right-acting scholars, and those who struggle in the way of Allah. The earth will not be bereft of those who have the proof of Allah, outwardly and inwardly.

The realised Sufi has reached the degrees of perfection. He has taken from the station of *Islam* (submission) the perfection of fearful awareness and straightness. He has taken from the station of Iman (faith) the perfection of tranquility and certainty. He has taken from the station of *Ihsan* (devotion) and the highest degree, and it is eyewitnessing. The people of the outward have taken action with the limb while the Sufi takes action with the inward heart. Hence the Prophetic tradition: 'Reflection for one hour is better than worship for seventy years.' The worship of the hearts is reflection and consideration and acceptance of what comes from the power of Allah.

Some have said that the Sufi is the one who knows no one in either this world or the next except Allah. He does not witness otherness with Allah. Allah has made everything serve him, and he serves nothing. He has authority over everything and nothing has authority over him. He takes his due from everything and due is not taken from him. By him the turbidity of everything is purified and nothing clouds his purity. He is occupied by One above everything else, and One is enough for him.

# The Man in the Black Cloak Turns

This article is based on excerpts from *The Whirling Dervishes* by Ira Friedlander.

*I am neither from the East or the West, no boundaries exist in my breast.*
Mevlana Jalal al-Din Rumi

For over 700 years the man in the black cloak turned toward Allah in a continual remembrance of his Creator.

Ever since the passing of the Sufi poet and mystic Jalal al-Din Rumi in 1273, in the Anatolian village of Konya, Turkey, the dervish order known as the Mevlevi has made their dhikr in a whirling fashion.

In 1925, with the overthrow of the Ottoman Empire, the Turn was interrupted for over 25 years. Then a small group of dervishes convinced the local government in Konya that it would be harmless to introduce the Turning 'as a historical tradition' to the new culture of Turkey. UNESCO invited the Mevlevis to Paris in 1964. In this their first European trip, Selman Tuzon and Suleyman Loras sat on the post as nine semazen (whirlers) turned to the music of several dervish musicians. They have since travelled to England, Germany, Spain and America.

Following is a description of the Mevlevi turn.

The dervish performs ablution, then proceeds to dress in the whirling costume unique to the Mevlevis. His attire is influenced by the mourning clothes that Rumi ordered after the death of Shamsi Tabriz. The *sikke*, the tall honey-coloured felt hat, represents the tombstone of man. The *tennure* (long white skirt) represents the shroud, and the *khirqah* (black cloak with long, large sleeves) symbolises the tomb.

The dervishes enter the *semahane* (dance hall) led by the *semazenbashi* (the dance master), and slowly, with heads bowed, line up on one side of the hall. The dance master, who is closest to the shaykh's post, wears a white *sikke*. The shaykh is the last to enter the hall. He stops to bow at the axis line to his post and proceeds to walk slowly to it. The musicians are at the opposite end of the hall on a raised platform, facing the shaykh. The *hafiz* (one who knows the Qur'an by heart) begins the ceremony by chanting a prayer and a surah from the Qur'an. Then the sound of the *kudum* (kettle drums) breaks the silence. The dervishes, now seated on their knees, listen to the piercing sound of a single *ney*, the reed flute which plays the *peshrev* or musical prelude.

The dervishes slap the floor with their hands indicating the day of the Last Judgement and the Path from this world to Paradise. It is said that this bridge is as thin as a hair and as sharp as a razor.

The shaykh takes one step to the front of his post and bows his head. He begins to slowly walk around the *semahane* followed by all of the dervishes. They circle the hall three times, stopping to bow to each other at the shaykh's post. As they bow, they look between the eyebrows of the dervish opposite them. This is known as *Mukabele* (to return an action) and has become the name for the Mevlevi ceremony. This part of the *sema* is known as the Sultan Veled Walk, in honour of Rumi's son, and symbolises man's identity and his place within a circle. The *halqah* (circle of dervishes) is used in many of the Sufi orders.

After circling the hall for the third time, the last dervish bows to the post and turns to complete the walk as the shaykh takes his post. They now all bow and in one motion remove their cloaks, kiss them, and let them drop to the floor. As they drop their cloaks, they leave their tombs, their worldly attachments, and prepare to turn for Allah. The shaykh and the *semazenbashi* keep their cloaks.

The musicians on the platform are playing as the dervishes, with their right hand on their left shoulder and their left hand on their right shoulder, slowly walk to the shaykh's post. The *semazenbashi* is the first to arrive at the post where the shaykh is standing. He bows to the shaykh, his right foot over the left and his arms crossed at the shoulders. He kisses the right hand of the shaykh, recedes backwards from him and, standing five feet from the post, is in a position to begin directing the *sema*.

Each dervish approaches the shaykh in this manner. He bows, kisses the right hand of the shaykh, the shaykh kisses his *sikke*, the dervish bows again and turns toward the *semazenbashi* for silent instruction. If the foot of the *semazenbashi*, who wears white shoes, is extended outside of his black cloak, it is a signal for the whirler that the outside area is blocked to him, and he must begin to turn on the inside of the dance master. If his shoe is hidden, the whirler continues to walk past him and begins to unfold and turn on his outside.

All the dervishes unfold and whirl as the musicians play and the chorus chants. The turners extend their arms, the right palm faces up and the left down. As they turn the dance master slowly walks among them gesturing with his eyes or position to correct their speed or posture. The shaykh stands at this post. They turn counterclockwise, repeating their inaudible *dhikr*, 'Allah, Allah.'

After about ten minutes the music stops, and the dervishes complete a turn that will face them toward the shaykh's post and halt. The movement is so quick that their billowing skirts wrap around their legs as they bow to the post.

This *selam* is repeated four times, each about the same length of time. It is only in the fourth *selam* that the shaykh joins the dervishes. The shaykh whirls slowly along the equator line to the centre of the *semahane* as a single ney sounds a distant wailing sound that leads him back to his post.

When the shaykh arrives at his post, he bows, sits on the post, and kisses the floor. All the turners sit, and their cloaks are put on them by those who did not turn in the fourth *selam*. They have returned to their tombs but in an altered state. The shaykh recites the *Fatihah*, the first surah of the Qur'an, and all the dervishes kiss the floor and rise. The shaykh then sounds a prayer to Mevlana and Shamsi Tabriz and begins the sound 'Hu.'

This concludes the ceremony and the shaykh leads the dervishes from the *semahane*, stopping to bow opposite his post at the far side of the hall. Each dervish does the same.

Why does the soul take wing, when from the glorious Presence
A speech of sweet favour comes to it, saying 'Aloft?'
How should a fish not leap nimbly from the dry land into the water,
When the sound of waves reaches its ear from the cold ocean?
Why should a falcon not fly from the quarry towards the King,
When it hears by drum and drum-stick the notice of *'Return'*?
Why should not every Sufi begin to dance, like a mote,
In the sun of eternity, that it may deliver him from decay?
Such grace and beauty and loveliness and bestowal of life!
O misery and error, if any one dispense with Him!
Fly, fly, O bird, to thy native home,
For thou hast escaped from the cage, and thy pinions are outspread.
Travel away from the bitter stream towards the water of life,
Return from the vestibule to the high seat of the soul.

by Jalal al-Din Rumi from the Diwani-Tabriz

# Urs of Sayyid Bukhari

## By Hajj Mustafa Shawqi

Looking ahead of us, the oasis village of Uch Sharif, nestled deep in the eastern Punjab of Pakistan, emerged from the desert. As we entered, it was throbbing with people. Today was not only Friday, Jum'ah, but the Urs of a famous saint, Sayyid Bukhari.

An *urs* is a yearly celebration of the death date of a famous *wali* (friend) of Allah. In Pakistan and the Indian sub-continent Islam was spread, upheld and revitalised by Sufis. The people who loved and followed these men often built beautiful structures around their tombs, sometimes with an adjoining mosque. These *darbars* as they are called became places for Muslims to come to, and by the life-example and *barakah* of the dead *wali*, to remember, possibly with greater humility and awareness, their relationship to Allah.

Our van headed into the bazaar, becoming a wedge parting a sea of people. The colourful clothes and flowing turbans blended into one another. A collage of living colour and movement. The road began to climb up into a narrow, winding street of walls and doors leading onto courtyards. We went as far as we could, stopped, and began the walk to where the main gathering was taking place, at the tomb of Sayyid Bukhari.

All around us were graves, lumps of mud piled up in shifting lines spread out over a continuously rising area. We were now several hundred yards up the hill. Later, I learned that once there was no hill at all, and that over the years it had been gradually built, one grave over another, the final resting place of more than 100,000 people.

Uch Sharif is an ancient city. It existed as a trade centre during the lifetime of the Prophet Muhammad (peace be upon him). Later, after the arrival of Islam, it became a centre for religious teaching with universities and schools of Islamic knowledge. Sufis from many parts of the Muslim world came to teach and live in what was one of the most beautiful cities in the world. Now there remains only reminders of that time.

The Urs was being held in the courtyard of the mosque built in honour of Sayyid Bukhari. We were now on a path leading to its entrance. In front of us was an arched door. I could see only slightly through the door, as there were many people stopped at its entrance removing their shoes. But what I could see was fantastic: a courtyard spread out across the very top of the hill. Arriving at the entrance, I removed my shoes and entered.

There were people everywhere; men, women and children, all dressed in an array of colours like so many flowers gleaming in the sun on a bright summer day. I put my shoes down on the ground where they soon disappeared in the pile that grew at every moment. But I didn't care. No one did; it was taken for granted that everyone would find their shoes later. We began moving through the crowd stepping over people, each foot searching for a piece of ground to balance on before going on. Hands stretched out from every direction helping our balance until we found space to sit.

I sat enthralled by the mass of people praying, singing and crying to their Lord: their faces as timeless as their worship. Time had stopped. My sense of being a tourist or visitor fell away and my heart began to open to this experience.

The Qawali singers began to chant songs about the Prophet (may Allah bless him), and his noble character and qualities, as well as songs about following the path of love for Allah. The sounds of their drums and musical instruments filled the air. With each breath we imbibed a portion of their intoxication.

Looking around, my eyes fell upon what seemed to be the vortex of the gathering across the courtyard; I moved towards it. It was the door to the tomb of Sayyid Bukhari.

I had never been in a tomb like this before. Upon entering it, I remembered the tomb of the Prophet Muhammad (peace be on him) in Medina. There was a similar taste, but reverence for the Prophet and his unattainable station forbids further comparison. I entered the tomb and immediately felt cooled from the desert sun. It was just the dark coolness of a mud building, but felt like entering a garden.

The tomb of the saint was lit up and the inside covered by mounds of flowers that sparkled in contrast to the deep green cover over the stone grave. I had no idea of the correct courtesy, of how to approach the situation I found myself in. Suddenly I was compelled to touch the green cover. I buried my face in it. I felt as though I were being brought through a tunnel whose end was complete darkness. For a moment there was nothing but cool, uninterrupted blackness. Tears burst from my eyes and a hand tugged at my shirt, indicating it was time to move on.

Finally, the celebration ended. From death had come life. People began to disperse and we headed back to the village of Ahmadpur from where we had come. On the journey I remembered a saying that my shaykh so often repeated: From the womb to the tomb; what is in between is nothing other than realising our ultimate fate and by this realisation discovering our beginning.

# SECTION 9

## On the Light Side

*Behold, Allah does not disdain to propound a parable of a gnat, or of
something even less than that. Now, as for those who believe, they
know it is the truth from their Lord, and as for those who disbelieve,
they say: 'What is it that Allah means by this parable?' . . .but none
does He cause to err by it save the transgressors.* (2:26)

————★————

# Bustan of Sa'di

Shaykh Muslih al-Din Sa'di was born in Shiraz, in Persia, CE 1175, 571 years after the Hijrah of Muhammad (peace and blessings be upon him). Imbued from early childhood with an insatiable thirst for knowledge, Sa'di eventually journeyed to Baghdad, then at the zenith of its intellectual fame. The young aspirant progressed rapidly along the path of learning, and at the age of twenty-one made his first essays in authorship. Soon after, Sa'di was admitted into the University of Baghdad.

His scholastic life did not end until he had reached the age of thirty. Of the value of this prolonged period of study he was fully aware. 'Do you not know,' he asks in his well-known work of spiritual teachings, the Bustan, 'how Sa'di attained to rank? Neither did he traverse the plains nor journey across the seas. In his youth he lived under the yoke of the wise; Allah granted him distinction in the life to come. And it is not long before he who is submissive in obedience exercises command.' No better example of the truth of this passage could be cited than that demonstrated by his own life.

On leaving Baghdad, he travelled with his teacher, the great Shaykh Abd al-Qadir al-Jilani, on a pilgrimage to Mecca. This was the first of many travels extending over a period of thirty years, in the course of which he visited Europe, India, and practically every part of what is now known as the Near and Middle East. Sa'di's travels brought him into the company of numerous men. 'In every corner,' writes Sa'di, 'I reaped gain, and gleaned an ear of corn from every harvest. I did not wish to return from the garden of the world empty-handed. Travellers returning from Egypt bring sugar candy as a gift to their friends. I have no candy, but the words I bring are sweeter, and are to be taken away by those who know the truth.' Thus Sa'di describes his reasons for writing the *Bustan*, which means 'Garden.'

After his thirty years of travel Sa'di settled down in Persia, where he was favoured by the ruling prince, from whom he received not only the dignity and the tangible advantages of the rank of honoured poet, but his titular name of Sa'di. He died at the age of 116, and was buried in his native city.

If the *Bustan* were the only work that remained of his genius, Sa'di's name would assuredly still be inscribed in the roll of the great. One aspect of his vast intellectual faculties needs to be emphasised, and that is the increasing power which they assumed as he advanced in years, the truth of which can be understood when it is stated that he composed the *Bustan* at the age of 82, and the *Gulistan* twelve months later. Few, if any, instances of such sustained mental activity are to be found anywhere in the entire world's history of letters.

Stories selected from the *Bustan* follow.

*The Story of Majnun and the Sincerity of his love for Laylah*

Someone called out to Majnun,
'O illustrious fellow,' he said,
'What would it be like for you in this life,
Should this longing for Laylah depart from your head,
Should desire for her leave you and your thoughts be fixed on
Something else instead?'

When the poor fellow heard this, he began to weep,
'Don't speak to me like this, the very idea is so cheap,
My passionate heart is already painful and aching,
Don't pour salt in its wound, wide open and gaping.
The cause of my patience is not far away,
For that which I need in the distance does stay.'

'O, dear smiling friend!' Majnun cried,
'These greetings of mine take to Laylah' side,
But before my love don't mention my name,
For it's shameful to mention me in the place where she remains.'

### The Story of the Glow-Worm of the Night

Haven't you seen in the garden glowing,
A worm shining in the night like a lantern showing?
Someone asked it, 'O little bird that lights up the night,
Why is it that you don't appear in the daylight?'
See the little glow-worm born of the dust,
What an answer of knowledge and light he gives us;
'I am always in this desert both day and night.
But I cannot be seen for the sun's so bright.'

### A Story of Self-Esteem Among People

A dog bit one of the desert dweller's feet,
He bit with such fury that venom dripped from its teeth;
At night the poor wretch was unable to sleep.
And his face was distraught with tears and grief.

'Where were your teeth when this happened',
His rude young daughter cruelly cried.
With a peal of laughter, he then replied:
'I could have fought back my delightful child,
But even were you to strike my head with a sword,
God forbid that I would use my palate and teeth
Upon the feet of a low and despicable dog.
One can act with determination with the mean and the base.
But a dog is not a member of the human race.'

### The Story of a Pearl

A single drop of rain fell from a cloud in the sky,
But was filled with shame when it saw the sea so wide.

'Next to the sea then, who am I?
If the sea exists, then how can I?'

While looking down on itself
With the eyes of contempt,
An oyster in its shell,
Took it in for nourishment.

And so it was, that its fate was sealed by this event,
And it became a famous pearl fit to adore a king's head.
Having descended to the depths,
It was now exalted to the heights.
On the portal of non-existence it went knocking,
Until it finally was transformed into being.

### Story of Sultan Mahmud and His Love for Ayaz

One of his subjects found fault with Sultan Mahmud, saying, 'Ayaz, his favourite slave, is no beauty. How strange that a nightingale should love arose that has neither colour nor perfume.'

When Sultan Mahmud heard this, he said, 'My love is for his virtues, not for his form.'

The sultan then related this story. Years ago, while journeying in a far land, the Sultan and his entourage spied a caravan ahead. As it entered a narrow pass, one of the camels stumbled and a chest of pearls fell open. The Sultan gave the signal for plunder and urged his horse onwards. His horsemen race forward and, leaving the Sultan behind, gathered up the pearls. No one remained with the Sultan but Ayaz.

'O you of quiet demeanour!' said Mahmud, 'What have you gained of the booty?'

'Nothing,' he replied. `I followed in haste behind you. I do not occupy myself with riches away from your service.'

If, in the Palace, a place of honour is yours, do not neglect the king on account of gain elsewhere.

*Discourse on the Education of Sons*

If you wish your name to be remembered, train your son in knowledge and wisdom for if he does not possess these, you will die in obscurity with no one to remember you.

Teach him a skill, even if you are as rich as Korah. Place no hope in the power that you have – riches may vanish from you.

A bag of silver and gold is emptied. The purse of a tradesman remains filled.

Do you not know how Sa'adi attained to rank? He journeyed not over the plains, nor crossed the seas. In his youth, he served under the yoke of the wise: Allah granted him distinction in the Next Life. It is not long before he who serves obtains command.

A boy who does not suffer at the hand of his teacher suffers at the hands of Time.

Instil in your son moral character and independence so that he may not be obligated to any man.

Protect him from undesirable company. Do not pity him if he brings ruin and dishonour upon himself, for it is better than a son who is without character should die before his father.

# Two Parables

## by Jalal al-Din Rumi

*The Caged Bird's Escape*

Once upon a time a bird in a cage
sang for her merchant master.
He took such delight in her song day and
    night
that her feelings began to matter.
He grew so fond of her that he brought her
    water in a golden dish,
and when he had to go on a merchant's
    journey he asked her for her wish.
'I will go through the forest where you were
    born
past the birds of your neighbourhood.
What message should I bring them
for news of your present good?'
'Tell them I sit locked in a cage,
singing my captive song.
My heart is grieved
and I hope it won't be long before I see them
    again
and look on their faces
and fly in freedom through the trees.
What message do they have for me
from their lovely forest
that will set my heart at ease?
Oh I yearn for my beloved,
to fly with him
and spread my captive wings!
Until then I sit disconsolate
separate from all sweet things.'

The merchant went on his donkey through
the thick and melodious wood.
When he got to where his bird was from
he stopped and pushed back his hood.
'Oh birds, one and all, greetings to you
from my pretty bird locked in her cage.
She sends her love
and wants me to tell you of
her condition and ask your sage
for a message to take back
that will ease her heart
and turn over a brand new page.
She is all alone with bars all around her – she
    wants to join her beloved
and sound her song through the air –
for her heart to be free again.'
All the birds listened to his tale,
then suddenly one bird shrieked
and fell from its branch to the ground, dead.
The merchant froze to the spot he stood on.
Nothing could astound.
him more than this did.

He went to the city and traded his goods,
Then he returned to his house and went
    around in a mood unable to speak.
Finally his bird asked him what message
    came from their beaks
and he stood before her cage and said, 'Oh,
    nothing to speak of.'
'No, no,' she cried, `I must know at once!'
'I don't know what happened,' he said, 'I'm
    a dunce!
I told them your message and just like that,
    one bird fell dead at my feet.'

Suddenly, his own bird shrieked and fell on
   her head
onto the floor of her cage.
He let out a cry
'Oh, what have I done?' he wept,
'What have I done?
Now my moon has gone out
and so has my sun.
Now my own bird is dead – my life means
   nothing.
I will have to bury her now, dear, dead
   thing!'

He opened the door and reached in and took
   her
into his hand, careful not to drop her,
but, once out in the air,
she flew up with one swoop
and flew out of the window
onto the nearest roof slope.

'Thank you, merchant master,
for delivering my plea.' She sang out,
'Those birds sent me a message
that instructed me
on how to win my freedom
and fly quite free.
So I go now to my loved one
who is waiting for me.
All I did was play dead.
All I had to do was die.
It's easy once you use
your heart and your head.
Goodbye, goodbye, master no more.
I will fly into space,
to my beloved I'll soar.'

She returned
no more.

# The Gift of Obedience

## by Ali Asghar

Once upon a time, somewhere in the land of the Prophet (peace and blessings be upon him), two young men set off in search of a Shaykh who would teach them the way of the Saints. They travelled for many days and nights. One of them was the son of a beggar. He was called Mikal and wanted to learn about his faith Islam, so he was very enthusiastic about finding a Shaykh to teach him. The other was the son of a rich merchant. His name was Hakim and his desire to learn was not his own but that of his father who wanted his son to become versed in the sciences.

On the twentieth night of their journey they came across the hut of a learned and well-respected Shaykh called Ahmed. Hakim knocked on the door in anticipation. When Shaykh Ahmed opened the door Mikal fell on his knees and said, 'Oh wise one, we want to become your pupils. Please invite us into your home.' The Shaykh looked at them and said, 'Before you can enter my home, you must climb that mountain over there and bring me the egg of an eagle.'

The boys set off and searched for the nest of an eagle. But when they reached the foot of the mountain, Hakim, said, 'I refuse to climb this mountain for an egg. I shall wait here for you to return.' Mikal looked at his friend and said, 'Be obedient Hakim so that we may both become pupils of this wise Shaykh.' But Hakim sat by a tree and closed his eyes, pretending he had fallen fast asleep.

Mikal climbed and climbed, encountering many wild animals and becoming hungry on his way. However, he still persevered with his journey and finally came across the nest of an eagle. In it he found an egg which he took and began his long trip back to the hut of the wise Shaykh.

When he finally reached the tree where Hakim was waiting, he ran to him showing him the egg. 'Look Hakim, I found an egg!' said Mikal excitedly. Hakim asked to have a closer look at it so Mikal gave it to him. Hakim said, 'Mikal, you must be tired. Why don't you rest under this tree for a few moments?' Mikal did so and soon he fell fast asleep.

Hakim smiled and left him there, taking the egg to the wise Shaykh who sat waiting for him. Approaching the Shaykh, Hakim said, 'I have done as you requested, now please tell me the secrets of all things so that my father will be pleased with me.' The wise and softly-spoken Shaykh asked, 'How many eggs were there in the nest?' Surprised by this question, Hakim became nervous and lied by replying that there were two. The Shaykh then said to him, 'This is not the one I wanted. Take it back to the nest and bring me the other one.' Hakim became angry and shouted, 'I will never climb that mountain for you, old man!' And he threw the egg to the ground.

At that moment Mikal came out of the forest and threw himself at the feet of the Shaykh, saying, 'Sir, I have failed in my task!' but the wise Shaykh answered: 'No, you have done well for the scratches on your knees and the tears in your clothes prove to me that you did complete your task.'

The old wise Shaykh invited Mikal into his home where he was greeted by a host of pupils, all of whom, like Mikal, genuinely wished to learn about Islam.